Jacques Salomé is a psychologist. He is founder of Le Regard Fertile, a training centre in human relationships at Roussillon in Provence, France, and has led training sessions on communication and personal growth for many years. He is the author of many books, including the bestseller about couples, *Parle-moi ... j'ai des choses à te dire*.

Sylvie Galland is Head of the Psychotherapy Centre for children at Lausanne Hospital, Switzerland. She has co-written with Jacques Salomé the book *Mémoires de l'oubli*.

If Only I'd Listen to Myself

RESOLVING THE CONFLICTS THAT SABOTAGE OUR LIVES

Jacques Salomé and Sylvie Galland

ELEMENT

Shaftesbury, Dorset • Rockport, Massachusetts
Melbourne, Victoria

© Element Books Limited 1997
Text © 1990, Les Editions de l'Homme, a division of the Sogides Group

First published in the USA in 1997 by
Element Books, Inc.
PO Box 830, Rockport, MA 01966

Published in Great Britain in 1997 by
Element Books Limited
Shaftesbury, Dorset SP7 8BP

Published in Australia in 1997 by
Element Books
and distributed by Penguin Australia Ltd
487 Maroondah Highway, Ringwood, Victoria 3134

Translated by Geraldine Le Roy and Jocelyn White
Cover illustration Françoise Malnuit
Illustrations by Françoise Malnuit
Cover design by Mark Slader
Page design by Roger Lightfoot
Typeset by Bournemouth Colour Press, Parkstone, Poole
Printed and bound in Great Britain by
Creative Print and Design, Ebbw Vale, Wales

British Library Cataloguing in Publication
data available

Library of Congress Cataloging in Publication
data available

ISBN 1–85230–971–7

Contents

To all those whose true freedom of being is based on respect, listening, tolerance.

Introduction

Nothing in the world seems more important and essential to our existence than communicating, being involved in relationships with others and sharing.

It is one of our most vital and deep aspirations to feel related to something larger than ourselves, to be recognized, identified and to belong to a group and a community of people or language.

But nowhere in our family life or at school are we taught how to communicate, either with others or with ourselves.

School systems base communication on specific dynamics, those of questioning and answering. The child cannot give his own answer; the only acceptable answer is the one in the book or the one the teacher wants. So for some fifteen to twenty years most of us are conditioned to produce answers for and to respond to the expectations of others.

No wonder we become handicapped in our relationships.

When we become aware of our shortcomings, it takes us time to learn anew; to reinvent practical ways of feeling better, of sharing more with others and of listening to them and to ourselves with greater care.

In this book, we intend to reveal some of our discoveries, as signposts that can help the reader to be heard and to hear others. These will lead to more lively communication and healthy relationships. Above all they will help us to listen to ourselves and to relate to the best in ourselves – those parts hidden and unknown to us.

We are going to suggest that it is essential for all of us to take responsibility for improving our relationships both with others and with ourselves. To do that, we need to understand some of the mechanisms that govern communication and intimate relationships. We also have to avoid the traps that consist of

'We seem to be a bit blocked when it comes to communicating.'

either blaming others for what is wrong, or of taking the blame in a way which is denigrating to ourselves.

We shall also describe the most frequent relationship traps and suggest important guidelines and basepoints. These may not lead to complete solutions, but they may help to keep us on the right track in handling our relationships.

A last word about gender. We have tried to use the he/she form as often as possible but it has not always been practical. Sometimes we have been compelled to keep 'him' and 'his' forms to refer to both men and women so as to avoid the awkwardness of continual dual reference. No offence is meant.

1 Communication

*Before being born into words, the unspoken must gestate in the
womb of the mind.
Then it gathers meaning, sonority and life.*

Alain Bosquet

We all know the vague feeling of communicating badly, both
with ourselves and with others. Daily, we face difficulties in
expressing ourselves and getting through to others. If we want to
improve the way we communicate, we must first question how we
learned to communicate. We might find out that we had learned
not to communicate. We might discover that very early on in life
we were deprived of our own words by those who loved us, and
who, believing they understood us, spoke in our place.

ANTI-COMMUNICATION

Parents and teachers more often criticize than help us to speak
freely. And even more seriously, they often distort the meaning of
our words rather than listening to what we are actually saying.
They talk *for*[1] us instead of letting us speak for ourselves. Thus,
worst of all, they deny our own self-expression.

'I'm afraid,' says a child. 'No, you're not,' answers the father.

'It hurts,' says a child who scraped his knee. 'No, it's nothing,'
answers his mother.

These examples seem harmless enough. They spring from the
good intention of reassuring the child. Wanting to rid children of

their fears is a common cause of parental distortion. Such messages nevertheless really mean: 'You can't trust what you feel. I'm the one who knows what you should feel'. They impose on the other the emotions and feelings he/she should have, or should not have. You can order or forbid an action (if the balance of power allows it) – 'I don't want you to hit the baby's head' – but, whatever the stage of life, any injunction concerning feelings – 'You must love him' – is inappropriate and creates confusion. Anybody who feels an emotion doubts it when a significant person (a parent for example) denigrates and denies it or tries to dictate to him what it should be.

'You must love him, he's your brother, he doesn't know what he is doing when he breaks your toy . . .'

'But, darling, you know that I love you both equally. I treat your sister and you the same.'

'You known, he adores you, even if he's angry. Anyway, you should stop contradicting him, he doesn't like it!'

In fact we mostly learn to communicate by being denied our own experience by those who love us. And of course we also see them deny their own feelings.

'Are you sad, Mummy? Are you crying?'
'No, don't worry, it's nothing.'

Nothing indeed!

'Grandma doesn't like Dad. What does she have against him?'
'What's the matter with you? Of course she likes him . . .'

If we do not try to find the basic principles of healthy communication we run the risk of spending our lives subjected to the sort of conditioning that ruins communication and makes an intimate relationship difficult and painful.

'She says that she loves us equally, but we're different.'

BASIC PRINCIPLES

The basis for real communication is simple to describe and infinitely complicated to apply. It obeys three fundamental rules.

- Recognize and acknowledge the others person's words, feelings or opinions as his own.
- Express ourselves by talking only about ourselves and stating only our own position.
- See both points of view, rather than opposing or confusing them, but don't be shy of comparing and challenging them – sharing and communication arise out of this process.

These rules have immediate corollaries.

- Don't let the other person talk *for* us.
- Tell the other person to talk only about themselves.

- Remember that listening to each other does not mean having the same opinion, feelings or point of view.
- Separate the other person's feelings from our own.

It's better to agree with a frightened child when he or she says 'I'm afraid', and to let him voice the fear. But you can then say: 'I'm not afraid'.

If a friend says: 'You ought to be interested in things other than comics', then I might respond by saying: 'Don't tell me what to do' or 'If you want, tell me what you are feeling when you see me with my head in a comic'.

We talk for others because we do not know how to talk for ourselves. The effects of other people's talking for us will last all our lives if we do not take the risk of reclaiming our own words. Reclaiming our own language is one of the major things at stake in any process of personal growth. Every move is a difficult and painful birth which gives us access to our *own* words, as distinct from the words of all the people who brought us up and cared for us.

COMMUNICATION AND EXPRESSION

To communicate means to share. But is it our differences or our similarities which we have to share?

Expressing oneself is not yet communication. It is only one stage. Real communication involves the following stages:

- expressing ourselves;
- receiving confirmation that what we said was heard;
- listening to the other person's words;
- confirming that we heard the other person properly.

These apparently simple sequences comprise innumerable traps. People do not react to what we say, but to what they think we say, or to the totally personal effect our words produce in them. In the

'Don't you think it's too hot?'

same way that there is sometimes a huge difference between what we said and what the other person heard, the reverse is of course also true.

In a difficult and important discussion we should check with the other person to see what he or she heard. When someone talks to us, we should make sure that what we heard is what he/she said. We do not have to agree with the other person nor to acknowledge the validity of his opinion. All that is required is to register the other person's point of view.

'Scientists say that there might be life on Mars. Imagine how extraordinary it would be to be able to communicate with Martians! I'd love it.'
'Well you're entitled to your opinion. But for me, I can do all the talking I need to do with people on this planet!'

This could stop the conversation . . . or alternatively we might suggest that the other person expand on his opinion. In the following sections we are going to try to pick out attitudes that hinder or facilitate communication. To do that, we need to look at the four processes involved in any act of communication:

- saying;
- not saying;
- listening;
- hearing.

Saying

Words know things about us that we do not know about them.
René Char

The most difficult thing for any of us to do is to talk about ourselves instead of talking about others, the world or life. But when we do manage to do it, it opens on to our own unique perception of reality, our own feelings and our own experience. In conversation we can never insist enough on the importance of speaking in terms of 'I', instead of 'one', 'we' or 'you'.

Verbal expression (we will not mention here the numerous languages of body and action) may involve at least five different levels. These are: facts, sensations and feelings, thoughts and ideas, resonance and imagination.

The level of facts

This is the anecdotal level, where we tell what and how things happened. Some people insist on doing it in a detailed and accurate way. For instance, I can describe the film I saw last night about a divorced father travelling with his daughter. I can recount numerous incidents with more or less detail about this or that aspect of the film.

The level of sensations and feelings

This level concerns the sensations and feelings related to an event, situation or meeting. These sensitive areas are never missing. They touch an emotional turbulence which bubbles in each of us. It is the source of an inexhaustible fountain of words – personal words. These will only come if we take the trouble to express our intimate experience. But this might depend on how the other person hears and encourages us to talk at this level.

I might say how moved I was by the film and distressed by certain scenes. My eyes filled with tears as I saw the father's effort to make his daughter love him. I experienced both laughter and joy at the mixture of complicity and tenderness which flowed between them. I felt sad during the moments when they were separated by mutual lack of understanding . . . If I am talking to somebody who is important to me, I do not need them to listen to what I express.

Many misunderstandings and frustrations in relationships arise out of the other person not listening to us. This might be because of his or her low tolerance, insensitivity to emotion, various fears, blindness or deafness; when this happens he/she cuts us off from the vital dimension of experience and feelings – or denigrates it. This is the root of an amazing number of misunderstandings and sufferings in family life. We all seem to have this magical expectation that others (mother, father, brother, sister) should share our feelings and emotions without appropriating them.

Among difficulties which could arise, the other person might answer at a level which differs from mine.

'You know, Mum, it was very difficult for me when I was six and you cut my hair so short.'
'But there were lice at school. You understand that, don't you?'

'*But there were lice at school ...*'

No, we cannot understand if we do not first feel heard. The child is talking about feelings and the mother is talking about facts.

Words can throw light on something but they may not resolve it.

The level of thoughts and ideas

We often start talking to others in a logical way, and a lot of what we say is generalization and normalization.

Be they discursive thoughts, orderly thoughts that conceal our inner chaos or thoughts that jump from one subject to another, ideas link and underlie our more colourful emotions. Thoughts help us to sort out experience and assimilate it; they protect us – even sometimes from feeling!

Thoughts are essential points of reference, necessary signposts in the chaos or multiplicity of human situations. Words mean that thinking can escape towards limitless horizons. It means the expansion of man within the cosmos.

I can criticize and assess the film I just mentioned: I find it beautiful and subtle. I can then express my thoughts on the father–daughter relationship, on the differences between generations, films about intimate relationships or on the art of communication!

I derive so much pleasure (or suffering) from expanding my thinking, building or destroying worlds, inventing relationships or letting them die, linking or separating possibilities.

The level of resonance

Present experiences resonate with older ones, taking us back to those engraved in our past to which we do not always have direct or immediate access.

If I feel confident, I might say that the film reminded me of my divorced parents, of my father's visits and of so many hopes and disappointments. Thus I might get in touch with my personal myths about my father, home or family life.

Each present occurrence strikes a chord in a near or distant past. This more or less conscious reactivation affects our relationships and communications here and now.

'A woman talking to me for the first time at a meal with friends reactivates something that occurred in my life when I was eight years old, at elementary school. I had a sadistic teacher with exactly the same crease around her mouth as this lady . . .

Without realizing why, I want to attack and humiliate her. In a bad-mannered way I dispute her point of view, which in fact is not all that different from mine. I become nasty, fierce and ruthless. In this absolutely friendly gathering all I want to do is reduce her to nothing. Naturally my friends are all surprised at my outburst.'

The level of imagination

Fantasies, wishes and all the personal imagery that goes with them can be shared, though not in all cases.

 For instance, I had imagined that I would make a similar kind of film to the one mentioned above, but different in some aspects. I would have emphasized the couple's relationship. I would have been the director. The leading actress would have been so-and-so, etc. I then start an internal dialogue with Julia Roberts or Juliette Binoche.

Used in this way, imaginary life, which is so essential for each of us, is a privileged source of creativity in dialogue, if we accept to share it and if others are able to hear it as 'an imagined life'. They should be able to understand that the translation of our imaginary world into words does not mean that we are going to act it out. Imaginary life needs to be heard. It can be revealed to others, but not lived by them. It needs respect.

To communicate fully means that, at various times in our relationships, we need to express ourselves, listen and be listened to at the above five levels.

Our words often remain stuck at one of these levels. We rigidly favour some and relentlessly avoid or reject others according to situation, person and topic, according to our ease or fears. But much depends on the kind of listening we receive. Fruitful communication involves free movement between all the above levels: it lets words flow. Actually every communication should be fruitful, that is to say bring about growth and amplification. Free relationships – those allowing us to be who we are – are ones where we can say everything. This does not mean the terrorism of *having* to say everything. The mere knowledge that everything can be said makes us feel amazingly confident in ourselves and in the other person.

We sometimes hear: 'It's so difficult. I can't tell him things like that . . .' or 'He/she just refuses to hear what I'm saying' or 'I daren't tell him because I'm afraid of his reactions'. The fear of saying, of expressing ourselves without constraint, exists in many close relationships. It blocks off enthusiasm, spontaneity and creativity. It holds us back and perpetuates the resentment and frustrations of unsaid things.

Sometimes we expect words to be right and true, whereas they mean different things to different people.

We often expect that words will give us access to the full and enjoyable communication we all hope for. Our natural expectation of achieving perfect and absolute communication often leaves us, after a conversation, struggling with anxious disenchantment, a gnawing anxiety or an inexpressible anger that looks for a way out, often through violence.

There are gaps between our experience, what we say, what we intend to say, and what is actually on our lips. There is another gap between what we say and what is heard. Others hear according to their own perceptions and references. We do not even know what they understand or hear, and sometimes we discover it with delight or horror days or weeks later.

Other people's thoughts and secret images are as utterly beyond our grasp as ours are beyond theirs. It is even true for the woman with whom we share bed and bread, and for the child we have been supporting with loving care since birth. So much remains a mystery; we do not communicate about the most essential things.

Verbal expression involves the risk of distortions and misunderstandings between:

- What we think or experience . . . and what we can say.
- What we say . . . and what others understand, choosing among the numerous meanings of our words those which touch, seduce or threaten them most.
- What we believe others heard . . . and what they think we believe they heard.

Of course we try to accept these inevitable gaps before

attempting to reduce them. We have to recognize the incompleteness of all verbal communication before striving to make it more fruitful.

Not saying

By trying to reach the unreachable, we make it impossible to reach even what is reachable.
P Watzlawick

This may appear to contradict what has just been said, but 'not saying' should be understood as a choice (and not a restraint). Communication will only satisfy us if we accept its limits. It is not possible to say everything. 'Saying everything' remains an illusion and a trap, a temptation of fusion. Sometimes 'not saying' means marking out our territory. We might not wish to mention a topic with someone, even though he/she questions us. Some questions are intrusive and we are entitled to feel that we are not obliged to answer them. For instance I am telling a colleague what I discovered on holiday:

> 'Who did you travel with?' he/she asks.
> 'I feel like telling you about Prague, not about my present emotional life.'

'Not saying' is also part of paying attention to other people's needs ('He's tired this evening') and choosing the right moment to be listened to ('He really wants to talk today; there's no room for my words'). Sometimes it is better to wait for suitable circumstances or to have clear ideas before insisting on talking about how we experienced a situation.

Not saying, or at any rate not saying too much, helps us to avoid a sort of 'pollution' in relationships. We should be careful not to use the other person as a dumping ground, not to dump our worries, depressions, angers and frustrations. Many people seem to think that the closer they are to somebody, the more they can tell them about all the things that go wrong.

We keep the worst of ourselves for the people we most care about. This is especially true in love relationships where we do not hesitate sometimes to pour out our worries or misfortunes. It is as if love entitled us to 'pollute' the person we love. 'Does he/she have the right to be joyful or happy when I'm sad and unhappy?'

'Not saying' should not be confused with 'the unspoken'. It is a kind of self-regulating process in communication which enables everyone to preserve areas of privacy.

> 'When you were away, I discovered the importance of being alone, even when we are together. Moments when I feel your closeness most, when you are present and absent at the same time, are as intense as those before nightfall when the sun is still shining.'

Being alone with another person is a subtle communication between two people who withdraw inside themselves, allowing magnetic forces to surge from two parallel and distinct poles.

It is sometimes like that after lovemaking. Each person is alone, happy to be alone and satisfied and does not want any interaction or active communication. Yet, in this purposeless state where no demands are made, the other person's presence is essential. It makes us feel our own presence and expands our deepest being. Long-term relationships need such a silence, made up of the intimate pleasure of experiencing our own sensations alone and feeling in harmony with the other.

This delicate balance often seems difficult to reach. Too often the other's presence and look – even if he/she is not looking at us – become so important that they impinge on our relationship to ourselves. We are more conscious of others than of ourselves. It is easier to enjoy solitude when nobody else is in the room.

The proximity of parents seems to hinder the possibility of happy withdrawal even more than the presence of a companion or of children. It is however in their mother's proximity that infants build their capacity to be alone with others. Secure about their mother's availability, they can exist, dream or play alone.

They experience a space where paradoxically they can forget their mother because they know she is there. It is a space where they can separate from her because they know that they will not lose her.

Many mothers intrude into this fragile space and thus jeopardize the fundamental experience of solitude. They intervene, comment on play, ask questions and, with good intentions, destroy the timeless moment the infant was experiencing without them. He might have been on a razor's edge between solitude/abandonment and relationship/dependence, exploring his own ability to exist as a whole, undamaged by another presence, however essential it is.

In close relationships, moments of shared solitude appear very precious, because they are usually prevented by differing expectations. Some people feel too invaded or interfered with by others to relax into solitude.

> A man is driving through a snowy landscape. He lets the soft motion of the car lull him. He is relaxed, half-dreaming and half-thinking, withdrawn into himself. He is happy to feel his partner near him without having to think about her. But she is anxious about his silence, which she understands as an expression of withdrawal, embarrassment or refusal. Moveover, she would like to take advantage of the moment and continue an earlier conversation. She would like to tell him at last what has been in her heart since yesterday, and to hear him say how he felt. She may break the silence with a reproachful, anxious or expectant: 'You're not saying anything?'

Free communication rests on the acceptance and pleasure of leading two lives: one with others and the other our own, in which we are emotionally self-sufficient.

'Not saying' is sometimes grounded in a capacity for mental isolation, an ability to be immersed in our own secret world. Then we can share the completeness of solitude with others.

Listening

*For the whole of a man's life among his fellow men is nothing else than
a fight to be listened to.*
Milan Kundera

It is difficult to listen to someone without taking his or her words
and reacting to them. True listening implies availability and focus
on the other person. To listen means welcoming what is
expressed without being judgemental while trying to understand
the other person's inner world in terms of his own system of
references.

Active listening means allowing the other person to say more
and to listen to himself while I repeat or summarize what he has
just said, what I heard or, at least, what I understood. It also
means suggesting open questions which cannot be answered by
yes or no but perhaps asking *how* instead of *why*, which helps the
other person to focus on himself. 'And you? How did you feel
about it? What did you experience?'

We usually ask questions that induce answers: 'Didn't you find
that unfair?'; 'Why don't you leave him?'

Reacting

'My boss made an unpleasant remark to me . . .'
'Oh! you know what he's like! He'll never change.'

'I feel discouraged and weary tonight . . .'
'Of course you do. It's so hot.'

To listen, I must first keep silent and stop reacting because
reacting is the first obstacle to listening. If I feel moved by what
the other person says, I will want to express myself, explain,
convince, be judgemental, tell about my feelings or ideas. The
closer the other person is to me, the stronger the reactions
aroused by his words will be. If he/she is talking about his

relationship to me, my listening will be hindered all the more by my fears, wishes or projections, and by the way his words resonate in me. It is what makes intimate communication so difficult and so fragile. Each word of the other person may reactivate fear of not being up to it, of being rejected and of not being loved. To listen means, at least for a while, to give up answering and grabbing what the other person said only to express my own opinion. An example might be if someone is telling me that he did not like a book and instead of listening to what he disliked, or what may have hurt him, I take up the topic to elaborate on my own enthusiasm for the book.

Allow room for the other person's experience before telling your own.

Dialogue

Simultaneous expression on the part of both speakers is impossible, there can only be alternate listening. But a good many dialogues look like fights to be the first one to be listened to.

'For the last few years I've started talking to my mother again . . .'
'Oh! that's impossible with mine; she never listens to me . . .'
'I saw her yesterday and we talked about our beliefs.'
'It's easier with my father.'

In this example, each person is hoping the other will pay attention and listen.

We ourselves may often have to accept responsibility for not feeling listened to and heard. Sometimes we do not express ourselves clearly or directly enough, hoping that the other will guess. Perhaps we do not dare say what we want clearly like: 'I would like to talk to you'; 'I would like you to listen to me'; 'I would like to tell you about my experience'.

Somewhere inside we all want to be able to talk about

ourselves without being judged, taken over, reassured, rejected or labelled. Everybody just wants to be listened to so as to listen to himself better.

Listening is a beautiful gift to offer, to ask for and to receive.

Hearing

In order to hear, we need to empathize with the other person and listen to how he is speaking.

We should hear what the other person is saying and also pay attention to his smiles, look, gestures, breathing, acts, pain, energy. Hearing is a matter of attention, of being able to pay attention and wait. Moreover the quality of a relationship is perceptible in the active availability of both partners as manifested through minute signs: a certain way of looking, relaxed breathing, an inviting gesture, a silence that bids the other one go further.

Hearing means going beyond listening to catch the essentials.

- At which level is the other person speaking?
- Is it a realistic, symbolic or imaginary level?
- Is it a mental, emotional or anecdotal level?

If we really want to hear the other person, not only do we have to hear them at the level at which he or she is speaking, but we also have to understand that this level may hide another one. We have to go beyond 'screen words' and discover the real words which are like a spring that surges up after a long subterranean journey. To be able to hear fully, we have to understand what is said, not always at the level at which it is said but *at the level on which the words arise.*

Conversely, if the other person is talking about his imaginary world and I hear him at a realistic level, then I have misunderstood him. Such a misunderstanding is a frequent cause of frustrations and sufferings.

> When I tell her: 'I feel like taking a sabbatical' and she answers: 'But how are we going to pay the rent?', I do not feel understood at my imaginary level.

> When a woman who has been living with a vasectomized man for several years softly whispers one evening: 'I would like you to give me a baby', her wish to have a baby and all her imaginary world about playing mother want to be heard. His answer: 'You know very well that I can't have children anymore' comes from the plane of his reality and will not make her feel understood.

Imagination helps to deal with the distortion between outer reality and our inner world of wishes and ideals. Parents often desperately try to curtail their children's imaginary world.

> 'If I find the treasure in the cave, I'll buy a plane.'
> 'You know very well there's no treasure. What would you do with a plane?'

When caught in their emotions, children – and former children – do not hear rational arguments. They hear only that they are not understood.

If the other person is talking at the level of thoughts, if he is trying to clarify an idea or a concept and if I only hear the emotional aspect, I do not understand him. He may also be trying to express his emotional experience under cover of a generalization. If I pursue the idea at a mental level, I do not understand him either. If he is telling me about his physical ailments, should I hear him at the level at which he is talking? Should I understand that psychosomatic illnesses are a symbolic language and devote my interest to the meaning they have in his story? 'I've got backache', he says, and I think that it may mean 'I'm sick and tired of . . .' Shall I invite him to change levels or shall I stick to the level he has chosen?

For hearing also means understanding, on the one hand, the chord that has been struck in me and, on the other hand,

the meaning I attribute to the message that reaches me. If he says
'I've got backache', the chord struck may be 'So have I' or 'I don't
want to hear him complaining'. The meaning will either be
centred on me: 'He is reproaching me about something. I weigh
on him' or on him: 'Does he have too much to bear? Is he asking
for a massage?'

Hearing does not mean answering. However, my answer will
show what I did or did not hear. Beyond my answer, the quality
of my *presence* will give strength to my listening. If I want to try
and improve the way I communicate, it is essential that I am able
to hear a request, a wish or a need without feeling that I have to
respond to it; it is essential that I am able to hear about a problem
without thinking that I ought to find a solution. I should simply
be able to hear and acknowledge that I have heard.

Sometimes it is also necessary to indicate to the other person
how I would like to be understood.

> 'I would like what I am saying today, at this precise moment, to be
> understood, but I do not want to be completely identified with what
> I express.'

Something like this would make it clear that I do not want my
words to be cast in stone.

'I hate my job!' I can shout when I feel fed up, discouraged and
overburdened with my everyday occupation. If the other person
then takes my exclamation too seriously and suggests a change of
profession or argues that I do really have a passion for this one,
then I might resent him, or afterwards be careful not to show the
fleeting moods that pass through me.

I would like to be understood without having to explain 'I'm
just feeling fed up, I'm only saying that to relieve myself of a
passing feeling.' All I want is really for the other person to say
something like: 'It's an awful job, much too tiring . . .' Or he/she
might share my dream of immediate holidays for a while, or pity
and comfort me with tenderness.

What I am saying at a precise moment is only one facet of an
immense complexity full of contradictions. What I am saying in

a necessary outpouring is only a minute part of me: 'Don't confine me in my words.'

> Someone said: 'I was born indignant, and my indignation is vital for me. Many people think I am always unsatisfied; I just need to moan to feel I exist.'

Feelings and sensations are related to the moment when I experience them. They are similar to the colours of a landscape that change according to the light.

> 'I don't like chocolate pudding,' claims the little girl who has just devoured three full bowls of chocolate pudding. 'I won't ever eat it again.'

The right listener might allow the little girl the range of weakness and enthusiasm. We all need to show ourselves as we are at that moment, but we only feel free to do so if the other person does not take the part for the whole and does not bring us back to our contradictions. We know them well enough and we have the right to express absolutely opposite ideas and feelings about the same topic. We like relationships in which we can be contradictory, unreasonable and absent-minded in what we say.

DISCREPANCIES

Sometimes words cannot act as a bridge between two people; sometimes words separate.

I feel hurt and not listened to when the expression of my feelings is met either by a value judgement or by rational logic. How many fears and wishes are met by 'shoulds': 'you should', 'you shouldn't', 'you should have', 'you shouldn't have'?

> 'I'm not good at finding my way; I'm not sure I'll be able to find again the cinema where we're supposed to meet . . .'
> 'But you should know where it is! We've already been there three times.'

Value systems have no hold on feelings. Sometimes they enable us to repress, hide or deny feelings but they do not suppress them. Does a jealous person become less jealous when he or she is told: 'You shouldn't be jealous'? Does a child feel his fear decrease when he is told: 'You're really stupid to be afraid of that'? All the same, the absence of judgement about feelings may seem unacceptable.

'After all, there is such a thing as objectivity. One person is right and the other is wrong. If I phone my ex-wife's house to talk to my daughter and my wife's boyfriend answers and hangs up the phone, he's in the wrong, not me!'

'She inflicts her parents on me but can't stand mine; she only thinks of herself. She was a spoilt brat, like all only daughters. Don't try and tell me it's fair!'

Rational logic does not shake emotional logic, it speaks a different language; they are irreconcilable.

'I'm afraid to go to the big school.'
'But there's no reason to be afraid. All the little boys of your age go. The teacher will be kind, you'll be glad to have friends . . .'

This well-intentioned mother has cut herself off from the dialogue started by her son; she has refused to understand. The child will have received this message: 'You're silly to be afraid without any valid reason; not only are you timid, you're also stupid.' We make these kinds of indirect comments every day, several times a day. We give stereotyped answers instead of stepping into a lively, actual and stimulating dialogue that might bring about changes.

These three levels – feelings, rational thoughts and value systems – exist in us without meeting each other. When they meet in communications, they produce numerous misunderstandings. They also create insoluble debates in our inner dialogues.

- Emotional level: 'I'm afraid of giving birth.'
- Logical level: 'There's no reason. Billions of women have done it. Statistics demonstrate that the risks are minimal in our countries.'
- Prescriptive level: 'It's childish and cowardly to panic like this. I should be calm and relaxed.'

Which level should I obey and be faithful to? To which level should I be unfaithful? How can some kind of unity be achieved? What a relief when there is neither opposition nor discrepancy between the diverse voices of feelings, thoughts and values:

- 'I don't love him anymore.'
- 'It isn't normal to go on living like strangers spending evenings without anything to say to each other. It's more sensible to split up.'
- 'It's important for me to be faithful to what I am today.'

So we long to recover a consistency and a sense of unity where there is no conflict between these different dimensions.

META-COMMUNICATION

To 'meta-communicate' means stepping aside from the content of a dialogue for a while to move on to the form, the way communication works or does not work. We can express our need to be listened to, and to ask for what we hope and expect.

> I think of telling my mother how I experienced an event which involved her. Of course she will react by justifying herself or talking about her own experience. But I need her to hear me first and I am going to ask her to listen and understand me.
> 'I need you to listen to me without interrupting, I need you to understand how I experienced this moment. My own experience may have nothing to do with the way you experienced it.'

A woman might say to her husband: 'I know that you don't like to talk about it, you don't like to go back over that situation. But all the same I need to tell you about my own experience – what I underwent fourteen years ago when you asked me to have an abortion and I agreed. It's true that I was helpless. I was afraid of my parents' standpoint on my sexual life, on our relationship. I was panic-stricken and I would have liked you to have taken more time then so that I could tell you all this.

I would have liked more support and, although I know that you were as lost as I was, I need to tell you this and above all I need you to understand. This is not an accusation but an attempt to overcome silence. I'm trying to put words to what was unspoken, to share my burden, my emotions and even the regret that still lives on in me. You see, I need this kind of understanding.'

Meta-communication is often needed to renew relationships that have gone wrong with our own parents.

A 38-year-old adult might say to his father: 'I don't find it easy to talk directly to you about what I'm experiencing today. The most important thing for me is to dare tell you, if you could only agree to listen, without answering, and without wanting to explain. I rely on your support and I ask you to accept without questioning or saying "I knew it would happen". If you only knew how much I dread this sentence. The worst thing is when you know for me; I feel so helpless then. Today I'm asking you not to know in advance, but rather to wait and hear what I'm going to tell you . . .'

COMMUNICATION WITH OURSELVES

Each step towards improving our communication with others will also lead us to question our relationship to ourselves. In this questioning, the first and never to be completed step will be to acknowledge what we are feeling just when we are experiencing it: pleasure or displeasure, sadness, anger or joy, happiness, love or despair. All these feelings are not as easy to identify as we might think because we have learnt to deny, hide and censor our feelings and emotions. Moreover emotions mix wildly together and intertwine so as to confuse our perceptions. My displeasure when I accompany a friend to a meeting that bores me will be mixed with the pleasure of pleasing him . . . Sadness is linked to the sweet happiness of letting my tears flow and letting myself go. Anger may produce the strong and pleasant feeling of existing, asserting myself or fighting.

We often delude ourselves about our real feelings. Anger, for instance, is first of all a signal: it tells me that there was an expectation followed by frustration or disappointment. Beyond anger, I may have to deal with the initial expectation.

'Did I expect something impossible, unattainable?'

'Do I expect too much from the other person? Do I expect him to fulfil me, to calm me, to understand me . . .?'

To give up this expectation, this impossible hope, would prevent me from experiencing a feeling of injustice and deprivation. Giving up does not deprive me because deprivation is precisely related to not giving up. When I give up an expectation, I only deprive myself of the frustration.

To be as close as possible to my real feelings and to listen to the feelings that flow in me will require a lot of attention and careful awareness.

I have a vague feeling of guilt lingering in me as I go out for a beautiful Sunday's skiing. Where does it come from? Of course, my mother had suggested that I visit her this Sunday! I discover that most of the time my guilt feeling does not come from what I have done as much as from what I have not done, what I should have done, been, felt or said.

Such thoughts as 'I could have', 'I should have' are infinite, inexhaustible.

Acknowledging my real feelings helps me to be more in harmony with myself. It makes me feel that I can rely on myself. It also enables me to be more consistent in my behaviour and in my attitude towards other people.

In the following chapters, we will suggest some ideas that will

'I should be working instead of wasting my time skiing ...'

pave the way to more open and lively communication and help
create healthy relationships.

**Lifting the stone of vengeful fury, we discover lacks, griefs,
wounded or ill-treated loves, feelings of failure . . . and many other
shoots that have been crushed or slumber in darkness. Close by are
also to be found the seeds of future flowers, and the as yet hidden
sun of a morrow that is drawing near.**

2   Relationships

Making the present come alive with laughter will help us to truly meet each other.

Having dealt with communication, we must now investigate what a relationship is, that is to say the fact of being linked and attached by emotional ties. Actually we hardly know what our relationships are made up of. We often confuse them with the feelings we experience for someone. This confusion between feelings and relationships is fairly frequent.

In our training sessions, we often suggest making a distinction between feelings and relationships. This helps us to recognize and accept the feelings we experience for someone and to define what is acceptable and not acceptable in a relationship. Too often, we tolerate intolerable, unbearable or alienating relationships in the name (or under the pretext) of feelings.

The level of feelings differs from that of relationships, in spite of their obvious correlation. For instance:

> 'I feel a lot of love and tenderness towards my adolescent son and yet I have a difficult, impossible and hateful relationship with him.'

> 'I love my spouse dearly and yet I communicate worse with him than with anyone else.'

We have to assert our position more clearly on these two levels.

> 'My love for you remains whole and is not called into question, but my relationship with you is too painful or unbearable. I need to make some space . . .'

Based on attractions and repulsions, affinities and incompatibilities, feelings do not help us to find and keep the right distance between fusion and differentiation.

LINKING

We establish personal ties so that we will not float around too much on the uncertain sea of life, at the bounds of an incomprehensible universe. Our ties are grounded in our inner world of wishes, lacks, fears, needs and expectations. All these appear so confused that it is usually impossible to understand what is truly at stake in a bond. All we can see is that it is a living organism that comes to life, develops, dissolves and retains its mystery. It can be wounded, well or unwell, or fade away. However, a seemingly dying link does not disappear altogether; it subsides and comes to rest in the memories or in the unconscious on which it has left its mark. The good things others have given us will build in us many foundations and anchors for life's adventures.

A link is a living organism, a subtle structure that requires a lot of energy and information. It acts as a sort of third party between two or more people. Each person looks after one aspect of the relationship and nourishes it.

The link may be called our love, our friendship, our relationship, our attachment, our group . . . If we take the example of marital life, we notice that the whole story of the couple's relationship lies in the difficulty of moving from being *one* (union/fusion) to being *two* (being differentiated in a 'we') and then being *three* (she + he + the relationship that links).

One 'I' + one 'I' do not just make two but also make three for they become a 'we', which does not mean fusion but the expression of a differentiated whole made up of the two 'I's of the relationship brought together by a link.

Be it fiction, metaphor or mysterious vibratory substance, this unit will take on a life of its own, like a being in its own right, an objectivized being.

'The nature of our love has changed.'

'Our relationship was meant to last for ever.'

'The quality of our relationship deserved attention and choices, but you mistreated it by spreading your energies all around the place.'

'Our love was unique; few women were loved as I was.'

The relationship sometimes devours individuals. We have seen people who were completely alienated, not by another person, but by a relationship which required unbelievably complex care, preoccupations, rituals and attention.

'Family union is more important than the individual interests of each member. Christmas gatherings are a burden to everyone, but if we don't keep them up, the family feeling will be lost.'

The working of the system seems to take precedence over people's needs and wishes.

'It's not a question of looking for what you or I want. Our marital relationship must be successful at all costs.'

When only one partner puts energy into nourishing a link which is not reciprocated, the 'we' is usurped.

A woman recounts the amazing devotion and absolute self-denial she developed towards he husband: 'I paid for his studies. I helped him financially to set himself up as self-employed. I never took a holiday. I acted as a mediator between his mother and him. Now he has suddenly left me in a state of need. But I'll do everything I can to save our love.'

What the woman calls 'our love' seems to be an imaginary construction, a kind of inner motto which she cannot bring herself to call 'my love for this man'. This love is all that is left to face her husband's twofold guilt: the guilt of owing her everything and the guilt of leaving her.

On the other hand we have noticed that many people give little significance to the link itself. This is particularly true in some couples where the concrete commitment of marriage or living together seems to be enough to keep the relationship going. In such instances, the relationship, given neither care nor nourishment, deteriorates. We need only look around us to see that sometimes only the shape, envelope or institutional appearance of certain marital or parental relationships remain: the actual core of the relationship is empty.

Both in therapy and in training sessions we have started to consider the relationship as a third party that has its own needs, demands and changes. If a relationship is important, we must take care of it, respect it and do something for it (and not only for ourselves or for the other person). Therefore, when involved in a relationship, we can question our own ability to take care of it and revitalize it.

In this connection, we know that every living organism produces waste, exudes residues. If a relationship is alive, precisely because it is alive, it will also produce waste: we call this 'pollution in relationships'. If we do not take the pollution into account (and the means of evacuating it), it will clutter up the relationship which, like a blocked pipe, will not let anything through, whatever the intentions and good will of the protagonists.

So we sometimes see people who are deeply committed and attached to each other but who are unable to remain linked in a 'tolerable' way because they cannot 'share' anymore; the 'pipes' of their relationship are either too clogged up or too porous to let anything pass from one partner to the other.

> 'I love him, but so many resentments, small misunderstandings, fleeting humiliations and unspoken words prevent me from accepting him altogether. My tenderness for him is mixed with repressed anger.'

Nothing is more difficult than to agree on a definition of a close relationship, on a shared description of this third object born of two individuals, which seems to have its own existence and power but cannot be separated from its creators.

However, in some instances, the relationship seems to fill up the whole space, leading an autonomous life, independent of its protagonists, whose activity is entirely reduced to 'feeding' the relationship, like a mythical object.

What induces us to become linked, attached and at times to lose touch with ourselves, to commit ourselves blindly or to free ourselves from a relationship which once seemed vital and essential? Looking at what is common to all relationships, we discover a very complex combination of four simple positions:

- giving;
- receiving;
- asking;
- refusing.

The numerous interactions of these elements develop into a more or less stable pattern of relationship between two individuals, or in family or social relationships. Actually we find these four positions in every relationship, from the most intimate to the most functional (professional, social), from the most fleeting to the most lasting. To shed some light on how we stand in any relationship, we can question our resources and deficiencies in each of these four positions.

Giving

I believe that giving love is essentially paying close attention to the other person and to oneself.

Few words are as equivocal and misleading as 'giving'. The word only derives its meaning from its object: what do I give? I can give kicks as well as solicitude, worries, orders or attention. I can give or give off my own negativity, anxieties and fears, all the things I feel that are 'not good' and which I often try to dump . . . onto others. For instance, after some phone calls we feel we have been used as little more than a dumping ground.

When I am lucid and aware, I can discover what lies beneath my good intentions: some of my gifts are disguised requests and refusals.

Giving what I would like to be given

I do to others what I would like them to do to me. I start with the idea that the other person has the same wishes, needs and tastes as myself. One of the most obvious traps in any relationship lies in the temptation to deny differences.

> 'My mother seemed indifferent and distant; she never asked what I was doing or experiencing. Now I love it when people ask me questions and show an interest in me, the more so as I find it difficult to express myself spontaneously. I like to be welcomed by such words as "How was your day?" or "What did you do this afternoon?"
>
> Knowing how good it feels to be welcomed in this way, I question my husband when he comes home. I ask him about his day. But he never asks *me* any questions. He seems indifferent to me, as my mother was.'
>
> As for the husband, he says: 'I had an intrusive mother. She was constantly asking me questions; I always seemed to owe her an explanation. Now I don't like questions, I find them indiscreet and disturbing, therefore I never ask my wife any questions so as not to appear to be controlling her freedom. I would like her to behave with me the way I behave with her.'

Each partner has managed to find the climate of his or her childhood: both complain and, out of good faith, they each offer the other what they consciously want for themselves.

Let us emphasize here the idea of 'good faith'. In love relationships we often see men and women offer each other harmful gifts, simply out of 'good faith', without any malice or aggressive intention. A similar process occurs in parental and sibling relationships. Good intentions fall short only because of the deafness and blindness of both parties: the one who does not listen as well as the one who does not express himself or herself clearly.

> 'I must have told my sister a hundred times that I hate sponge cakes. And what does she bring every time she visits me? Sponge cakes . . . and she goes on regardless to tell me that she tried them out beforehand in some new cake shop she has discovered.'

A man told us – he had not told his partner – how guilty he felt about having had less desire for her for some time. That very evening, he touched his girlfriend in a sexual way: 'I wanted to give her some pleasure.' She pushed him away and burst into tears. It was only the following day that she managed to tell him: 'You don't understand anything, you think I want sex. I just wanted to talk to you and I wanted you to talk to me, too. With so much silence between us, I can't feel any desire.'

Giving to get

Much of what is believed to be giving is in fact a form of demand. For instance, parents think they are taking care of their children when they give them a series of orders. 'Put your cap on. Don't bite your nails. Do your homework before playing. Kiss me. Listen to me when I'm talking to you. Lend your toys to your brother.' What are these parents giving their children?

By saying this, we run the risk of shocking or hurting many parents. Yet nowadays children have little space for receiving as they are taken up with endless demands or requests, often seen as signs of attention or parental intervention. Also children are invested with many expectations which they cannot always meet. In this way misunderstandings are produced in an endless circle of 'expectation–request–frustration'. Parents are convinced that they are giving time, attention and concern, but children receive these as yet more demands.

This is also true in couples. Many women say that they receive their partner's cuddles or tenderness as sexual requests. Some even add: 'I don't have time to give him anything . . . he's already taken it.'

Requests for approval or for confirmation of our self-worth underlie most of our gifts. We need to feel we are a good mother, a good husband, a thoughtful godmother, a generous friend. So we offer presents, give food, lend money, and are careful of others so as to live up to this good image. We try to increase our sense of self-worth by giving what we have, or what we are. Sometimes children steal so as to have the pleasure of giving . . . and of being recognized.

It is as if what the other person gives us is actually less important than what he does not give. We are more aware of being deprived than of receiving.

Giving to equalize

I hate feeling that I am in debt, so I return what has been offered to me: an invitation, a present ('He remembered my birthday, so I should remember his'), a compliment.

The need to return is part of the difficulty of receiving; it may also be a way of refusing. Children sometimes throw up the food that their mother has given or imposed on them. Similarly, a pleasure that has been received can be returned by imposing pleasure on the other person!

To give can also lead to putting other people in your debt, and keeping them in a state of dependence.

'When my daughter decided to become independent, I helped her a lot,' tells a father. 'I bought her furniture. I found her a flat. I gave her a car.'

'When he went to live with another woman, he left me everything: house, furniture, books, records. Only years later did I understand how all this had kept me in a state of dependence. I wasn't in my own house, I was in his house. One day, I sold everything. It was then that I really separated from him, from his shadow and his presence.'

It is when we deprive ourselves so as to give something that we put others most in our debt.

'All the things I sacrificed for my children . . .'

'All the things I gave up to marry you . . .'

'I sold my boat and bought this house that you wanted so much, and now you want us to move to another area to be nearer to your mother, because she's alone . . .'

Giving and offering

We have all heard or said in the playground during our childhood:

'To give is to give; to take back is to steal.'

'I offered her a record of Mozart and, two weeks later, I asked her if she had listened to my record. . . My record!'

If I really give something, I must completely forget about it; not record it in a secret account. As the word indicates, a present only exists in the present. To give is to give freely, without any expectations, any kind of self-interest. It is spontaneous, which means that it comes from my innermost being, be it received or not. It is a total offering, as when the flower gives its fragrance or the sun its warmth, without depriving themselves of anything.

A true gift is an offering which is free of demands. A gift that comes with conditions is a deal, an exchange. We all long for unexpected presents. What we then receive deep within is the happy laughter of the person who offers and gives his innermost being.

Receiving

In long-term or short-term relationships, there are many levels at which we often find it difficult to receive. It is as if we oppose other people's propositions and impulses by refusing, by being unreceptive or reluctant, or by misinterpreting intentions. We react as if we were 'crippled' and unable to receive.

This may affect areas as different as receiving, approval, expressions of interest, presents or declarations of love, or even when we are asked to call into question certain aspects of our lives.

Receiving approval

Compliments, praise, signs of love or admiration could satisfy our need for recognition. But often in the course of a conversation, our first impulse is to reject or minimize them.

'You're wearing a nice dress.'
'It's the third time I've worn it!'

The person who pays the compliment is rejected, or even accused (of not having noticed the dress earlier).

'I really enjoyed the talk you gave this morning.'
'I didn't develop the third point enough.'

What is this mechanism? We denigrate both ourselves and the other person's impulse. When a present is not well received, the giver feels hurt. He is reminded of his own inadequacy, of his helplessness or solitude.

Is the way we look at ourselves so severe and demanding that, in the name of perfection or of an absolute ideal, we cannot acknowledge our own reality?

'Your eyes are beautiful today.'
'Aren't they on other days?'

'I like this blouse. It suits you particularly well.'
'Oh, I bought it in the sales.'

Our search for absolute love can sometimes make us reject what is on offer because it does not fulfil our ideal. False modesty can sometimes betray an ideal image of ourselves to which we do not correspond.

Receiving refusals, being called into question

Refusals seem as difficult to receive as approval. Yet they could awaken us, stimulate us, and open the door to discoveries.

'Our son doesn't really seem to have understood your position about his going out. In my opinion it isn't clear . . .'

'Don't interfere! I know what I have to tell my son!'

Sometimes the best present others can give is precisely to call us into question. 'A true friend is a friend who tells you that you have bad breath. Other friends leave you smelling bad.' Our reflection in someone else's eyes can question us, sow seeds, and initiate a process of change.

When you look at me, I exist more fully and grow. Other possibilities open up.

Instead of feeling like losers, we could feel like winners when someone takes the trouble of questioning us, offering a criticism, a different point of view, or making a remark: 'I don't share your point of view on . . .', 'I've got a different perspective . . .'

Receiving new ideas and unexpected propositions

Our first reaction is often defensive. We cling to what we have and know, and summon up our forces of resistance. Receiving something new means risking change, risking a transformation, however minimal, and human beings have a great fear of transformation. Being open to other people's influence jeopardizes our fixed identity, our familiar references and sometimes our priorities.

Receiving expressions of interest

'Have you changed your hairstyle?'

'How is your daughter?'

'You look tired.'

We may feel that such comments threaten our need for distance, reserve and private space. Our great fear of intrusion will make us look away or answer evasively so as to break off the conversation or refuse the invitation. Many people do not want to receive. They prefer to give again and again. It seems easier.

By giving . . . I keep people away from my own needs.

Receiving can arouse the fear of being dependent and indebted.

'If the other person does too much (for me), then I owe him something . . .'

To receive reawakens the fear of 'not deserving'.

'Each time he offers me something, I feel that he's wrong, that he hasn't really seen who I am, that I don't deserve so much attention. My discomfort is so great that I don't even know how to express my gratitude. In fact I can't feel any gratitude when I am embarrassed by his presents.'

Receiving objects

Objects will also arouse fears: I shall owe something, I shall have to give something back in return. And giving in return is precisely a way of not receiving.

'I've received an invitation from the X's . . . I shall have to return the invitation!'

A gift of an object can represent a kind of intrusion. Part of the other person will enter into my private space, and, who knows, may disturb my familiar images.

'He gave me this statuette. It's here, on the bookshelf. He has put a part of himself in my home.'

'She gave me this book. I'll have to read it, but I'm not interested in this topic at the moment.'

'She has a hold on my appearance because of this tie she chose. I'm wearing something of her . . .'

Receiving is a double-edged process which brings fruitful openness but also involves a risk of intrusion and penetration into our private world. Receiving means taking the risk of being influenced and therefore of changing.

Receiving means opening up, letting go, welcoming and keeping. It means unleashing an anxious tension that reveals an effort to keep control, to protect our integrity under whatever pretext.

'I don't deserve . . .'

'I want to do it myself.'

'I don't want to owe anyone anything.'

To receive gracefully we have to find a delicate balance between allowing ourselves to be open and maintaining control, protecting ourselves. The more differentiated and 'centred' as individuals we are, the more able we will be to receive without becoming alienated from ourselves.

Receiving freely

Resentment is the ruthless enemy of receiving.

'I've had too many disappointments to be able to receive what he's offering now.'

How many caresses, and how much love and attention gets lost, because they cannot be received!

It is empathy with the other person's wish that enables us to really receive what is being offered.

'For instance, you suggest going to the cinema and the movie which is showing is the one I wanted to see with you tonight. My wish may not have been expressed before your suggestion, but I let it be awakened, revealed or created by it.'

We can receive two kinds of gifts:

- those which answer a consciously felt wish: a little boy wanted a car operated by remote control and got it;
- those which awaken a wish, a potential or an unsuspected interest: 'I never thought I could become so interested in Native American beliefs before you took me to this lecture.'

Therefore, we can only receive what is in line with our conscious or unconscious wish, with a more or less buried wish. Giving and receiving can merge when such concordance exists.

A fully received gift also gratifies the giver.

When we receive, we can also amplify what has been given. Have you ever felt this while listening to an aria? The voice ventures out in search of the music, rushes out and rises up. Your whole body, your sensitivity and your wonder amplify it, and prolong its vibrations in all the unlocked recesses of your memory.

The emotion of certain encounters, the intensity of certain exchanges takes root and germinates. A time of receiving begins.

Asking

Each one of us has many requests of himself or others. These requests may be linked or compete with each other. They may be expressed or unexpressed, clear or confused. And yet, these numerous requests require listening, attention and sometimes gratification.

Asking means running the double risk:

- of meeting a refusal;
- of being satisfied.

In the following chapter we shall look at the various forms our requests may take when they are mingled with fears, wishes, needs and lacks.

Quite often in a relationship, we do not know whether we are giving, asking, responding to a request or receiving. Nor do we know what the other person's view of our conversation is. All kinds of misunderstandings can occur.

> 'I am talking about my experience. I share it. I reveal myself. I have the impression that I'm giving my innermost being. The listener is a bit bored and thinks that he's giving by paying attention to me.'

> He wants to please his mother and offers to take her to see an exhibition. She does not feel like it but interprets his offer as a request and does not dare refuse . . . so as to please him.

> 'Is this caress a gift? Can I be happy and relaxed, or should I consider it as a request?'

Approval lights up a face, refusal gives it beauty.
René Char

The most fearful requests for the person who receives them are those which directly or indirectly aim at making him feel guilty. Such requests are frequently heard from parents.

> 'Your brother wants to invite me for the Christmas holidays, but I don't know what to do this summer . . . it's so hard staying on your own when everyone else has gone away!'

Neither words nor actions can be considered as gifts or requests in their own right. This depends on the context, on the relationship in which they appear, and on the present situation. Moreover it depends on each person's lacks, wishes, needs or absence of wishes.

> When a young man is in love with a girl who does not share his feelings and offers her a trip to Italy, the offer will look like a request. If she accepts, will the trip be a gift that is accepted or given?

On the doorstep, a 50-year-old executive 'receives' a ten pound note as his mother says goodbye to him. The mother is anxious that 'he won't lack anything' on his way home. By accepting this gift of love, he is the one who gives her a marvellous present.

Any request will be more readily understood in relationships if it is turned into some kind of concrete proposal.

'I want to talk to you about our collaboration and I suggest that we have lunch together on Wednesday.'

Making an acceptable proposal involves:

- not trying to control ('I make you listen by speaking to you whenever I want to');
- not making it into a command ('I must talk to you!');
- avoiding complaints ('You've never got time to listen to me');
- not leaving yourself dependent ('Tell me how I can get you to listen to me').

The person who receives a proposal can then either simply accept or refuse. Too often, requests are demands that do not leave any choice, and trigger discomfort in the person who receives them. We can all learn to ask freely, with a kind of relaxed ease, as an invitation or as a proposal of something that is possible.

We can dare to ask in a way which leaves it open for the other person to say yes or no.

Refusing

The more pain we attach to receiving a refusal, the more difficult it will be to say a clear no to a request or proposal. Many irrational beliefs surround the act of refusing: it may destroy the other person, damage the relationship, provoke aggression or massive rejection. However, in all relationships clear refusals could be important indications. Because, for want of these, people put up fences, erect walls of silent refusals and barriers of secret fears.

We might thus come to avoid certain people for fear that they will make requests, for fear of feeling obliged to do what we don't want to do. A general indirect and disguised refusal will then replace the localized and precise refusal we have not been able to utter.

There are three types of refusals.

- a refusal of some action that another person asks us to undertake;
- a refusal to accept feelings that arise from what others say or do;
- a refusal prompted by fear of the consequences, which may involve repression or patterns of self-deprivation or, on the contrary, may demonstrate our own freedom of choice.

So many actions are done grudgingly, dragging our feet or even sabotaging, for want of being able to refuse or express annoyance.

'Do you mind driving me to the station?'

'No, I don't . . .', and I sigh as I put my book down. I would have felt more comfortable if I had answered: 'Yes, I do mind, I've just sat down to read, but I'll drive you to please you.'

It is even more difficult to express refusal when people throw their anger, despair or helplessness at us and try to make us feel responsible for them.

'You didn't do anything to help me.'

'You didn't understand.'

'You weren't here, so . . .'

'Your sister came to see me last Sunday. As for you, I haven't seen you for at least three weeks.'

We risk letting a feeling of guilt or inadequacy get hold of us instead of giving back to the other person what belongs to him – his anger, his failure, his passivity. A lot of time, personal clarification and courage are often necessary to know how to formulate clear and structured, though maybe hurtful, answers.

'I don't feel responsible for your suffering.'

'I realize that you're angry, but I can't feel guilty about not having the feelings you want from me.'

'I understand that you're disappointed, but these are my limits.'

'Your threat to commit suicide belongs to you. I can't do anything about it.'

It will thus be possible to return to the other person messages that do not belong to us.

'I sometimes return a letter to its sender, or at least the part of the letter where I strongly feel that the other person's projections do not concern me. I do the same with letters in which I feel imprisoned and "polluted" by words.

I've discovered that I don't need to keep what isn't good for me. There is no need to make myself suffer by holding on to the other person's negative thoughts or violent feelings.

Over the last few years I have also been able to return phone calls whose obvious aim was to make me feel guilty or to denigrate me.'

'I learned to say yes by daring to say no. It took me ages to discover that I could answer "no".

Saying no meant being bad, nasty, unlovable, impossible to love. And I wanted to please the other person at all costs, to fulfil him and to show him how important he was for me.'

Through refusing, through saying no, I open the door to differentiation and thus assert myself as unique and responsible.

'I'm the only one who knows what I feel.'

'No, I didn't like the film. Some scenes were very beautiful, but the whole thing seemed confused and melodramatic.'

'I don't feel the same as you about your mother. I like her firmness and clarity; you can't get confused with her. Her outlook on life suits me . . . but I understand that it's different for you.'

It is not easy to distinguish in our behaviour between refusals meaning opposition and refusals meaning self-assertion. A refusal should be more than just a reaction and should be meaningful in the relationship.

When I say no to someone, I say yes to myself.

TOWARDS A POSSIBLE BALANCE

We consider a relationship to be balanced and healthy when these four polarities exist, and when each person accepts that they can ask, refuse, receive and give.

The majority of couple or parental relationships are mostly made up of mutual requests or demands. We are convinced that we are giving while we are actually asking! To balance a relationship requires flexibility and fluidity.

We should create our lives with the best in ourselves. The quality of our presence to others and to the world can be used to communicate better and to communicate about ourselves.

3   Wishes, Requests, Needs and Lacks

We enter into each relationship with our wishes, fears and needs on a background of what we lack. But we also bring into it our resources, intuition, interests and impulses. Sometimes we even bring an amazing ability to create the unexpected, to introduce surprise in our certainties, and to weave dreams into reality.

We have the fantastic power, as man or woman, to make life richer and more meaningful and to extend it to the bounds of the universe. How? Just by taking part in the communication networks that dwell in us or pass through us.

We have to handle all this unwittingly, preferably without thinking, reflecting or analysing. We can manage this by initiating a more intimate communication with ourselves as well as with others. Alas! The myth of spontaneity in relationships often leads to a sort of blindness that triggers off discomfort and suffering.

In this book, we want to signpost a way that would help us to live more freely, avoiding both blindness and over-analytical lucidity and yet being vigilant enough not to stagnate. For life is movement: the eagle's flight across the sky, the tiny steps of an old lady on a pedestrian crossing. It is a long journey from a baby's first steps towards his mother's outstretched arms to the raised fist of a successful politician on polling day.

WISHES

We tend to confuse a wish with its realization. This prevents us from recognizing and dealing with our own wishes and makes us intolerant to those of others.

'When I grow up, I'm going to marry Mummy …'

A mother is talking about her nine-year-old child: 'I don't understand, David keeps talking about a house where we would live together, the three of us, although his father and I have been divorced for five years. Doesn't he understand that we are separated?'

David certainly understands, especially if it was explained clearly to him, but he still wishes to bring his parents together, regardless of the reality.

What happens to an unfulfilled wish? It goes its own way, far from answers and constraints, sometimes so far it becomes pure spirit. What about a wish that has not been heard? It never dies. It escapes all traps, bypasses all obstacles, and interferes with our slightest thought. It goes on leading its wish life, and becomes either creation or madness.

Every wish has the right to exist as a wish, however unlikely it is to be realized. Though very often, parents in particular try to annihilate those of their children's wishes which they cannot satisfy.

'I can't bear to hear my sons say they would like to live in a house that belonged to us, because I can't afford to buy one. I've asked them to stop thinking about it.'

The father could have suggested to his children that they describe, draw and tell him about their imaginary house. This evocation of their unrealizable wish would have brought him closer to them. But children's wishes hurt parents for they are afraid of feeling inadequate; so they try to suppress such wishes rather than frustrate them or even simply listen to and recognize them.

'My daughter always has impossible wishes. They shock me because I can't fulfil them. I want to strangle her when I hear another one of her fancies.'

Confident in our own power, we retain a kind of infantile omnipotence. To satisfy wishes gives us a means of control, but when we cannot control, we can become tyrannical and violent.

'I want to satisfy his wishes, therefore I won't allow him to express wishes that I can't fulfil; I won't even let him feel them.'

'You must only feel wishes that I can satisfy, that is to say control.'

An unsatisfied wish is experienced more peacefully and less crazily if it is recognized. Of course frustration does not disappear, but the dialogue can be more real.

A wish that is expressed is not necessarily a request; it is a wish of the present moment, which may not want to be trapped into a realization.

'When I grow up I want to be a clown!' exclaims a little girl, very happy with the funny faces she has just discovered. Very anxious not to bully his daughter as he himself was bullied in his childhood, the father immediately says, very seriously: 'Alright, I know a school for clowns. I'll find out what age you can go there and how you have to prepare for it.'

The little girl becomes gloomy and stops her pirouettes: will she *have* to become a clown?

'Now what shall I do! I only said I wanted it, but he's taken my wish seriously.'

Parents and adults often jump at wishes expressed by children, misinterpret them by treating them as requests and give totally inappropriate answers.

A little girl of 12, dazzled by her father's fluttering sleeves when he was preaching, said admiringly: 'I want to be a pastor when I grow up!' Her name was immediately entered for the Latin class. Years later, she was still having to fight to shake off this 'vocation'.

Desire: we use the same word for two different movements in the dynamics of a relationship with another person.

- If I feel a desire for the other person, it is an urge in me, a recognition, an emotion awakened by him or her, an inner movement which is sometimes shaped into 'I love you'. But we should remember love means surrendering rather than conquering, letting go rather than calculating and manipulating. If we do we can avoid the failure of Solal in Albert Cohen's novel *Belle du Seigneur*, who persistently tries to prove his love to 'get rid of the boredom of everyday life', but loses it, and ends up killing it by chasing one woman after another.

- If I feel a desire related to another person, I would like him or
  her to give me something – attention, care or consideration.
  This inner movement should really be expressed with the
  words 'Love me', but it too is often expressed in terms of 'I love
  you'. What I want is not the other person but his/her desire.

'I wanted to put my hand on his, but didn't do it, because I wasn't
sure that he would like it.'

This frequent confusion between desire for and desire related to
often leads to 'terrorism' in relationships. We shall explore some
aspects of this in chapter 9.

The person who answers 'So do I' to the 'I love you' said by the
other person dramatically short-circuits the offered impulse. He
does not welcome the other person's emotion, but in a way
returns it. He cancels it to leave room for his own emotion. Or
maybe he rightly understands that this 'I love you' means 'Love
me' and answers the implicit request. Or perhaps he understands
the question 'And you, do you love me?' that follows his 'I love
you' as an expression of fear and a violent desire to have the
love returned.

Children are very often invited to satisfy their parents' wishes
rather than respect their own, and perhaps even help to realize
them.

We do not agree with the conclusions of some sociologists who
think that the children of the last three or four decades were
spoilt. On the contrary, we think that childhood is often a time
of frustrations, a school of dense and closed 'uncommunication',
where awakening potentialities are permanently thwarted.

Family and educational systems that bring about a real
blossoming of resources and potential are few and far between.
Not only do we suppress future Mozarts, but also billions of Jules
Vernes, Thomas Edisons and so on. What will the survivors
become, lost in the swirl of time?

Where are you now, Chinese friend whom I saw on
Tian'anmen Square stopping 17 tanks with outstretched arms? I
want to meet you. And you, the woman in a diaphanous white

dress, for whom I felt an acute desire, and whom I followed for a whole day and lost in a museum in Florence?

Never forget your wishes, respect them as dear and precious friends.

Be it small or great, realistic or not, each wish deserves consideration. It deserves that we ask the question: 'What am I doing for my wish?'

Sometimes I can play with my wish, look at it and fulfil it in an imaginary or symbolic way. Or I can try to understand it better, listen to its message. I can ask:

- What is important for me in this wish?
- What part of me would be hurt if I did not get the answer I expect?
- What does this small and incongruous wish tell me?
- Which door does it open for me?
- Which path is it trying to show me?

Wishes that are strange and difficult to understand also go through our minds.

- the wish to suffer, to be ill;
- the wish to inflict pain on those we claim to love, to denigrate them and even to see them die.

In some instances we undertake action which would be a step towards the realization of a wish.

A father answered his ten-year-old son who wanted a horse with the question: 'What are you ready to do for your wish?' A few months later, the boy laid down a pair of gloves, a cap and a riding crop on his father's desk. He had invested all his savings in these first elements of his riding fantasy.

You are taking a powerful step when you ask: 'What are you ready to do for your wish?' If I am a young girl who wants above all to meet an interesting and cultivated man, I can take care of my wish by cultivating myself. If I am a man who wants to meet the woman of my dreams at all costs, then I should first of all enter into life . . .

Whatever its aim and object, my wish will be appeased or reinforced by any practical action I take towards it. I can sometimes gratify my wish slightly to pacify it, in the same way that I would send a down payment to a creditor so that he would not bother me again – for a while.

There is one overriding wish in the human heart: the wish to be happy. It can take on a thousand shapes. It can make use of a whole labyrinth of disguises. It can be present in many mistakes, or get lost in trial and error.

A wish is like a series of tensions that drives us to act and to annihilate it by gratifying it. Deep down inside us, we aspire to an absence of tension which we confuse with an absence of wish. When a wish has been fulfilled, we wish for something else – an endless chain of reactions. Some people invent symbolic mediations to deal with unrealizable wishes, be they their own or those of people they are close to.

Words, art, symbols or games can have their roots in unsatisfied desires.

A mother had established a ritual to help her young son deal more easily with separations: 'I have started a training course and I have to go away every month. At first my son resisted and made a scene when I had to go. I tried to explain to him the dates and times, where I was going and what I was doing. I thought that I was reassuring him but it didn't improve anything. I then bought a nest of Russian dolls. There were five of them fitting together. I kept two and gave him three, and we each wrote our names on them.

When I go away, I tell him: "Lend me your doll and I'll lend you mine." Sometimes I put sweets in the doll I lend him, and I put his on my bedside table at the hotel. He understands that sort of talk very well. It's easier for him to let me go now that his anxiety and frustrations will be relieved by playing and verbalizing his feelings through talking with the dolls. He told me about all kinds of games,

'I haven't lost you, Mummy, if I still have you in my Russian doll ...'

tender and aggressive, played out with "my doll", the one that symbolizes me during my absence. Talking about them, and naming the feelings related to them has a very liberating effect.'

Another woman, to calm down her husband's anxiety (and aggression), gave him a sort of security blanket each time she was away. 'I'll lend you my scarf, and I'll take it back when I return.'

Scarfs, handkerchiefs and all kinds of threads represent links that bridge together, over a period of absence, the moment of separation and the moment of reunion. Such moments are very important for both young and old.

A woman who was going through a difficult time of solitude and deprivation had sewn a small bag on which she had embroidered the words 'bag of wishes'. She wrote her wishes and frustrations on tiny pieces of cardboard and slipped them into the bag hanging in her kitchen. From time to time, she would look at its contents and throw away the pieces representing outdated, outmoded or satisfied wishes. She told us that this practice had helped her to distance herself from her sufferings and even laugh at them.

It is better to recognize a wish, to listen to it and protect it from possible mistreatments than to place it into someone else's hands.

Don't put your needs, and even less your wishes, into someone else's hands.

A man devised a kind of Ali Baba cave for his wishes. Each wish was symbolized by a single object that was linked to a story, an event or a relationship. 'On evenings when I had the blues, I opened the chest, sparkling with memories, and I was able to work through my nostalgia.'

The negation of wishes is more harmful than their frustration. To refuse to see, hear or recognize wishes in ourselves or in others, to repress, censor or even conceal them with fake detachment, may lead us to lying and alienation.

Every wish is associated with one or more fears which we also have to face.

'How do you make babies ...?'

Fear of frustration, disapproval and change overshadows our wishes.

'Many years later, I understood that I had got married to please my mother, but it did not satisfy my own wish for a different way of life.'

'I wanted to sit on my Dad's lap and, at the same time, I was afraid of doing so.'

'For years I lived with someone on suffrance, lacking everything. I didn't dare have any desires of my own, and in fact it would have seemed indecent to have requests under the circumstances.'

Those who succeed in burying or denying their wishes and needs, in the belief that it will somehow reduce the intensity of conflict, often look more dead than alive.

REQUESTS

Just as easily as we confuse a wish and its realization, we also confuse wishes with requests.

Requests directed to other people

One man said: 'I have an insatiable wish to be listened to, to be heard, understood, accepted, loved and helped. But I don't want to burden my wife with this immense desire so I turn it into polite requests. It's not the same. For instance, I ask her to give me half an hour or a moment of her attention.'

A wish mainly needs to be heard, a request requires a reply. To ask means to take a stand and for the other person to take one, be it acceptance, refusal or negotiation. Some people discover with surprise that they dare to make requests.

'This afternoon, I was able to tell a friend of mine, a doctor with whom I have a close relationship, that I would like to see him more often and that I wanted to share a project with him. He was happy about my request. I don't know if this project will lead to anything, but it was so important for me to be able to express it. I felt very lighthearted afterwards. I felt I had regained my confidence in him. It was a discovery which led to increased hope and confidence.'

To ask however does mean giving up that deep hope of receiving without asking, of being understood without needing to express ourselves.

'When I was dreaming of an imaginary husband, I always told myself that he would have to be kind. I think it meant that he should guess and meet my expectations without my having to formulate them. I realize now that it is impossible. I have resigned myself to communicating and asking. What a pity!'

Many people prefer to express their requests:

- by accusing;
- by complaining or making others feel guilty;
- by asking negative 'why' questions.

A request can be disguised as an accusation or blame. It is easier to say 'You're not listening to me' than 'Listen to me'. Innumerable attempts to communicate fail immediately because our first impulse is to denigrate the person of whom we would like to make a request.

A father, having problems with his adolescent son, now feels the need to at last begin talking to his own father. He decides to go and tell him about his experiences. He manages to meet him alone and presents his request to share experience in the following terms: 'You have never let me express myself and talk. I know you're going to tell me again that I'm stupid . . .'

It is a bad beginning. The father will in turn become defensive. He will justify himself, return the accusation and the requested conversation will get bogged down in mutual blame.

Requests disguised as complaints or psychosomatic illnesses are even more indirect and concealed.

'I feel useless and my headaches prevent me from doing anything.'

'Nowadays, people communicate less and less, and what they say is superficial. It's depressing.'

'I'm completely overwhelmed with work. I can't stand it any more. We don't even have time to talk to each other.'

'On Sundays, I'm exhausted. I don't feel like doing anything. She's just like me so we both have nothing to do and we kill time by staying in bed.'

'The best thing we've managed to do between us is to get rid of desire. We haven't been making demands on each other for years and it's better like that.' Yes, but at what cost!

How do you recognize the precise requests beneath these demands that dare not be said or even thought?

In everyday language, a useless 'why' question often stands for a request.

'Why don't we ever get on to this issue in our work meetings?'

'Why don't you say anything?'

'Why don't you take my advice?'

'Why haven't we been to the cinema lately?'

The 'why' question is a fake question above all others. It calls for justification and explanation, and buries any possible communication beneath empty talk and false answers. Many of us have been brought up to censor direct requests. Consequently we have learnt thousands of ways of expressing them in a concealed way.

When we want a request to be fulfilled, we must give ourselves the means:

- first, make sure it is heard;
- then, if it meets a positive answer, further it.

Let us consider the example of a marriage proposal! It is not enough to declare one's love and to set a date. We often forget there will be new discoveries and we must say:

- what we expect from this new situation;
- what we want to bring to sustain it;
- what we cannot tolerate (what is not negotiable), our limits, our constraints;
- our utopian ideals or at least the ideas that lie at the surface of our imaginary world.

The most difficult thing about certain requests is when the other person answers 'Yes'!

This is true of any request.

Sometimes, the most difficult thing is when the other person answers 'Yes'.

- If I phone, I must have something to say.
- If I ask for a meeting, I cannot turn up without bringing my resources and interests to sustain it.
- If I ask for help, I have to help the other person help me.
- If I ask for attention, I have to be able to accept it and sustain it.
- If I ask someone to switch the television off, I may have to be ready to make conversation.

The person who is making the request takes on a sometimes formidable responsibility. He is the one who is making a commitment.

> A man who was slightly afraid of his wife's reactions told us that he never took the initiative in sexual intercourse. 'This way,' he said, 'if it doesn't go well, she will only have herself to blame. I'm not the one who asked.'

Some people are skilful at making the other person be the one who asks. In this way they maintain a position that seems to reassure them. But then they sometimes complain that the other person is demanding too much.

Other people's requests

Often when people ask things I find it triggers off an inner conflict.

> 'My mother invites me for the week-end and I have another, more attractive, plan.'

> 'She asks me to bring flowers and this spoils the pleasure I would have had if it was my idea.'

An inner conflict is an unpleasant tension, hence my wish or even my request that the other person does not ask for what I do not feel like giving, or even that he or she does not want or expect it, because silent requests can be as burdensome as expressed ones.

'I feel like staying at home tonight. I hope my wife won't ask me to go with her to the cinema, because this would create a conflict in me.'

'I really don't want to spend ten days of the holiday at his parents' home. Let's hope they don't ask me like last year if it would make me happy! Too often they confuse my happiness with their expectations.'

Ideally, the other person's requests should fit in with what I can give: there should be some sort of miraculous coincidence between the request and the response.

'Our sexual life is a real issue between us, difficult to tackle without a lot of emotion. His desires are too strong for me. My desire vanished because there is no room for it. Anyway it's so much easier to pretend than to risk a quarrel or put up with his expression when I say no.'

Sexual requests are the ones that give the roughest time in some marital relationships. Because the request mainly entails asking for the other's desire: 'I want you to want just when I want . . .' Endless discrepancies, belated desires, competing cravings, everything is at work to make the encounter impossible. He will never express his fear of losing his erection or mention that getting older has always frightened him.

I become alienated by the other person's request because of the conflict it creates in me between my wish to answer and my refusal or inability to do so.

'Shall I give up an aspect of me, and believe that if I do I'll satisfy my wife's expectations?'

'He wants me to change and become the woman of his dreams, but I can't.'

Very often, the other person's request stimulates two antagonistic or contradictory aspects of ourselves. Trapped in the desire to satisfy and in the fear of not satisfying, we often have to balance our desire to satisfy and our fear of not satisfying. Otherwise, conflicts we don't want will crop up and cost us a lot of energy.

NEEDS AND LACKS

'I need . . .': what an ambiguous and hackneyed phrase covering so many different levels! Does it mean 'I want' or 'I feel a lack of', or 'It would help my development to . . .', or even 'I feel compelled . . .'? Beyond our physiological needs, what are our true needs?

I sometimes unconsciously change my wish into a need, which then demands urgent and pressing satisfaction.

> 'I need him, I can't do without him. If he left me, I wouldn't exist any more.'

This woman in love has enshrined this man into her life as the only possible way of filling a lack in herself. Of course, her choice has fallen on an inadequate object, which is reactivating and keeping open a weakness or wound from her past.

In our attempts to gratify our ill-differentiated needs, we often knock at the wrong door. We ask someone to give us what he does not have. We are like a customer who insists on having bread from the shoe repair shop. 'It's bread I need', we insist, and our anger rises against the shoe-mender who is not satisfying our immediate need. We perpetuate these dynamics in many relationships, asking with stubborn or fierce insistence for what the other person does not have (he might have it – but only for himself or someone else).

The link here is created by a lack – what he is not giving me – and it is this lack which ties me most to the other person. And in this way attempts to control the other person develop. But control has its cost. So what can be called 'the link created by the lack' persists. Disappointed hopes and unanswered expectations become the glue in many a relationship.

'Everything we haven't found or been able to achieve together attaches me to you more than our pleasures and encounters.'

'It's our failure to communicate which prevents me from separating from you. I'm searching over and over again for a way to reach you, to get in touch with you. I will not be able to leave you until I have achieved that.'

'I can't bear the idea that my father might die, because we never really talked to each other.'

The unspoken rigidifies family life. Silence binds people together. The most obsessive fixations are articulated around a lack that frantically seeks to be filled, and this desperate quest aggravates and solidifies a death-like dependence.

She clings to him like ivy and pretends to be nurturing him. He is addicted to drugs and drink. She is controlling him with her anxiety. Her own life is fading away. She wants to save him. He will give up alcohol and drugs for her; she will be unique; she will be the only one who has been able to help him.

Her life has acquired meaning and direction, and found an anchor. She seized the hook he threw and she cannot let it go. She is obsessed by him, permanently worried about him. It is like a taproot grown into her, that sucks up her marrow, her life, most of her energy. Because of him she is getting depressed and yet he is her antidepressant.

The link created by the lack is expressed by 'if' sentences that tell of the hell of vain and ever recurring hopes.

'If only he would talk.'

'If only she appeared to be more available . . .'

'If only I understood better what he wants . . .'

'If only I were more self-confident, more mature.'

'I would be so happy with you if you were not the way you are, or if I were not the way I am!'

We should briefly explain here that the concept of lack is used in psychology in reference to the past: painful experiences in our childhood leave rifts and fragile areas in us. Some of the fabric of the human condition is woven by the tragedies of separation, of loss or abandonment.

A lack is fundamental and cannot be filled; life gets organized with and around it.

When we transform a desire into a need, we are prey to the illusion that such a person, such a situation or such an achievement will erase our lacks.

> 'I would like you to give me all the love I never received from my mother, but I know I could never get that even if you tried to give it to me, because the lack is so great that it can never be filled.'

> 'If I get my degree, I shall at last become self-confident.' But the piece of paper obtained will never be good or big enough to hide the recurring lack.

> 'My feeling of emptiness would disappear if I had a child.'

But, in the last example, the child's entire life will never be sufficient to fill up this empty space. Some of these children become obese or anorexic. They desperately try to fill, with extraordinary courage, the known and named emptiness, by eating (bulimia). Or, on the contrary, with just as much courage, they resist by not eating (anorexia), putting their life in danger so as not to be drawn into this huge emptiness: they reduce themselves to their simplest expression to escape from the attraction of the lack or emptiness.

When the needs for physical survival are not taken care of, then other needs disappear or lose all significance. In our abundantly satiated society the jungle of needs takes root, and these needs conflict in us with each other.

> 'I need solitude and I need relationships; I find it difficult balancing both, paying attention to these two vital needs and reconciling them'

'I need to read in the evening, and yet I miss being out in the twilight, which gave me such joy as a child.'

'I need you of course, and also many other people whom I don't yet know but who I know will bring me closer to you, though it may be hard for you to accept that.'

The needs that we cannot satisfy make us dependent on others. A link, an attachment, is created, when we see the possibility of having our needs met by someone else. Attachment begins when we believe, rightly or wrongly, that the other person has the power to satisfy our needs. This keeps them going rather than subdues them because the link focuses on someone whom we see as essential, significant and maybe irreplaceable.

Love often focuses on specific people and we feel that no one else could take their place.

'I need to be seen as a son by my mother. She is the only one who can confirm this for me.'

I then lose my autonomy; I cannot satisfy my needs myself, but I have no control over their gratification. I become attached to the other person.

Is love only the fact that I need someone else to hear and understand all my hidden expectations – in addition to the more obvious ones? Of course not, but there are aspects of love that remain a mystery, not to be revealed for a long, long time.

The paradox is that only auto-erotism (eating, smoking, wandering alone, reading, indulging in pleasures) keeps me free of a dependent relationship. Indeed a link created by a lack focuses on someone who seems to have what we lack. If vital, reactive needs are the main reason for a relationship, we can become excessively possessive. But using other people just to fulfil our own needs alienates them.

To protect themselves from possible suffering and dependence, some people go so far as to deny their needs, or they deprive themselves by becoming rigid and ascetic in their relationships. Others try to overcome their needs, to master them, sublimate

them or transfer them onto another level. Others still try to
become freer by transforming their needs into desires: they grow
desires on the compost of their needs. And so we get people who
write about needs: the poets of life and the wise.

Caution does not engender life, it holds it back.

It is a lifelong task to discover our own true and evolving needs,
those that favour growth, at all stages of our life. They are usually
buried under layers of fears and desires.

> 'I want to be cared for,' said a young woman. 'I want someone to
> guide me in everything, and for years I have managed to find this
> support. This desire for dependence remains in me, but I'm
> beginning to see that my real need is to learn to stand on my own
> feet.'

A mother who knows how to respond to her child's true needs
certainly does not satisfy all his wishes. She understands that
what the child likes (stuffing himself with chocolate, going to
bed at midnight, sleeping with Mummy) is not necessarily good
for him and his development. So many of our adult desires and
requests go against our best interests!

**If we can be less affected by the urgency of our needs, we will find
the traces of happiness they leave in us.**

4 Reactional Chains

The difficulty of changing from reacting to relating

How much violence there is in denied or repressed aggressivity,
how much violence in inflicted kindness.

When we go through a small or large crisis in our relationships,
we sometimes feel drawn into a deadlock, as if confusion and
anxiety swallowed us up. We do not understand anything
anymore. We see no way out other than depression, anger, guilt,
loss of self-worth, even war, separation and madness. When
relationship and communication are blocked, every attempt at
communication exacerbates both protagonists' automatic
reactions and makes them sink into feelings of rage and
helplessness.

In the course of our lives, we have all experienced the violence
we inflict on ourselves when we just react, with mixed feelings of
malice and bitterness, and without being able to control in any
way what we say – of course to the detriment of our relationships.
We know that some words will estrange and hurt us, and
contribute to a lack of understanding, yet we cannot help
uttering them. What is worse, we often have a deep-down strong
but erroneous feeling that there will always be time to sort things
out or that the other person will understand, adjust or come back.

These emotional dynamics are more apparent in couples,
although they exist in any personal or professional relationship.

Any discussion leading to a stalemate generally starts with
denunciation. One of the partners points out that something is
going wrong for him and makes the other responsible for playing
a part in his discomfort. This start to the discussion is like a spur
that provokes a strong reaction in the other person, because it is
aimed at their weak spot: an area of immaturity or guilt, a more
or less hidden fragility, or an area of low tolerance. In this

'If you only knew the fears and uncertainties hidden beneath my shouts and complaints.'

sensitive area, a tiny trivial-sounding phrase will act like a detonator and sometimes bring about a whole range of reactions, hurtful to both the person who is reacting and the other person subjected to them.

I have often been struck by the constancy, fierceness and despair with which we develop and nourish cycles of these reactions, often lasting for several days, or even weeks.

'When I was young, I specialized in such attacks, such wounds in my relationships. With a kind of fierce (I would say today masochistic) will, I would corner the other person and make him feel inferior, or punish him . . . for not having understood, heard or simply listened to me.'

A man complains one day that he does not have enough time and his girlfriend retorts: 'You've got time for lots of things, but never for me!' The man is stung to the quick in his self-image. He needs to be seen as a satisfying companion, as someone who gives a lot. He feels judged, denigrated and guilty. A surge of irrational violence sweeps through him and overwhelms him. Out of this swirl can only spring aggressive claims or justifications.

'You never suggest anything.'

'But I often take you out. You've nothing to complain about. You're just never pleased about anything!'

'You know very well that I have too much to do. Everybody is making demands on me and blaming me. Are you going to join in as well?'

Hurt in turn, his girlfriend can give up and even denigrate herself: 'I'm perfectly aware that I'm not an interesting person. I really wonder why you stay with me!' Or she will confront him and attack again. 'You never do anything for us. You take what I give for granted and you neglect me totally!'

He might then retreat into heavy silence, feeling guilty, furious and depressed, and brood for hours or days, attacking her all the while in his mind. 'She's insatiable. She never appreciates anything I give. The tokens of concern for her that I give don't count; nothing is enough for her; she's always throwing accusations at me. She'd like to be the only one in the world. She's like a leaking barrel. I'm wasting my time and energy with her. She's so immature . . .'

As for her, she will ruminate and might also be afraid, feeling the violence triggered off by her aggressive claim. She will then talk to him with a nice smile and become submissive and conciliatory. For a long time, they will speak to each other with caution and they will not dare talk about their relationship.

In a lifetime, an unbelievable amount of energy gets wasted. It is the same with time. Time is wasted when it is not fully lived but consumed, and frittered away in struggles with our discomforts.

. . . and her fury at knowing that she had been caught out just drove
her mad . . .
As usual, to defend herself, she attacked . . .
G G Márquez, *Love in the Time of Cholera*

Sometimes it is only many years later, at the beginning of the
autumn of life, that we can at last hear what was at the same time
both necessary and in vain in these bellicose reactions. It is as if
they had been a chaotic, violent or perverse test.

   This beautiful quotation by Gabriel García Márquez about
Dona Fermina Daza discovering her dying husband expresses the
core of our regrets and attachments:

> She prayed to God to give him at least a moment so that he would
> not go without knowing how much she had loved him despite all
> their doubts, and she felt an irresistible longing to begin life with him
> over again so that they could say what they had left unsaid and do
> everything right that they had done badly in the past.

When a relationship is hindered, it is always difficult to
determine if it is a deadlock in communication or a real dead
end. The deadlock resulting from a way of communicating
where reactions abound could be broken by using ritual and
taboo. (Each person talks about himself and not *for* the other.
When a person expresses himself, the other one listens and
controls his emotional reactions. Both try to take responsibility
for their own feelings and to pay attention to their projections,
etc.) The real dead end consists in excessively ardent and
irreconcilable wishes about the other person and about the
relationship. In that case both parties' needs and positions are
incompatible.

The terrorism of a desire for something *from* the other person
leaves no room for the wonder of desire *for* the other person.

She says: 'I need you to devote more time to me and become more
committed to me.'

'I need ...'

He says: 'I just need to feel free with you, to withdraw, and devote less time to you. I can't bear your needing me.'

If the person who asks for more cannot change his existential stand and get closer to the other one who has a different request, then separation will be a necessary way out. Otherwise the relationship will become pathological because both partners' stands are too different.

For us, pathological means 'obstructing development'. In the above example, the man avoids feeling and recognizing his own areas of immaturity since he sees them in an obvious way in others. The woman remains stuck with her unsatisfied needs, avoiding the need to develop her own emotional autonomy, for she feels that this dimension is the other person's prerogative. Frequently, we come across these dynamics in couples where one partner, if not both, acts as a point of fixation for some part of the personality which is unacceptable to its owner. By fixing or fastening it on the partner, he can thus see it, reject it and treat it as if it were not part of him.

These polarized dynamics where something is seen in the other are all the more powerful when this mirroring game begins very early on in relationships. Sometimes only a third party can help us to reframe or readjust, and this should lead to more lucidity and therefore increase real sharing. In this way our projections prevent us from enlarging our consciousness, unless we detach them from the anchoring point we have found in the other person and reintegrate them as something that belongs to us. Indeed it is as if our unconscious were trying to become conscious by projecting its contents onto others. And those who are close to us become, in spite of themselves, invested with some feature or behaviour whose meaning does not belong to them. Pursued by our ruthless projection, they will struggle with it and try to escape it.

The fundamental faults in a love or couple relationship are embodied in the phrases:

- 'You've changed.'
- 'You haven't changed.'
- 'You changed when I wanted you to remain the same.'
- 'You didn't change when I wanted you to evolve.'

SPONGE-LIKE DYNAMICS

Some love relationships seem essentially grounded in suffering and in maintaining the suffering in oneself or in the other. For instance, a woman will offer her suffering to a man, and the man will seize it to take care of it. He will become very much involved, out of a sense of duty and out of a wish to heal her suffering.

'I can't possibly leave her alone in such a state. If I left her, she wouldn't get over it.'

Another man will only be able to offer his depression, his complaint, his bitterness towards life or his alcoholism which will be taken care of generously (at least at the beginning of the relationship) by a devoted and tireless woman convinced that thanks to her love he'll recover.

So one person produces suffering and spreads it while the other absorbs it. This 'absorption' becomes the recognizable sign of love.

'I feel loved and accepted when he takes care of me. When he listens to my sorrows and does everything he can to help me, I experience loving feelings.'

The obliging sponge-like person does not realize how much he or she maintains the other person's game and keeps it functioning at its maximum. It feels so good to be listened to in one's unhappiness and deep anxiety, so the so-called victim is not ready to jeopardize his stand by giving up suffering. You do not come across a persevering saviour every day.

The sponge-like person may become overwhelmed by the other's anxiety and doubts, and frustrated in his own need to make himself whole. The situation will deteriorate. The man will begin to inflict suffering on the woman whose unhappiness he wanted to relieve: feelings of estrangement, rejection, impatience, veiled threats of breaking off, search for other partners, and blame or accusations will appear.

Henceforth the woman's suffering has found its point of fixation, its obvious cause: it is him, her unsatisfying partner. He is the one who constantly reactivates the wounds he pretends to heal. The princess feels tortured by the hero who came to set her free.

'You who helped me and promised to restore my taste for life, you know very well what my anxieties are and you do everything you can to exacerbate my feelings of abandonment, my anxiety, my sense of worthlessness.

You're never there when I need you and I see very well that you are fed up with me. You don't really love me, and you let me get attached to you by helping me.'

If the man who is made to feel guilty keeps his commitment, the mutual dependence increases: neither of them takes care of themselves because they are both so centred on the other and worried about the other's misfortunes. The woman tries to be taken charge of. She asks the man to do things for her; the man tries to heal the wounds he is inflicting. He is doing things in her place and in this way she becomes alienated. As he becomes at the same time a persecutor and a helpness saviour, he too begins to see himself as a victim plagued with impossible demands or starts to feel guilty just for hoping for change. He begins to have the painful realization that he has his own needs and expectations.

In different ways the dynamics are similar in each partner evading and betraying themselves. Such dynamics are common in the caring professions, where there are many self-denying people.

The game can get even more out of control and head for an acute crisis. The woman suffers more and more, until her suffering goes beyond her partner's capacity for absorption and he becomes ill or leaves. At these stages we witness spectacular acting out (serious accidents, acute psychosomatic illnesses). The woman may attempt to commit suicide or may also be a victim of accidents. All this will serve in two ways: to retain him, and at the same time drive him to abandon her. To be abandoned is wished for as a relief, as a way out of this mad relationship. If neither of them has the courage to give up, there may be at this stage symbolic murders and deaths.

One day, the man is overcome with rage against his wife's car, which is blocking his way. He drives straight into it and of course damages both cars.

A man unloaded his shotgun into the front seat of his wife's car. Then, full of remorse and distressed, he expected understanding and support.

The double 'mission' that this man and woman have mutually assigned to each other is incredibly violent: 'My happiness depends on you, therefore you are responsible for my unhappiness'. It is as terrible an injunction as the other's utterance: 'You should be happy because I'm taking care of you'. The development of such a game may bring about physical acting out on oneself or on the other person so as to escape and go away.

We often see that our choice in love falls on the person who is most able to exacerbate the flaws and characteristics of our own internal structure. It is as if we were trying to be touched where it most hurts and to be stimulated where we are most immature and aberrant. Perhaps our unconscious is thus trying to bring to light and to test its most fragile areas, to work on them, and in this way to transcend them, transform them and allow us to become more cautious in our future choices.

For a long time, I believed that my dreams were also his.

FALSE COMMITMENTS

Which aspects of ourselves are involved in our links with others? After 15 years of marriage, I may discover that I brought into play a 'false me', perhaps an idealized image of myself, based on ideological patterns or unreal characters. I may have seen myself as part of a beautiful image of a couple – but then I might begin to wonder where the me is in all this.

I may also have called into play an injunction that I made mine.

'When you go out with someone for a long time, it has to turn into something. It has to become serious. If you go on seeing him, it means that you want to marry him.'

'In this way I felt that someone made a commitment for me, someone who thought for me, who knew what I should be and what I should do.'

We agree to some commitments so as not to hurt others or trigger off conflicts, or because we feel obliged to conform.

'I ought to be pleased to be invited. If I'm not, it means that I'm not normal. Therefore I have to behave socially by accepting what I don't like.'

In the labyrinth of false commitments and parasite-like loyalties, I lose touch with my true self and forget about it.

'That 23-year-old helpless and dazzled young woman who became involved with a man 15 years her senior is no longer me. Now, at the age of 40, I have other aspirations, but I am linked by a debt of gratitude and I can't free myself.'

Some loves are like nurseries that enable a person to grow and blossom and thus offer him or her the possibility of finding love somewhere else, further away.

To be honest in my relationship to my partner and to myself I have to say that my commitment is not real in the sense that it does not involve my deeper self. If I persist in maintaining it, I shall make the other person pay for it and I shall sabotage and disparage our mutual experience.

We all have in mind examples of commitments made at a time in our life when they symbolized the person we were then.

Some commitments are made at times of crisis.

'Promise me that you won't disappoint your mother when I'm no longer here any more.'

'I'm counting on you to continue my work if I ever pass away . . .'

Requests for commitments from the deathbed are among the most harmful and can become a lifelong burden.

'If you marry again, choose a Christian wife.'

Other commitments are made in the course of the development of a love relationship, in more or less obvious power struggles.

'I promise you that I'll never do it again.'

We should know that when we do something against ourselves, we will make someone pay for it. The paths towards truth and real commitment require great faithfulness to oneself, through recognition of one's own shortcomings and increased clear-sightedness about one's authentic feelings.

'I once felt like having a cat. This wish really concealed an unexpressed wish to have a child. Wishes are like Chinese boxes: each may conceal another one. I displaced it by buying a very beautiful black and white china cat which I put on a small table near my bed.

A few weeks later, thinking that it would please me, a friend offered me a little black and white cat whose presence did not suit my way of life since I was often away.

Touched by his thoughtfulness, I accepted the gift and conditioned myself to thinking that it pleased me. So my cat and I had a dreadful relationship. She mewed so much that my neighbour offered to get rid of her for me. It took us years to get used to each other and to acknowledge each other's needs and requests. Today, I feel committed to her.'

Many relationships might follow this path and develop, not under the constraint of a commitment made in the past, but in the freedom of a choice made in the present with the perspective of a near future.

Being loyal to myself goes far beyond my immediate experience. It concerns who I am deep down.

THE NEED TO RESPOND TO THE EXPECTATIONS OF OTHERS

Many blocks in relationships are linked to a compulsive need to respond to other people's expectations, either by trying to satisfy them, or by deferring to them rather than leading our own lives.

> Talking about her lover, Catherine says: 'I know that he needs me. He's divorced but still lives with his wife. He's unhappy in the situation because he can't leave her. Each time he tried, he became impotent. I must accept the situation; he would be too unhappy if I refused.'

> Mark tells us with emotion about his wife's expectations: 'She wants me to accompany her two weekends a month to see her parents. She hates her mother and, as she knows that I get along well with her, she imagines that her mother will be less unhappy.'

> Louise eventually understood that the amazing birth of her daughter ('I had had an abortion and a curettage in a clinic. Two months later I was still pregnant') is her way of responding to her mother's expectations: 'I was 35. None of my brothers were married and she told me each time she saw me: "So, when will you have a baby for me?"'

To respond in spite of oneself, and sometimes against oneself, to the expressed or imagined expectations of others is a double trap. Firstly, because we do not know what the real and often contradictory expectations of others are. Secondly, because we cannot be truly ourselves when we condition ourselves to satisfy the expressed or assumed demands of others.

Without this need to conform to the apparent or concealed expectations of others, there would be no 'terrorism' in relationships. However much the other person might brandish his threats of suicide, his headaches, his despair or his judgement, he would not produce in us feelings other than, possibly, compassion. He could not awaken our guilt feelings nor our need to heal and protect him. Any explicit or implicit 'mission'

Louise, her daughter, her mother.

burdens us only if it fits in with our wish to conform to the other person's expectations.

If we take on 'selfless missions', they can become burdens.

A man feels that he owes an explanation for what he did in his friend's absence. He even describes the things that he knows will irritate her and estrange her from him. 'I can't help telling her about it.'

'My strongest desire is that my daughter should become really independent, take charge of herself and find a place of her own to continue her studies. I'm continually helping her, finding solutions for her, imagining what she should or should not do. Without realizing it, I force my wishes on her and I don't let hers come out.'

The obligation to respond to expectations in relationships and the need to satisfy the other person's emotional demands take root in us in early childhood. At that time, our survival depends on it. And we have no personal references or structures other than our survival instinct, our need to be recognized and accepted and our physical and intuitive sensations. Babies are incredibly skilled at stimulating people around them, at arousing in others the wish to take care of them, sharing gratification, producing anxieties, gaining and focusing their parents' emotions or those of the people who occasionally take care of them.

In adolescence, many people try to get rid of the need to respond to the expectations of those around them by doing precisely the contrary of what is expected of them. This may also be an attempt to be free from their own wish to please, though it is still conditioned by others.

> An adolescent girl will not be able to pass the competitive examination which would enable her to enter an elite Parisian school of higher education. It would mean leaving her home town and her mother. By failing, she remains faithful to her mother's wish to keep her near.

How many parents think that they are the only ones who can 'allow' their adolescent children to live away from home or differently from them?

Adults often retain this wish to hear, guess, sense and anticipate the other's expectation so as to conform to it in order to be loved, appreciated and admired, to avoid being disappointing and to exist by feeling that they are necessary and indispensable. This is like 'bein~ faithful' to a 'good self-image'. It is necessary for some people to live vicariously by introducing themselves into someone else's life and taking part in his needs. But to function like this leads to inextricable paradoxes and deadlocks. If I perceive that the other's request is 'Resist me. Don't obey me', I shall be tempted to disobey him . . . so as to obey him. When someone attacks me and wants me to be, at the same time, both

'If I were you ... .'

stronger than him so as to reassure him and self-denigrating so as to give him a sense of self-worth, then how can I make sense of it, if I do want to respond to his expectations? I may lose touch with myself in the wish to decipher and satisfy them, especially if they are idealized or more or less perverse.

'She ideally expects me to agree completely with her point of view, even when she is attacking mine! She denigrates mine and then she seems to want my agreement.'

'He provokes me by touching my weak points, my insecurity. Actually he is asking that I listen to his own doubts . . . or that I openly tell him about my difficulties.'

'She takes me to task because she needs a conflict, a good fight to pour out the aggression she has stored up.'

'If he criticizes my disorder, it's mainly so that I can admire his meticulousness.'

'She denigrates herself so that I can resume my role of intellectual guide which she will at the same time both follow and challenge.'

'He suggests that I leave him so that I can reassert my wish to live with him.'

'She talks me into leaving her to prove, once more, that she can't really be loved by a man.'

There are innumerable kinds of expectations. Some are idealized, others conceal fears, others still are requests for proof. And then there are the paradoxical expectations.

It is always the combination of two reaction points which causes stalemates in communication and intimate relationships.

'I often let myself be stopped by the other person's reaction. If he doesn't show signs of interest in what I say, if a shadow of irritation passes over his face, then I immediately fall silent. I tell him about my sadness and he answers: "I don't like you to be sad." I then try to change immediately to a different level of conversation. And I don't like it either when the other person takes my own reaction too much into account.'

'What he says irritates me, but it doesn't mean that I expect him to stop on the spot. The fact that I'm irritated will also teach me something.'
'Am I irritating you?'
'No, no . . . (I should have said: Oh! yes, but go on, I want to listen to your irritating point of view to the very end).'

'Have you ever been unfaithful to me?'
'Oh, yes, since you ask, once . . .'
'When? With whom?'
'It was last summer . . .'
And she starts crying out of anger and because she feels hurt.
'But you wanted to know!'
Yes, she wanted to know, but she did not want to deny or repress her reactions. She wants to know, even with her pain and with all the facets of herself. She wants to know with all her vulnerability.

'I'd never dare tell my mother that ...'

Many feelings and thoughts seem inexpressible because of the reaction we expect the other person to have, that is to say because of our reaction to the other's reaction and because of our fear of consequences. At certain times in a relationship, the unspeakable, which flows between two individuals who love each other, fills all the vacant space left by what was speakable. Thus silences set in, invade the space of love . . . and pollute it.

'I'd never dare tell that to my mother. It would risk hurting her too deeply. She's old. She has the right to end her life in peace.'

And this concealed and unsaid 'that', these unspoken words, will be a cancer, a separation, a redundancy – a major event which will not be shared by two people who love each other. It would be advisable one day to question this idea: 'I have the right to ...', 'What right do I have to tell her that?', 'He doesn't have the right

'I'll keep some things to myself ... and I'll not say how I'm suffering ...'

to . . .' How many deadlocks are created in relationships by this false idea!

We have noticed how old sayings weigh heavily on former children, now adults, and on their parents.

> 'Everything can't be said. Anyway it's the past (the remains of old disputes). They wouldn't understand. It would hurt them unnecessarily.'

And so the unspoken will go on because we take it upon ourselves to be silent, to keep things to ourselves and bury them. A psychoanalyst said: 'We're too often on the planet Silence.'

We suggest, on the contrary, that we should dare to say things, by sticking to our own experience and speaking only about ourselves.

> 'This is what I experienced and felt. This is how it hit me, and the

impact it had on me. Today it's important for me to tell you that, to let you know about this part of me which you didn't know about.'

We should dare to talk and remain loyal to what we experienced.

'She will be hurt if I say I'm bored. She will either feel obliged to make a tremendous effort to entertain me, or she won't invite me again.'

'It will make him angry if I say that I would like him to talk plainly. He won't tell me anything anymore.'

'She will be embarrassed if I tell her that the tobacco smell on her breath bothers me. She won't kiss me again.'

'It will block him if I say that I don't like the way he caresses me and he will lose his spontaneity. But can I let him hurt me and let him believe it's pleasant?'

'It will affect her if I tell her about my annoyance at seeing her so attracted by this dull and conceited man, and she will hide her feelings and impulses from me even more.'

'If he knew all the judgements and criticisms that go through my head when he talks, he wouldn't communicate with me any more.'

'If I say that I noticed she was lying, she will feel ill at ease and will hold it against me for having humiliated her.'

'If I express to him my wish that he phone tomorrow, he won't know how to refuse and I won't know if he is calling out of desire or out of duty. If he phones, I'll feel bitter.'

'If I told her about my other affairs, she would poison all our meetings by direct or indirect hints.'

'If he knew that I didn't go out during the whole weekend because I was waiting for his call, he would think he was being made to feel guilty . . . and under attack. He would reproach my lack of autonomy. He wants me to be independent, but I like to be dependent on him in this way.'

I remain silent so as not to do violence by being intrusive, inflicting wounds, demands, humiliations or making the other feel guilty. But my very silence does violence to myself and to the other person.

This is because our silence about some of our feelings will show through in a thousand signs. How many gestures, sentences with double or triple meaning will thus interfere when we meet! Sulky, accusing and heavy silences make the other person's presence and ours even more unbearable.

Knots are made out of excessive sensitivity and excessively intense reactions to the other person's reactions, and also out of intolerance to the other's suffering, disappointment or anger.

Passive dependence, weakness and self-sabotage can only have a hold on those who are tormented by their own guilt, bad conscience, or need to heal others before healing themselves.

The weight of silent or expressed expectations is a load only for the person who believes that he has to remedy the other's inability to take charge of himself.

'I can't ask him to go away', says a woman who took her alcoholic brother into her home, at the age of 40, after his divorce. 'He has nobody. If I let him down, there are only two solutions for him: my parents or becoming a tramp. I can't do that to him. And I resent my sister-in-law for having divorced him. She has been feeding him for 20 years; she could have gone on doing it. She didn't have to divorce him for that?'

And for several years she will endure all the burden and violence of living with an alcoholic in opposition to her own way of life. 'I'm losing touch with myself in this relationship.'

The other person's idealized or distorted image of me will only drive me insane if it matches my own deep wish to correspond to it.

If the other person dictates my behaviour, if he talks for me and says what I should be or do, his words only take on unbearable importance because of my own propensity to obey, and conform, and my need for approval. Otherwise, I could consider the other person's point of view as an interesting proposition (there may be good ideas in it) or as a sign of his interest in me (I am important for him). Or it might cast a new light on what I had not thought enough about.

By thus interfering with my life, he can broaden my horizon and show me other possibilities. Anyway I am the one who manages my life. The other person who gives orders only becomes a dictator by relying on my fear of being threatened.

In love, what we experience as a vital threat is the threat of loss, of the other person's withdrawal from the relationship. The withdrawal may be not only physical but also emotional. I become less present in him, less present in her. I become a casual passer-by. So, to maintain my presence in the other's mind, I shall not assert myself and I shall merge into what seem to be his expectations.

Fear of loss and abandonment make a strong cement in many emotional or love relationships. Such cement will keep together, for a very long time, men and women who are worlds apart.

It's not you I'm afraid of. It's my own fear I don't want to listen to.

The process of maturation that should lead the individual to become more truly himself goes through gradually relinquishing the need to be loved and approved and particularly the need to be loved for what he is not.

What is this young Italian woman actually doing when she dares not tell her mother, a practising Catholic, that she has for years been the girlfriend of a married man?

> 'I have a panicky fear of losing her love if she hears about the way I live. She would tell me: "You're no longer my daughter." She would reject me and stop loving me.'

Therefore, during her visits to Italy, she continues to present herself as a well-behaved virgin daughter who is uninterested in men. Whom does she offer her mother to love? She offers a pretence, an unreal image, a lie. But she is the one who is the loser, who is taken in and placed in an awkward position, believing in love for what she is not, for values she does not hold. She cannot feel really loved as long as she hides herself so as to avoid disappointing her mother. She is still lacking something while accepting her mother's love. She maintains an infantile pattern that keeps both her and her mother in infantile roles. By offering for love what is not herself, she does not receive anything except an illusion of love. This is how false feelings that spread out over several generations are created.

In any family there are 'out of the norm' emotions which are considered 'bad' (for instance, anger, sadness or sexual feelings). Children, like other members of the family, disguise their emotions because they feel that they cannot be loved if they have this 'bad' feeling. So it becomes an aspect of themselves to be rejected.

Sometimes the need to satisfy the other's apparent request may make us lose precisely what we are looking for: his love and esteem.

A young girl marries a farmer who plans to take over his father's farm where he works and lives. After six months together, the young girl has had enough of the countryside and presents her husband with an ultimatum:

'Choose. It's either your father's farm or me.'

'It's you,' answers the husband.

'On that day', she tells us, 'I lost all the admiration and love I felt for him. I had obtained what I wanted, but it was the acquiescence of a zombie. He wasn't himself any more. He had given up his life plan and wishes for me. I resented him for not sticking to his position and for reversing his decision to conform to my desire of town life. Moreover, he disappointed his father although I knew that he loved and admired him. It was as if I couldn't trust him any more. I understood too late, and much later, that I had trapped myself with my own request.'

Even if the husband had felt that his wife's hidden request was that he should not assent to her ultimatum, if he had behaved according to what he felt, he would still have been trapped.

The ultimatum presented to the other person is often just an attempt to persuade them to make the choice for us.

These dynamics are frequent in parental relationships.

The mother of a 25-year-old boy who was still living with her and was neither studying nor working exclaims: 'I would like him to take the decision to leave and find a room for himself. He doesn't even clean his own room; it's a pigsty.' She cannot take the decision to throw her son out, so she asks him to take it.

It is often the most powerless person who is asked to 'do something'.

Intolerance to the other's feeling of disappointment (I am seen as a let-down) disturbs our behaviour and desires.

'I have let myself be "polluted" by his disappointment at not having found the ideal woman in me. I tried so much to conform to his model, though it was vague and full of contradictions. He would describe it without spelling things out or he would talk to his friends about what he meant by "a woman"; he described a magical woman on which I tried to model myself. I felt at the same time the huge gulf, the unbearable gap between what I was and what I presented. I resented myself bitterly: this is the meaning that I give to the cancers I produced repeatedly for years.

Yes, for years, I lost touch with myself by trying to please him. What a relief and what a panic after our divorce when I had to try and find out who I was, without referring to his expectations.'

A man was perplexed and anxious on his hospital bed. After a minor surgical operation, he had insistently called for his wife's presence: 'Come just at the time when visiting hours begin. Come twice a day. Stay a little longer.'

She had suddenly burst out: 'Stop asking. I dream of giving to someone who wouldn't ask for anything. Your requests kill my spontaneity. I don't feel like giving you anything anymore. If I continue to come, it's out of duty and not out of pleasure.'

He mulled things over in his mind, feeling himself in an insoluble dilemma: 'She asks me not to ask, but I can't condition myself to her limits. I should stop asking so that she could give to me, but that's mad! It's another way of asking. She dictates to me how I should be but I'm not the way that suits her, so she rejects me and I can't bear it. What am I to do?'

Crazy dialogues lead to anxiety, uncertainty about how to be, and self-negation. Faced with the emotional demands of the other person, there is only one answer: to try neither to respond nor to oppose them. We should listen to them and confirm that we have heard them, that is to say acknowledge them.

A miracle then occurs:

- when I spontaneously give what the other person wants;
- when the discrepancy between my expectation and his answer opens unexpected horizons for me;
- when there is no need to think and analyse to live these moments;
- when the other person's expectations actually stimulate my potential.

The best way to keep or re-establish a relationship is to remain faithful to our own position, to respect deeply and fiercely what is at the root of our way of seeing and listening. We have to ask ourselves: 'Does it go with who I am, if I do this?'

We know that we are faithful to ourselves when we feel a deep respect for ourselves, when there is congruence between our actions and our convictions, between our feelings and our words. We should try and reach this harmony between these different levels in us, and hear the right note which resonates, rich and full, as an echo in the core of our being.

Some people speak with living words that enable us to listen to ourselves.

THE CULS-DE-SAC OF LOVE

When their eyes met, they were sure of one thing only, that everything was decided and that they were now indifferent to all prohibitions.
Robert Musil

Yes, my beloved, I love you in the past, now and forever; and forever is now.
Albert Cohen

And it is not enough to have memories. We should know how to forget them when they are numerous, and have the patience to await their return.
Rainer Maria Rilke

Love presents itself as an immense authorization, a universe of possibilities and a world of mutual acceptances to be amplified in all the days to come. Yet once the miraculous wonders and agreements of the encounter are past, love relationships often become a privileged area of subtle violence. A couple does not remain alive by adding feelings to feelings, but by having communication full of quality, by maintaining life in areas that not only enable them to share, but also link them to each other beyond the misadventures of life.

Delicate adjustments go wrong more or less quickly when a relationship becomes established over a long time. They give way to obligation, to dependence, to the discrepancy of desires and to oppressive demands.

A relationship based only on feelings and their fluctuations remains an uncertain venture whose balance is infinitely fragile. Many marriages find solidity in the functional area, in the mutual task of running a home and a family. They are kept going by obligations and rules which do not belong to the realm of wishes and fears. In such marriages, the life of feelings is framed in an organized structure. The couple is weakened each time the functional task is threatened (children who grow up and leave, the hazards of unemployment, illnesses ...).

We can distinguish four aspects of love which combine with each other and thus form complex dynamics in relationships.

Loving out of desire

My desire falls on you. It discloses aspects of myself which I did not know. I become different. I discover sides of myself that were slumbering and seeds which are enhanced by your existence.

To love out of desire is an invigorating feeling which carries me along, opens me up and leads me to become more fully myself, in

'My desire is larger than you!'

this movement towards another person. I go to him not to take but to offer, to give and welcome what he is. Love out of desire is a mutual expansion.

Loving out of need

Often, love is a request for love, an imperious demand which sometimes becomes imperialist. Love feels omnipotent. It can never really believe in non-reciprocity. It is as if we were thinking: 'My love is so powerful that it creates love in the other person.'

'I need you all for myself.'

'I love you and it means "Love me. I need your presence and attention. I mainly need to feel loved by you." You cannot not pay attention to me because I love you. My love should have the power to make you love me.'

Such a love leads to possessiveness, and very often the other person becomes alienated for the benefit of my own needs. I try to use him for my demands, expectations and fears. In a relationship, 'I love you' is often followed by 'And you, do you love me?', which introduces my own fear and doubt in the other person. He will immediately have to confirm, reassure, and give concrete evidence of the love that is requested and called for.

Where is,
The time of light requests
When you only wished for what I wanted?
At the time I responded unreservedly to your expectations.
(An Afghan poet married to a Western woman)

Consuming love

'I love the love you feel for me. It flatters my self-esteem. I love the image of myself reflected by your love. I feel unique. Your love gives me a sense of security and worth.'

The pleasure of being loved creates a real need in the person who is loved.

Loving to redress something across generations

"One love may hide another one". When this sentence came to my mind, it struck me like a thunderbolt. It was as if the clouds had separated and I saw more clearly through my blindness. The extraordinary and unshared love I had felt, and still felt at this moment, for this man suddenly appeared pointless, devoid of support, derisory and childish. I hesitated between laughter and tears. I felt both little and strong, desperate and calm.

So all the love, care and enthusiasm I had given him wholeheartedly were aimed at somebody else through him. It was the love I would have liked my mother to feel for my father. As a small child, I had spent a long time in my bed imagining how my mother "should have loved" my father. I fondly cherished this model for a long time. As an adolescent, every evening I added to this "Thousand and One Nights" dream a thousand variants, a thousand new splendours. I endlessly enriched these scenarios with all my tenderness and wishes of happiness for this wonderful and frustrated father.

When I met my husband, I hadn't understood the displacement I was making. He had indeed mentioned an unloving mother, but it hadn't caught my attention. I offered him a unique and unfathomable love and completely forgot that it was made to someone else's measure.

It took many years of tension, hindrance and avoidance of the real issues for me to discover this. I loved my husband with what I at least believed to be absolute sincerity, and yet I remained blocked in my body and senses. This should have warned me and made me aware. But no. We were both blind. He did his best to give me pleasure, accepted my limitations, and became twice as careful, while I felt guilty, closed yet perfect in so many other areas.

I stepped out of this love as you step out of a convent. It was a mistaken vocation, a mistaken object of love. I was able to say to my husband: "I've been imposing on you for eleven years a love that didn't belong to you, that wasn't intended for you." I really believe that he heard me.'

Loving to redress is a huge myth in relationships. Whatever the efforts, attention and quality of the relationship offered, they will lead to deadlocks and culs-de-sac. All the resources of communication, therapeutic help, marriage guidance counsellors and consultants will be thwarted because the real object of love has been displaced.

This loving to redress may exist at very subtle levels. It is usually grounded in something belonging to a previous generation.

'I was 44 years old when I eventually understood what I called 'my love for her', my wife, the woman I had married at the age of 22, when she was pregnant by another man. She was so lost, so hurt and eager for love and tenderness. I proposed to her on the fourth night of our embraces. I acknowledged the child, who wasn't mine. I gave him my name. My name, that is my mother's name, because she also (but did I know it at the time?) had been pregnant at 22 and abandoned. She had hidden my birth from her own parents. She had passed herself off as my aunt for ten years before telling me on the eve of my first communion that she was my mother.

Whose wound did I heal? My mother's? I don't think so. I think that I mainly tried to put right what my father had done. I did what he hadn't been able to do. Across the years, in the powerful anchor of anniversaries but mainly of loyalties, I inscribed the gestures, acts and words of an unfinished story.

Yes, 44 years to understand all that, to put commitments back where they belonged and not where I put them. At the age of 44, just at the moment when my son, the child I recognized as such, is 22 years old and attacks me with his violence, clumsily rejects me and imprisons me in his own suffering. There are so many silences to understand.

I am now entering into a new love. I embrace it to near suffocation so that it doesn't escape me, but I shall lose it through my excessiveness . . .'

This is the account of a man who took upon himself to put right his father's behaviour, and got involved in a love that was not his own. He tries to survive in this encounter with a woman who is already thinking of leaving him.

'Hold my hand, I want to be alone.'

Up to what point is the scalpel of lucidity powerless and inadequate to open, sever, and clean the cysts and inflammations of loves that are too old?

There are many facets, many secret things at stake, and disturbing repercussions in such loves. Sometimes, but only sometimes, there is no way out of them.

A love relationship in which love is given and received is a world in itself. No language can suffice to give an account of it.

However, in the infinite complexity of each love relationship, we can single out schematically a few processes which manifest themselves as inner and outer violence.

The violence of love

In many couples, there seems to be one who loves and one who is loved. But sometimes these apparent poles are reversed according to events or developments. The one who loves is more violently disturbed by his emotions than the other one. This inner violence is then externalized and inflicted on the other in a disguised and subtle way, as a pressure exerted by suffering, demands and weakness. Similarly, the need for autonomy of the one who feels less dependent does violence to the other.

The violence of dependence

'I can't live without you'. These words contain an extraordinary violence, the violence of a threat: 'If you leave me, I'll die'.

> 'Without you, life loses its meaning; I need you and you cannot leave me in a state of anxiety, and not answer my letters. If I'm unwell, you should rescue me. If I miss you, you should come and you should listen to me tell you about my love. You should because I love you. This makes you responsible for my moods.'

Do our needs create an obligation for the other person? Does love give us rights over the other person? The one who is in need feels like that and does not imagine other possibilities. 'I need him – or her – so it's up to him – or her – to respond because no one else can do it.' This seems perfectly obvious.

'It would be a crime to leave me in a state of anxiety, it would be failure to assist someone in danger of despair, and there is only one possible rescuer. Only the person who makes me suffer can comfort me.'

'I love you' can exert an intense pressure on the person who receives these words and hears them as meaning 'Love me'. Nobody is indifferent to the love that is felt for him or requested from him. But if he accepts the other person's dependence, he will find himself imprisoned behind the bars of the other's suffering as soon as he wants to draw away.

Forced or expected love is like hostage-taking. During a love relationship, many debts, duties and obligations are created which simply deaden communication (sharing) and produce tensions, violence and oppositions. These last constitute powerful separating elements that will become difficult to contain after a few years.

I can share what belongs to me, but it still belongs to me and I'm completely responsible for it.

If we add to this the myths and sets of beliefs brought into the love relationship by both partners, we must indeed admit that to keep a relationship alive while enabling love feelings to blossom is an arduous task for which few men and women are prepared.

The violence of change

At the beginning of any love relationship a kind of contract is established, sometimes tacit, sometimes hinted at in a few words and behaviour, or even explained at length. The contract can range from 'exclusive until death' to 'brief encounter'.

'I told her from the beginning that I didn't want to get attached, that I liked her presence and our meetings and that when she didn't want me any more, well, I wouldn't make a fuss . . .'

'I have set you the task of looking after my needs ...'

'She told me: "Each of us remains free. I won't ask any questions, and I don't want to be asked any. As long as we are happy together, it's all right."

'I would like us to have the freedom to tell each other everything without getting hurt, to share everything, to be really ourselves without the other feeling hurt.'

Freedom is one of the topics which most often recurs as a preamble to a relationship that will lead to dependence. The opposite topic is fusion, resemblance and looking in the same direction.

'We'll take every decision together. We'll take each other's opinion into consideration.'

'I'll try to understand him and by doing so I'll be at one with him.'

'What is most important is to do things together, to share the maximum of experiences.'

Thus very quickly 'one', 'we' and 'I' appear, to seek out, find, fight and do violence to each other. Often, one person in the couple will define the kind of relationship he wants. The other person submits or accepts, which is not the same thing. In fact, we cannot really agree to step into a plan suggested by another person unless this plan is in accordance with a similar and latent wish deep down in ourselves.

Sometimes we submit because we do not know clearly what we want, because we do not want to lose the other person, because we want to prove our love for her or him, or even because it is impossible for us to influence him the way we want. But then, later on, we shall always indirectly sabotage this pseudo-agreement without even wanting to.

If we side with someone, we risk putting aside our own opinion and not giving it up on a deeper level. But it will find a way of manifesting itself and of hindering the relationship.

In this situation, the powers are unequal. Those who have experienced it often say: 'I loved him. It was that (what he offered) or nothing. So I said yes.' The feeling of love invoked here is felt as an irrepressible, almighty force. 'I loved him' means that, at this stage of the relationship, he or she could have asked us anything. Many have experienced this, for love wants to be the absolute gift, the offering and surrendering of oneself. But the use that the other person makes of this gift may produce violence and suffering.

Starting from an agreement or pseudo-agreement, each person will evolve in different directions, but if changes are not synchronized and complementary, both partners will experience the other person's changes as a betrayal. By using emotional pressure, the one who will have changed least will attempt to bring the other one back to his initial position.

A woman began studying psychology after many years of a marriage in which she had sincerely shared her husband's views on women staying at home. She became very engrossed in this field which was so alien to her husband's interests. At this point he lovingly expressed his desire to have a third child. He slightly denigrated the path she had taken and repeatedly told her tenderly: 'I don't want you to change. We're so happy together.' She was fond of him and ambivalent regarding the third child. She could hear her husband's anxiety which meant: 'Are you going to choose your studies or me and my family life plan?' She accepted but was not able to prevent the existence of this new child from sabotaging her current training. Apparently her husband had got her back; he had concealed his own dependence by stimulating hers, but she resented him and her resentment estranged her from him. The seeds of this ongoing disagreement were already present in their respective positions when they first met. She had sincerely believed that she had given up her personal desires out of love for him. Actually, he was only leaning on one side of her own ambivalence, for the wish to have at least three children and to devote herself to them was also present in her, together with her wish for a professional occupation.

'Yet I did repeatedly tell her', complains another man, 'that for the time being I wanted a sporadic and light relationship, from time to time, without possessiveness or control. She agreed and accepted. She said that it suited her because she was afraid of attachment and needed solitude. Now, after several years, she is asking for more and more; she even talked about us living together, can you imagine! She has become so attached to me that her demands have become unbearable. Yet she had agreed to the type of relationship I suggested. Now I can only threaten to break off with her so that she'll come back again into my idea of living in a relationship.'

'We had everything we needed to be happy; I loved this man and felt loved by him. At the beginning I had been attracted by his uncouth appearance: he was silent and didn't make any concessions. When he talked, he brought things to an abrupt conclusion and it sounded right to my ears. Later on I couldn't bear his silences any more; I really needed to exchange and share. I wanted him at all costs to tell me about himself, about us and about what he felt.

I realize that this is paradoxical. It was as if at the beginning his silence had given me confidence and I felt that it confirmed what I said. And this was true: I gained more and more self-confidence, I talked more freely and became more open. I wanted to share all this. He became more and more withdrawn. During the last stages of our relationship, I constantly battled with him and harassed him. I continually attacked him to shake him out of his silence so that he would talk to me. He was silent, eluding and rejecting me; it was unbearable. Any real encounter was evading us because I was destroying unacceptable possibilities.

During that time, I inflicted so much violence on myself and on him. There was nobody to tell about it. All my friends confirmed that their husbands didn't say anything, that husbands were like that ...'

And this, almost a mirror reflection of the above, is the account of a man who is silent, hurt and violent at the same time:

'I was seduced by her gentleness and understanding. I was amazed at her ability to understand everything without ever uttering a judgement. With her I had the impression of unconditional acceptance. This was what I had been in search of for a long time, I think.

As the years went by, I don't know what happened, I wanted her to assert herself more and even contradict me. I couldn't stand any more what I took to be passivity. I wanted her to assert herself, and I had before me an unbearable person who accepted everything. During this period, our life became a nightmare of incomprehension. I took pleasure in humiliating her, rejecting her, and she bore it all with this air of always understanding which drove me mad. I didn't want to leave her. I wanted her to change. The arm-wrestling lasted about three years.

One day she announced that she had a boyfriend, but that this relationship which was important for her did not mean that she questioned her commitment to me. It was like waking up from a drunken binge. It was as if I had just come out of a state of deep inebriation.

Well, I sobered up, and my demands vanished as if by enchantment. The way I looked at her changed and so certainly did the way I looked at myself. A change had begun; it was as if I was released from shackles.

Today we are still together, a man and a woman so different from the two people we were when we first met.'

'If you understand me too well, we're too close . . .'

'If you give me positive feed-back, it upsets the image I have of myself.'

Often it seems as if the central element on which a relationship is anchored is precisely what will split or even destroy it.

A woman's second marriage was with a man who was an adventurer, an international businessman dealing with China as well as Brazil. During the first meal which brought them together at a mutual friend's house, she was seduced by his account of his travels. As for him, he was touched by the woman's calm and intense presence. She knew how to listen and stimulate him, she enabled him to really be himself.

'I hadn't thought of remarrying after the failure of my first marriage', he said, 'and this woman, who was also afraid of commitment after a failed marriage, really made me want to start something anew. I was convinced that with her it would work, whatever happened. We very quickly became involved and got married. It took me three years to realize that she couldn't bear my travels, my absences. I had indeed suggested taking her with me. My position as a self-employed person enabled me to do so. But she never accepted.'

Years later, on her own again, she said: 'My great dream was to have him accept a sedentary position. I believed my love to be so strong and beautiful that for several years I was convinced that "his love for me" would make him change his way of life. That's what led us to marriage. That was the misunderstanding that separated us.'

In the struggle against change, as well as in the efforts to change the other person, the violence exerted by love is an attempt to reduce the other person to the sole dimensions that please and suit us. If the other person cannot be tailor-made, then the violence becomes mutual: it develops into an awful war. If he conforms, then the violence is internal because he faces a heart-breaking choice: submit or lose his partner.

The violence of idealization

In the pursuit of love, too often we look for what does not exist while refusing to recognize that it does not exist. We therefore burden the other person with the awful task of helping us achieve unity and completeness. Some men and women endlessly look for the unreachable presence of an idealized person they have cherished within themselves for a long time.

> **At what age did I conceive this image of a woman with wonderful breasts, blue eyes and laughter deep in her belly?**
> **Were you born with this fragrance, this burning mother-of-pearl skin and the force of absolute surrender?**
> **It was so long ago that both of us have forgotten, but what does it matter . . .**
> **And this doubt that dwells in me, mixed with the pleasure of being with you, is it really you, is it really me?**
> **Yes, it is you, it is me.**
> **Let's rejoice in our meeting. Let's promise ourselves everything.**
> **Let's enter the intensity of love.**
> **Let's create a fragile eternity.**

To continue idealizing a person, we sometimes have to resort to self-sabotage or to accusation. I am the one who does not know how to see, recognize, hear, appreciate, receive . . . I am the one who is 'bad' so that the other person can be good. I am the one who does not know enough, who does not understand anything. I am the one who must change and improve. I am the one, with all my strength, who must carry my failings and the shortcomings of the relationship. I am the one who must overcome obstacles, smooth away the unexpected and expose misunderstandings. It is on me that today's future rests.

The omnipotence of imaginary life here takes on its full

'I often get backache when I am torn between several desires.'

scope at the expense of real life or of the reality of the other person.

Conversely, when I become accusing after being disappointed or frustrated, I build an imagined portrait of the other person which explains the failure of the relationship. I back it up with numerous justifications.

> 'He's so self-centred, I believe he's incapable of really loving. He doesn't see himself as he really is, but I have noticed a thousand times that it is unbearable for him to take others into consideration.'

> 'She mainly needs to complain and chew over her childhood dissatisfactions. So she blames me for my attitudes whatever I do. If I'm silent, she tells me off. Whatever I say is the wrong thing.'

Thus, displaced onto expectations in love, the idealization and search for the absolute lead to the denigration of oneself, of the other or of the relationship, and sometimes of love itself.

Truth, to tell the truth . . . is what everybody requires, especially those who love you . . . But how can you tell the truth to those who cannot bear its glare?
Alice Rivaz

5   Personal Myths

Tales I Tell Myself and Other Fictions

Too often we ignore what we can't understand, in others and in ourselves.

Early on in life each of us builds a network of personal beliefs or myths about life, death, love, men, women, relationships and ourselves.

Sometimes our most significant relationships are rigidly moulded by these myths. Unfortunately, they prevent us from gaining access to the richness of the moment, because they impose themselves on us with a kind of omnipotent obviousness. They deny the unexpected that has emerged, and block the way to the wonder of miracles. Our certainties prevent us from being surprised anymore. But any encounter, any relationship, brings change, disruption or evolution; this is what we must be prepared for when we relate or communicate.

There are two kinds of myth:

- *pseudo-realistic myths:* They concern what I am like (not worthy of being loved, unhappy, a winner, attractive, etc.), what others are like (threatening, benevolent, indifferent, superior, inferior, etc), what men are like (they're all the same), what women are like (they're all the same), life (a valley of tears, a marvellous adventure), death (a scandal, a blessing) and relationships (impossible, vital, disappointing, etc).
- *normative myths:* They define how I should be (perfect), how a father, a mother should be (not like mine), how a lover, a child and relationships should be (healthy, lively, reassuring, stable).

Both kinds of myths are prefabricated images, pre-established patterns that lead us, without our realizing it, to deny the

If the people in our imaginary lives never get it together it must be because they are miles apart!

permanent and vital evolution of people, feelings and relationships.

'I expect criticisms, compliments and demands from my boss. He expects conformity and goodwill from me. All hierarchical relationships are like that.'

'In bed, it's the man who should know what to do and how to do it. It's up to him to awaken and satisfy the woman's desire.'

'Mainly, parents should be fair and give each child the same thing.'

'When you love someone, it's for life.'

'If you're really fond of someone, then all obstacles will be overcome.'

'I have never been unfaithful to my husband; if I were, I wouldn't stay with him.'

These beliefs sometimes take on the force of injunctions, of rules to be kept, of life lessons: 'If I conform to them, everything should work out well, there shouldn't be any problem.'

Even repeated experiences that strongly deny our intimate theories have no hold over these last, which remain inflexible. Myths come unharmed out of most experiences and are perpetuated over several generations. They are used as codes of references for a lot of our behaviour and confirm the validity of our actions and thoughts.

A FEW BELIEFS

Our reactions are determined by the interpretation we give to events, far more than by the events themselves. It is sometimes useful to see them from a different perspective, the point of view of a third party. Accepting the need to question our beliefs is the only possibility of progress towards evolution, maturation and growth.

Reactional beliefs

Our beliefs are constructed out of our emotional tendencies:

- either to confirm them;
- or to fight against them.

  A man who finds it hard to express his emotions insists on the importance of decency and reserve in relationships; he advocates respect for the other person's privacy and his own. He has turned his temperament into a general ideology. His way of relating is in accordance with his belief . . . and doesn't take into account the real person facing him.

On the other hand, another man, who has the same difficulty to be spontaneous and open, advocates personal and direct communication as a major condition for relationships: 'I believe it is important, mainly, that each one of us be spontaneous.'

A woman who tends to let herself be influenced and invaded too much by others has built her ideal in relationships, her basic belief, on the importance of independence and autonomy.

A 50-year-old man, who advocates anarchy in relationships, has spent his life rebelling against taboos, rules of conduct, behaviour and limits imposed on family and friendly relationships. The only rule he acknowledges is that of each person's individual pleasure and he relentlessly champions his theory.

One day, feeling confident, he related with great emotion the event that had marked him at the age of 16: 'My mother had been paralysed for a few days. She had had a haemorrhage and in turn each member of the family sat up at her bedside. She couldn't talk but she seemed to have kept all her lucidity. I was an adolescent consumed with sexual curiosity and desires. In my family there was a heavy prohibition on any sex-related talk.

One night, when I was sitting by my mother's bed, I folded back the sheets, uncovered her body and almost without wanting to, touched her breasts and sexual organs. Then I caressed her. I was convinced that it did her good. But panic overwhelmed me and it even came to my mind to stifle her with the pillow so that she could never tell what had happened.

She died a few weeks later without having recovered speech. During all those days I was terrified by the idea that she might be able to speak again.'

Having transformed his guilt into an ideology of freedom ('Why not incest, after all'), this man does not at all realize that the transgression he committed may have moulded his beliefs. He experiences himself as the real inventor of a way of life. And in a way that is true, even though he is not able to recognize the forces at work in him.

False beliefs presented as truths

When we talk about ourselves, we need to produce a 'clear' description of the way we function. We offer it, apparently, to others, but it's really for ourselves.

Our descriptions are true in a way, because it is in good faith that we believe in this definition of ourselves. We support it by means of explanations and justifications.

Our images are characterized by their consistency: they are drawn without nuances and are devoid of contradictions. We impose them on the other person and on ourselves as an accurate, true and unchangeable representation of what we are. It is as if we were offering others our recognized or unjustly contested reality:

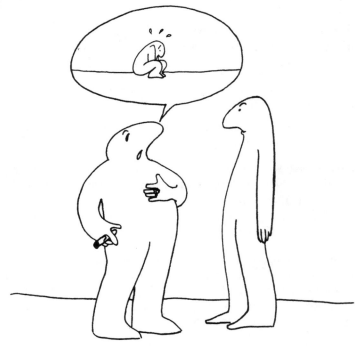

'Nobody ever loved me ...!'

'I'm very frank. I always give my opinion. It sometimes gets me into trouble, but I can't stand dissimulation or hypocrisy.'

The friend or the person close to us who listens to this statement will be puzzled. He is convinced that his friend is speaking in good faith and really sees himself like this. But this does not correspond at all to the image of the rather fearful and hesitant man he knows. Will he tell him, or will he let him go on describing himself the way he wants without contradicting him?

'As for me, I'm a very tolerant person; I easily accept ideas that differ from mine, but it's not like that around me.'

These myths we tell ourselves fulfil an essential purpose. They present us to the world and to ourselves in the light we have chosen.

Our images are not always flattering. Some people, on the contrary, cultivate the self-portrait of being unlucky, of being a victim or powerless.

'I have never been understood. Nobody has ever loved me; I made myself what I am; nothing was given to me . . .'

'I never had any luck in life. When something started to work, someone always showed up to destroy it.'

Our self-image will always be influenced by the desire to be good or reputable. Negative representations (I am worthless, I am incapable, etc) are simply the noticeable reverse of an ideal self-image. They are generally accompanied by explanations and justifications that tend to take away our responsibility.

'If my father hadn't had a drink problem, I could have gone to university, but I had to help my mother by working to support the younger ones. I promised myself that I'd never marry; I'd rather die. I had three abortions within five years, but it wasn't my fault. I couldn't stand the pill. It made me put on weight.'

We are often struck by the fierceness with which a person clings to the description of himself that he has elaborated with profuse details and examples. He does not allow the other person to see him in a different light if the latter attempts to oppose him:

> 'But I don't see you as someone who is exploited. You seem to be the one who calls the tune and you get what you want.'
>
> 'No, no, I'm the one who's taken in. I'm always the mug, because I'm afraid of taking advantage, of disturbing or imposing. You should have seen the way I got married. My girlfriend had left me a few months before, after I had proposed to her. She suddenly came back to tell me that she was pregnant by me. I was moved and happy. On that evening we decided to get married, and later on, she told me that she wasn't pregnant! So you see, she took me in!'

The false images which we produce have an outward function in relationships and also an inner function.

> **On a building site, three stone-cutters are hewing stones. Someone passing by asks them what they are doing.**
> **The first one answers: 'I'm cutting stones.'**
> **The second answers: 'I'm building a wall.'**
> **The third one answers: 'I'm building a cathedral.'**

In relationships the functions of false images are numerous. They are sometimes hidden from our own consciousness and it can be hurtful to discover them.

> 'I present myself as helpless, therefore I won't be criticized or attacked.'

> 'I describe myself as generous, giving and devoted; I hide my inner emptiness from others and from myself.'

> 'I explain that I'm totally able to love several women at a time and to give enough to each of them. I reassure the other person and myself by honestly denying the threat that weighs on our relationship.'

> 'I give the complete list of the merciless circumstances that obliged me to change work several times in the last three years so as not to confront my own responsibility.'

The inner function of false images consists in giving myself the impression of being balanced and self-aware, since I can define who and how I am in a simple and coherent way. Some people reassure themselves with a 'good' image of themselves, others with a 'bad' one.

'I'm faithful to myself' can mean 'I remain faithfully imprisoned in the image of myself I constructed, and outside of which I'm terribly afraid of venturing.'

> An altar boy sometimes dips into the collection box in the church, but he keeps an image of himself as a 'good altar boy'. He really believes this, and he mentally cancels out the action he has committed or finds justifications for it. His intimate conviction that he is good and devoted predominates.

> A man is convinced that he has done everything he could in planning his timetable so as to put aside as much time as possible to be with his girlfriend. He simply forgot to consult her and to take into account *her* timetable. He experiences himself as open and satisfying and is surprised and hurt not be perceived as such.

> A woman evokes a whole series of situations in which she sees herself as negative, trapped in repetitions and unable to experience pleasure and satisfaction. She is furious and rejects the other person when he says: 'Yes, you only see the negative side of what you're experiencing.'

> 'I resent you', she says, 'for seeing only what is wrong in what I'm saying.' It is as if she were saying: 'I give you the negative side. You should give me back the positive so that I can refuse it.'

> A social workers tells how she listened with astonishment to a woman whose circumstances had led her to abandon her three children. The woman described herself in this way: 'I never received anything from my parents; they didn't bring me up, so I don't want to do the same thing with my children. I do everything I can for them, I shall never abandon them. They have been put in residential care but I think of them constantly. I know that thanks to me they are well.'

The image of oneself as a 'good father' or 'good mother' is one of the most deep-rooted and keeps all refutations away.

Here, wish and reality are confused. All parents wish to be 'good parents', and they really mean to be. Some of them build whole strategies concerning their responsibilities, or how to control care, cleanliness, food, leisure or school – and, in doing so, will prove to be awful if not unbearable parents. This can also be observed in marital roles:

> 'I really believed for a long time that I was a perfect husband because I always agreed with her. I stuck with whatever she suggested. Years later, I at last discovered that she found it unbearable. The fact that I didn't take any personal stand about anything obliged her to make suggestions continually, which she admitted she hated.'

We keep our balance by refusing to see the unacceptable in ourselves. This mechanism of cancellation, of denial of reality, seems to obey a magical and infantile need:

> 'That's not fair, not wanted. It shouldn't be so, therefore it isn't.'

To create more space in myself and in my relationships, I shall have to give up the tales I tell myself, be they glorious, grandiose or unlucky.

These tales will be difficult to give up or modify, because they build a pattern in which I arrange the events of my life. This gives me a feeling of awareness and coherence. My perception of these events even distorts them so that they fit into the original scenario I built.

> 'I wasn't wanted, I was an accident. Therefore I'll never find my place in life. I'm always unwanted.'

> 'My mother wanted a boy and I wanted to please her so much that I was a tomboy till the age of 13. Afterwards I had my periods, but for me it was something dirty, a real drag. I was very happy when I became pregnant and had a boy, the first one in the family. I couldn't have tolerated having a daughter.'

But who can claim that a child who was not consciously wanted by his parents isn't loved? He might be an unexpected gift of life.

He might receive special tenderness since his existence, not having been planned, is miraculous. The unwanted child might be lucky to be born of desire. He might be less trapped by his parents' expectations, because he was not born to live up to someone else's expectations and meet his parents' needs.

Such changes of points of view or of perspective are a first step towards a relaxing of these false images which burden us and prevent us from meeting ourselves. In this way we will at last gain access to our own wish: a desire to exist for ourselves and not for others.

It is in the shadow of ourselves that we make the most luminous encounters.

DUES AND JUSTICE

Giving up what we don't have is more difficult than giving up what we do have.

One of the most difficult beliefs to let go of is the belief that there is or should be human justice, that reciprocity is owed in relationships, and that rights and duties are expected of both partners.

'I asked him a question, so I have a right to his answer.'

'I love you, so listen to me; read my letters, help me, love me.' This is considering love as a right, as a due.

'I take a lot of trouble to welcome my husband's son when he comes for weekend visits. I feel moved by him; I have a lot of affection and tenderness for him. So he should love me and not keep me at a distance the way he does. He should give me the love that I need to get rid of my guilt at having replaced his mother.'

'I deliberately sacrificed my other children's rights for my favourite son. He was the only one who could take over my business. I gave him everything. I even bought up my partner's share so that he could be sole master on board.

And now he has asked me to give him back the keys of a chalet I had bought with my own funds but which was, for tax reasons, in the company's name. He's dispossessing me of my own estate, although he owes everything to me . . .'

This father is not at all aware of the guilt he induced in his son, the guilt of having agreed to infringe on his brothers' and sisters' rights. He isn't aware that his son will make him pay dearly for this unfair gift of wealth, which deprived him of the pleasure of acquiring it. Vowing an unlimited hatred to the father who valued him too highly and made him be rejected by all his brothers and sisters, he will in fact completely dispossess him.

It is not within our power to modify, increase, diminish or transform someone else's feelings. It is difficult enough to keep power over our own feelings; with someone else's feelings, it's impossible.

Letting go of the wish to act on other people's feelings is an achievement. It is by giving up this infantile omnipotence that we enter into mature relationships. And yet we persistently try to act on other people's feelings.

'Don't be jealous; love me as I am; don't be frustrated; don't be angry ...'

'Knowing that I'm happy shouldn't make you suffer. You always told me that it was your greatest wish.' Of course, he meant that he wanted her to be happy with him . . . not with another man!

'Stop making a fuss about that loss of money; we're not going to die because of it.'

'If he loved me, he would take care of my anxieties, my feeling of worthlessness and my disappointments. He seems to think: "It's her problem, not mine." He refuses to take on my suffering, even when he's the cause of it. That's not love.'

As for him, his position is: 'When it's convenient for me, I listen to her. I try to help her see herself more clearly. I take care of her anxieties. It is intolerable that this should be considered as a due and an obligation, by her and sometimes by me.'

When the idea of owing something merges with a deeper feeling of being indebted, it acts as a detonator in some relationships and triggers off refusal, escape or aggressive behaviour.

'My husband only thinks of himself and I also only think of him, of making him happy. So if our life as a couple is a failure, it's because of him, because of his selfishness.'

She takes care of him and he takes care only of himself: they cannot really meet. Nothing can shake her theory that 'obligatory altruism' is the only possible basis for a relationship as a couple. She does not see that her altruism hides an intense request for reciprocity, a deep-rooted belief that what is given is owed in return. She unknowingly confuses gift with request. She gives him abundantly what she actually wants for herself, which means that he doesn't receive anything.

These dynamics are common in relationships. They would be unremarkable if they did not cause a lot of frustrations and therefore a lot of suffering. Many couples say the same: 'He gives me a lot, especially what I don't ask for. He's so convinced he knows what's good for me . . .'

Many woman are deeply convinced that their sexual partner owes them something: money, taking care of them, continuity, exclusiveness, attention, gratitude. Otherwise, they have the impression that they have been 'had', whatever the pleasure they received in lovemaking. Our culture discredits sexual relationships based solely on pleasure and physical harmony.

Our beliefs induce failures which we then use to justify these very beliefs:

'If they had been properly applied, there would have been no failure. If I had been more firm, this wouldn't have happened. Next time I won't let myself be taken in like that.'

'If the other person, especially, had behaved according to my beliefs, if he had been able to live the freedom of love without being possessive, well, then we would still be together; we would both be happy ...'

For frequently, the innermost belief which we call personal myth partly consists in thinking that the other person ought to adopt a certain behaviour in response to our own attitude.

The psychological theories of the first half of the 20th century were affirmative and anticipatory. Many people have distorted them and used them as a basis for their own beliefs. Scientific researchers modify their theoretical hypothesis according to their experiments and discoveries, not without trouble, certainly. For most essential discoveries, as we now know, are the results of mistakes or distorted manipulations.

In the emotional field of relationships, our normative and explanatory beliefs seem ineradicable and completely impervious to any proof of their inadequacy. Life has little hold on them. It is as if life had to adjust, not us! Our resistance to requests for personal change is mostly the result of our individual preconceived beliefs.

One must give up and mourn long-loved myths so as to develop and grow!

WHAT WE THINK WE OWE

I cannot hear and recognize another person's desires, demands, disappointments or sufferings if I am trapped into thinking that I owe something.

Some people feel invested with the 'mission' of healing someone else's wounds, of satisfying him and even taking his place.

'You know, I didn't tell her that her father was seriously ill as it was three weeks before her baby was due. I didn't want to shock her . . .'

'He is doubting and ambivalent. I ought to be able to deal with his questioning.'

'I ought to be able to understand what he is really asking for and find a way of giving it to him.'

'He's saying he feels very discouraged. I ought to cheer him up.'

A man might think he ought to quieten the fear and anxiety of a woman who says: 'You know, my mother had cancer at the age of 38. Yesterday I discovered a lump under my left breast. I'm sure it's cancer.'

The thought that we owe something is linked to a feeling of guilt, to messages we have received ('You should be less self-centred, you should think of others') or to 'missions' we are given by our parents or grandparents. All these messages confirm that, anyway, the other person is more important, and that he or she deserves all our attention and availability.

The thought that we owe something might be rooted in our infinite need to be recognized, valued or appreciated by doing good to other people or by devoting ourselves to them.

This belief that we have to satisfy other people prevents us from simply welcoming certain words. Instead of just listening and receiving, we launch into giving answers, searching for solutions and examining the problem closely. Wanting to avoid these predictable reactions the other person won't dare talk about him or herself and will stay silent.

'I'm disappointed that my husband had to cancel the weekend we had planned in Paris to celebrate our 20th wedding anniversary. It's nothing serious, but it was important for me and I don't want to tell him. He would feel guilty. So I say that it doesn't matter . . . and he might be disappointed by my indifference.'

When we abandon some of these 'missions', let go of received injunctions and give up the thought that we ought to do something, then paths open up that lead us to more possibilities and freedom.

We often think we should satisfy a wish and receive it as a request when it was really the expression of wondering, enthusiasm, or a dream.

To assert oneself and one's own position means to step out of the obligation of doing something, whatever its real or fantasized origin.

So during sessions of personal growth, we sometimes suggest the use of symbolic gestures and actions to reframe an old scenario, so as to move out of a repetitive game in a relationship.

> 'Mummy, for years I carried your anxiety about men. I made it mine. I was faithful to your version and your perception of them; I perceived them as you did, and saw them from your point of view, as bastards who had only one thing on their mind.
> Today, I give you back your anxiety; it's yours. I return to you your vision of me. You probably had good reasons to see them like that. Mummy, I give you back your message; I don't need it any more. I trust my own perception and my own experience of life.'

Through this gesture and statement, which can be accompanied by the gift of an object, the person recovers a more personal and more intimate vision of the world. We also discover that he or she can give up brooding, accusing, resenting, and put back into circulation energies that had remained blocked and immobilized by suffering, prohibitions and censure.

FICTIONS

Two friends meet again, three years after a long and adventurous voyage together. And they launch into memories.

> 'It's strange,' says one of them. 'We don't have the same memories.'
> 'But I assure you that it really was as I'm telling you,' retorts the other one.

And they will have an endless discussion to establish the objectivity of such and such an event or encounter, and the reality of such and such a danger. They will discuss it till they argue about it, and then suddenly start laughing: 'We travelled together, but it wasn't the same journey. Tell me yours and I'll tell you mine.'

We all build in good faith the story of what we have seen, felt, experienced or done; we all build our own fiction about each event. But it can be unbearable to hear the other's fiction concerning a mutual experience, especially if it destroys our own.

'I'm happy to have been able to offer you this training that opens up new possibilities for you,' says a husband tenderly to his wife.
'But I'm the one who paid for my training and I'm proud of that!', retorts the surprised and humiliated wife.
'But, remember, you told me about your wish to do this training and I told you that each month I would pay an allowance into your account.'
'But of course, I was working part-time because of the housekeeping and the children. It's with my salary that I paid for the training.'
The husband remains silent. He tells himself that it is very important for her to think that she herself provided for her training, and he doesn't want to contest her tale, and he remains convinced that it is his own view of things which is objective. He reinforces his opinion by adopting a paternal attitude: 'Yes, it's more vital for her to believe that than it is for me to confirm that it isn't so . . .'

In this way, it is possible not to accept the story related by the other person as a reality for oneself, but to hear it as an important reality for the other person. It is possible to give up the wish to convince.

It is by accepting the other's experience, and not by making it ours, that we find the sence of communication. Only differences can be shared. By revealing our own truth and letting the other person do so as well, we leave room for respect and sharing.

One of the ways of tenderness is to be able to listen to what comes from the other person without wanting to alter it for our own benefit.

Each of us communicates with and according to his personal myth and his representation of himself and others. Our self-image, our personal fiction, is intended much more for ourselves than for others. But I also need my myth to be believed, to strike a chord in someone else and be mirrored, even though neither of us is really taken in by it.

> 'Couldn't you lie sometimes', a husband asked his wife who was relentless in her quest for lucidity and truth, 'and let me believe that I'm a good companion for you?'
>
> Another begged a particularly demanding wife: 'You're so ruthless with yourself that I have no chance of escaping your fault-finding. I am doomed to complete imperfection.'
>
> A father often reminded his children: 'I'm only your father. That's all and that's very little, I know, but I'm the father you have.'

Through these few examples we realize the difficulty of sharing a mutual experience.

> When Mary and Paul try to recall their wedding day, they discover ten years later, with some suffering, that their experiences are so different, and sometimes so opposed, that for a moment they find themselves doubting the reality of their wedding day.
>
> In his perception, it was the radiant and full day of an overjoyed man marrying his beloved, surrounded by all the people he loved, including his son (born of a first marriage).
>
> For her it was a day of frustration and non-fulfilment, a day of violent emotions as she observed her husband busy with many others on a day that belonged only to her.
>
> They had believed for a long time that it was the same wedding, and that they shared the same vision, but that day had left two different impressions in their bodies and memories.

We can say that truth has only relative value. As far as personal communication goes, our experience is the truth.

'Yes, I dreamt that on that day you would really be mine ...'

When a child talks about an event, he or she seldom tells what happened. He usually gives an account of his experience, and his experience acts as a reference which links him to the event and to the people involved. The adult who, at the beginning, will try to contest his experience by relying on facts, will disturb him and cause him to doubt. It would also be suitable here to acknowledge the other person's perception and experience and to give up imposing one's own perception.

'It's true. You experienced it like that. That is the way it happened for you.'

'This is how you understood what was said on that day and what I did that time.'

A man and a woman who have known and appreciated each other for 12 years have kept different memories of their first encounter.

'I assure you that you were the one who invited me to drink coffee after the lecture.'

'Not at all. We were in the same workshop and at a certain point you asked me to be your partner in an exercise suggested by the leader.'

In this example, neither of them wants to keep the memory of being the one who asked; each one wants to believe that he or she was the one chosen. The fiction seems necessary for their relationship and must be maintained against all the evidence.

These fictions contribute to the inner regulation of our self-images; they serve as anchors in the complexity of life and of our characters.

Fictions about relationships reveal themselves in a tragi-comic way when you listen separately to two persons talking about what they experience together.

'I have such a marvellous and open communication with my adolescent son,' says this smiling mother. 'He has complete trust in me and I tell him everything about myself.'

'It's terrible with my mother,' says her son, 'she needs to know everything. She is continually questioning me, offering to listen to me, inviting me to express myself and worst of all, she tells me everything about her marital life. I've had enough, but I don't want to hurt her.'

Another mother declares peremptorily that she knows how to listen to her son: 'I do it all the time,' she adds. 'The other day he told me he didn't like school, he felt rejected and would like to train in a circus. I answered him that it was too soon to leave school, that he was imagining things about his rejection, that he had at least two good friends, Michael and John, who often came round to the house, and that I found circus work dangerous and unreliable.'

The woman is convinced that she is a good listener because of the validity (so she thinks) of her answers.

A number of parents are persuaded, like this woman, that they listen to their children because they don't 'hesitate to answer'.

If we want to communicate, that is to say to share, then we must not confuse answering and listening.

In a couple, the husband thinks everything is alright: their life is harmonious, they don't have any problems, and he congratulates himself because 'nowadays, successful couples are few and far between'.

But she tells her friends – and only her friends and never her husband – that her marital relationship has become dull, dreary, even lifeless, and that this make-believe desperately weighs on her.

Husbands would be astounded if they could hear their wives talking about their relationship and themselves the way they do at the hairdresser's.

In the interpretation and fiction through which we describe events, we tend to show ourselves in a good light, and to throw onto the other person the responsibility for that which affects us.

An 18-year-old student has been living for a short time with his father in a different town than his mother. He spends his weekends at his mother's house and when he comes back on Sunday evening, his father often finds him fairly depressed. 'His mother depresses him,' he says to himself. 'She lets her own wounds weigh on him. She doesn't let him become independent. When he leaves on Friday after five days with me, he's in the best of spirits.'

He shares his perception of the situation with his ex-wife and she almost laughs at his fatherly blindness. 'He doesn't even see that it's the fact that he goes back to his father that makes his son sad! Of course he's happy on Friday at the prospect of coming to me and of leaving his father for the weekend!'

Each of them attributes to the other the teenager's depressive state. As for the son, he probably has a totally different version that explains his changes of mood.

The meaning we give to events is the pivot of our everyday life and relationships; the fiction we tell ourselves creates our story with its dynamics and repetitions.

'My life really changed', says an old man, 'when I became convinced, really convinced, that my happiness didn't depend on others, nor on circumstances. I discovered that it was an inner state, which I could influence. It took me many years to believe this and to nurture this belief.'

Unfortunately this fundamental discovery usually occurs late in life. The inner state this man is referring to is like the beam from which our perceptions radiate, the rainbow where all the colours of life join, or the melting-pot where beliefs, events and relationships come to merge and be unified. It is a state of wisdom, plenitude or serenity towards which some of us let ourselves be carried, whereas others let themselves be drawn away from it.

We should love the other person because of our richness and not because of our shortcomings.

DEVELOPMENT

It is the modification of beliefs, the change of points of view, which forms the basis for possible development. We can exchange a myth for another more liberating myth, which will in turn be replaced by another version. We could substitute a more acceptable fiction for a painful one. That would simply be subjecting the same scenario to a change of meaning, as in *Rashomon*, a film where the same sequence of events takes on a different significance according to the perception and words of the person who is telling the story.

Usually, beliefs only evolve if they are shaken by serious crisis, shattering experiences, exceptional encounters or by an arduous, assiduous and painful search for oneself.

This is the characteristic of many discoveries in social sciences: they allow for new points of view, develop a new sensitivity, draw our attention to other signs, and thus help us build a theory and practice of life. But be careful! Personal myths become ideologies when it is considered that they can be applied to the whole world. They can become dangerous when they are used by uncompromising prophets who know how to impose their views on others. When discoverers become prophets, when those who are enlightened want to enlighten others, then the half-open doors to freedom get blocked and the announced movement gets paralysed, divided and lost because paths have been too clearly signposted.

Let us pause here a while and consider ourselves, we who are writing these lines, and you, the reader. We too in these texts bring in personal ideologies and myths about change, lively relationships and healthy communication. Our creed is continually updated by our practice of leading groups, enriched and structured by lectures, articles and books. Be careful, reader! We too convey our myths, our beliefs about love, relationships and life. Perhaps we are trying to offer them and not to impose them. But that too is a belief.

6   Major Sabotage Mechanisms

I'm open to everyone with the same sort of ideas as my own.

We all want healthy relationships and lively communication, and most of the time we are full of good intentions and good-will. So what is it that sabotages and invalidates our relationships and communication?

We all have inside us swamp-like areas of mixed feelings and deep-rooted attitudes which interfere with our efforts. We hope for dialogues which then don't get anywhere because of the irrational waves of emotion that overwhelm us. Our intentions and decisions to do the right thing are thwarted, and once again we are unable to stop the encounter being spoilt or damaged.

'I wanted to tell him quietly and deliberately what didn't work for me in our relationship. I had planned to talk only about myself and to make some propositions. As soon as I started to talk, everything became muddled. I heard myself launch into blame and judgements, then I made my point sound so trite. I withdrew a little and eventually burst into tears, having nothing further to say . . .'

'I only wanted my point of view to be heard. I wanted to tell him how important for me it was to be heard on this issue: I had felt deceived and not respected in our initial agreement. And he accused me and hurled at me in a nasty voice: "You only think of yourself. You always want to be right." His words resonated in me. They were unfair. I walked away slamming the door. Afterwards, I didn't know how to go back.'

The less we recognize in ourselves the sabotage mechanisms at work, the more their subterranean influence will be perceptible in our actions and words. If we want our relationships to become deeper, we have to face our inner demons and transform their energy by daring to look at them face to face.

We have to find out our areas of tolerance and particularly of intolerance. We also have to recognize as quickly as possible what is at work when we suffer. Three aspects can be involved. Is it:

- the invasion of our territory?
- a wound related to the image we have of ourselves?
- the apprehension of future persecution?

Each time one of these dimensions is 'touched', we react. We stop behaving according to the relationship and behave according to our gut reactions.

To illustrate such behaviour, we will mention seven families of sabotage mechanisms. We know that they have innumerable facets, that they are all double-faced and constitute vital forces that can be creative as well as destructive:

- self-deprivation;
- resentment;
- jealousy;
- guilt;
- judgement;
- comparison;
- projection and appropriation.

These poisons in our relationships come from the numerous fears that have been dwelling in us, tormenting us and working in us since early childhood. In fact they function like slow acids that chew over, corrode and destroy the structure.

We cannot prevent black birds from flying over our heads, but we can prevent them from nesting there.
Chinese proverb

SELF-DEPRIVATION

In the West we apparently live in a world of abundance and waste. But our inner feeling of deprivation is sometimes so important or so intense that we begin to deny our immediate needs and get carried away in an escalation of frustrations. We try and satisfy old deprivations which are really like bottomless pits and, in doing so, we forget the present and its immediate urgency.

Emotional deprivation in childhood marks us and induces self-deprivation in adult life.

'The sentences that I seem to have heard most often from my mother's lips are: "I don't have time" and "Don't disturb Dad". I realize that not only do I never ask anybody to give me any of their time, but I don't even give myself time either. I let other people's needs come first, and I hate to ask for anything.'

'All through my childhood, I heard: "There's no point in asking, if you are going to have the humiliation of a refusal." The fear of refusal is now so strong in me that it seems almost an obscenity to ask.'

Our feeling of emotional deprivation is often expressed in terms of possession: I want to have a lover, a wife, friends, a partner, parents who would be such and such a way, who would give me what I need. We often express this in the past tense, or in the conditional.

'I wish I had had a childhood which had given me a feeling of security.'

'I wish I had known a great love.'

'If only I had taken other subjects at university . . .'

This nostalgic fixation on past problems is a powerful means of nurturing the feeling of deprivation in the present. It is also associated with a wish to return to relationships of fusion which we had early on in life, when we were satisfied without yet being differentiated from our mother.

> 'When I was little, my grandmother heard me without my having to say anything. She even heard my silences. Then my parents took me back and life became as empty as a desert.'

> 'I wanted to be understood without having to resort to speech.'

Our feeling of deprivation is sustained by a magical expectation of satisfaction – 'I would like to be loved without having to ask for it or to prove anything' – and by an idealization of our own tyrannical demands.

> 'Something is due to me and I'm not getting it.'

We often think that our feeling of deprivation would be appeased by possessions, by having everything we want and don't have: a beautiful house, more holidays, Old Masters, sumptuous carpets, a computer . . . Some people repeatedly purchase and accumulate

'It's my fault I don't get any relaxation ... I don't allow any time for it.'

objects. They may even become compulsive buyers. Superstores make a fortune by selling stereo equipment, video-recorders, videotapes and sophisticated goods which fill up the emptiness of an apartment but add even more to the feeling of deprivation.

Although they know that money cannot buy happiness, some people do not believe it and deprive themselves of happiness so as to have money. The recent development of small-time speculation and the craze for playing the Stock Market illustrate this trend. To earn money with money, to be on the lookout for deals, requires sacrificing a lot of time that could be devoted to happiness. It is difficult to identify clearly what it is we feel deprived of and separated from. We can try and explore our wishes exhaustively by asking if they are what we really want. It is a long process that might lead us to what is essential. We might also get discouraged when faced with all the expectations that lurk in the shadows of our personal history.

For the feeling of deprivation is linked to expectation. In this sense it creates possibilities or puts a damper on them.

What do we expect from others, from ourselves and from life? What did we wait for in vain during the whole of our childhood? What fabulous expectations did we have during our adolescence? What is this need to remain tense and on the alert as if forever expecting something?

'I need tenderness, but I don't ask for it. It wouldn't be worth having, but I still expect people to come to me.'

'I can only be in love with men who are not available.'

'I expect the impossible but it's always the possible I get; it's quite disappointing.'

'I look for my perfect female image in all women, but I never find it.'

The path is a long one that begins with the opposition between the principle of pleasure and the principle of reality, and finally makes them coincide.

'I don't feel deprived if I accept what is available.'

'Each second, each moment, of happiness is worth receiving even though it is transient and short-lived. It is all the more miraculous if it is fragile and vulnerable.'

Happiness means daring to say yes. But happiness has its own unhappiness: being the only one who is happy.

There are also deprivations which we inflict on ourselves because we don't expect anything. We cut ourselves off from our own inner richness.

'I dispossessed myself of all the things that I didn't dare do.'

'Each time I answer a vital question with a ready-made answer, I cut myself off from my ability to listen to myself and create myself.'

'Each time I didn't dare step out of my fears, each time I didn't go for the unexpected, I deprived myself of a new possibility.'

All kinds of self-censorship limit our possibilities. Let us call this 'imaginary repression': we imagine the terrible consequences of an action which we are not going to carry out, of words which we are not going to say.

We use our imaginary ideas about other people to censor ourselves. We attribute to the other person all sorts of reactions that prevent us from doing such and such a thing. We think as if we were in the other person's place, so that we limit ourselves.

'If I tell him that I don't think like him, he'll be angry and the evening will be spoilt.'

'I can't tell her the truth. She couldn't bear it.'

'If he doesn't feel like going out, then I'll make myself stay in too.'

'I won't ask them to come. I know they wouldn't dare refuse and then they'd be bored.'

These projections are closely related to childhood experiences. Vagueness in education, the absence of clearly set limits, produce in sensitive children a strong self-censorship. They forbid themselves to do what other people have not explicitly forbidden. They create so many barriers as they try and guess and especially invent what would displease Daddy, Mummy or Grandma that any step into the future becomes too disquieting an adventure.

As adults, they continue to attribute to others imagined reactions and prohibitions. They avoid checking other people's reactions and simply pursue a sterile and inhibiting inner dialogue.

'I'm not going to show him how pleased I was to go out with friends; it would hurt his feelings.'

'For five years, I didn't dare separate myself from him for fear he would be too hurt and would become an alcoholic again. When I finally told him, with a lot of apprehension, I discovered that he too had wanted that for years but hadn't had the courage to tell me for fear of destroying me.'

Perhaps the most subtle and violent deprivation is the one that mutilates my imagination and limits it with prejudices and preconceived ideas. All I can do then is to conform to the norms of my self-images.

'I'm not educated enough to address this famous writer. You should know your place and not bother people.'

'I was convinced that I wouldn't achieve anything, as my father had predicted for years, so in secret I prepared for and sat a special university entrance examination. I thought they had made a mistake when I saw my name on the list of eligible candidates, and I let the registration deadline go by and had to wait a year before continuing my studies.'

We use our principles as barriers to avoid unexplored paths.

'A conscientious mother shouldn't give her children to a nanny so that she can take up studying, especially when she has the financial means (those of her husband) to stay at home.'

'You shouldn't leave a sterile woman, even if my wish to have a child has become so strong that sometimes I want to do myself in.'

We deprive ourselves of alternatives because we blindly believe that we are limited, and because of our inability to abandon a given frame of reference.

'I daren't love because I think that one should be loved by someone else first.'

'I don't sing because I don't think I know how to.'

We can deprive ourselves of all the things we know nothing about, of everything we think we don't like, just like a little child who does not want to taste an unknown type of food.

The worst thing is not what we lack but not really knowing all the things we have.

The absence of wishing is an even deeper source of genuine loss than the absence of expectation ('It would never be possible', 'I don't want it anyway').

'When I feel that I don't want anything, I ask myself what it is that is not alive in me?'

Not wanting anything is another form of trap. If we can force ourselves out of it we might discover marvellous things.

'I didn't feel like it, but I made myself go out last Sunday, and I rediscovered the wonder of the mountain meadows in June.'

'I didn't feel like going to the party because I thought I'd be bored, and that was the very evening that I met her.'

The absence of wishing could be a refusal to let ourselves be stimulated, out of passivity or out of a need to withdraw to be free for something else. Sometimes, at first sight, we get the impression that a person or a situation really does not interest us. But if we can find just one sign to open ourselves to stimulation doors might open.

'I treasure my wishes ... I nourish them, I even dream about them.'

'This woman doesn't seem very interesting to me, but she is wearing an unusual gemstone. I'm going to ask her which country it comes from.'

'I find this family reunion boring. But I suppose I could try to make contact with that nephew of mine, and find out something about his world?'

Creative people are dreamers who find the means to fulfil their dreams. We often lack audacity in our search for what we really want as well as the courage to let our imagination explore our wishes.

We so often say 'I would like to . . .' and so seldom 'I want'!

There is no cheating with the imagination, for the poet is free to invent. He imposes unconscious images and symbols that seem far closer to reality. Truth dwells in the imagination.
Eugene Ionesco

Some aspects of our personality remain inaccessible to our conscience. Some of them seem to be threatening or shameful and, unwittingly, we project them onto another person. They then come back to us like boomerangs.

> An affable and gentle father is completely disconcerted by his son's sudden aggression. The child is expressing through actions and words the violence that his father has always ignored in himself.

The basic deprivation concerns our innermost being. We long to experience an inner state of completeness and perfection. We feel that we shall never be in possession of our whole self.

> 'I sometimes have a sensation, as sharp as a stab, that leaves me with a feeling of nostalgia. It is the nostalgia of having too small and exiguous a body to contain the life that dwells in me. It is the bitter feeling of being restricted, of being in the wrong era and maybe on the wrong planet.
>
> Nowadays, especially as the years seem to have gone by so quickly for some time, I feel that there is not enough space for all my possibilities.'

I marvel at the mystery of man, at the fragility and beauty of each person, at the courage summoned by tenderness.
Marie Eve

RESENTMENT

All those who have experienced it know how terrible it is to be caught in waves of resentment. When we are, a kind of fierce will dwells in us and pushes us to refuse, reject, break or slowly destroy any relationship, however important and sometimes vital it is for us.

Resentment is like a jungle of feelings: 'Kill him', 'Revenge!', 'I'll make you pay for it', 'Don't think that you'll be happy if I'm unhappy'.

When we are resentful, we can become deaf, blind and violent, like a small child when it is distraught. We implode and we don't want anyone near our pain. It is our pain, and only we have the right to talk about it or deny it.

Violence is often helplessness expressed in action.

We all more or less tolerate frustration according to situations, people and sensitivities. Few of us really know our areas of intolerance (*see* Dyer, *Your Erroneous Zones*, Arthur Time), that is to say those parts of us which are always on edge, fragile, made up of wounds that have never properly healed and that reopen at the slightest provocation.

Resentment is like an attack of hives; it comes on when we feel out of balance, deprived of something, specially in relationships. We want to scratch it. Who has not known the dubious pleasure of reawakening a distant yet still present pain?

Resentment doesn't look for reassurance, it searches for confirmation. Everything must be accounted for. Resentment hunts down all those who might divert it from its ultimate goal: to suffer by inflicting suffering.

The deep roots of resentment reside in deprivation experienced in early childhood. This may be real or fantasized, because for the small child there is an infinite distance between his wishes and the violence of his needs. The source of possible answers is infinite.

Words, language, should be a bridge or a link that connects and brings people closer. In particular they can symbolize a possible approach to the unreachable, and where they fail imaginary life can take over. The absence of true words is certainly what brings about resentment and causes brooding, fantasies, confusion and distortion. True words name, tell and therefore link the child to the world. True words bridge the gap between the urgency of real needs and outward reality.

We do not have to make reality into threats. It is better to say 'There's a step by the door' than 'Mind the step!'

It is better to say: 'I felt hurt by your words', than silently accuse: 'Once more, he made me look like an idiot.'

Resentment comes from not accepting that our wishes have not been fulfilled, that our words have not been heard, that our expectations might not be met, that our plans might be countered or postponed, that life does not adapt to our point of view.

At certain times the world is like a minefield of frustrations. We advance and come across a belated refusal, an absence of answer, something that acts like a detonator and triggers off misunderstandings. Certain periods are fertile only for mis-understandings, conflicts and frequent frustrations.

The other person did not come up to our expectations. Reality proved to be different from what we had hoped, and this is intolerable. When the other person gives us a role that we do not want, or an answer that does not suit us, we feel destroyed because it destroys an image we have of ourselves.

'I wanted the role of the leading lady and he made me play the maidservant, or the bothersome wife.'

'I saw myself as a wonderful lover and she said I was taking advantage of her.'

'I wanted to be a kind father and he makes me behave like a cop.'

'I expected her to welcome me with a smile, to be delighted with everything I was bringing . . . and she's in a bad mood with me and blames me for always being away.'

The gap between our hope, our perception of the relationship and what actually happens produces a feeling of dispossession (dispossession of our omnipotence?) and we look for a way out to avoid depression. We store up blame, self-justifications and accusations so as to protect ourselves from rejection, denigration and distress.

Anger, rage and repeated accusations give us the opportunity to step out of ourselves. We say: 'I'm beside myself', because if we were inside ourselves, we would experience sadness and

'I am beside myself!'

bereavement. We produce anger so that we do not feel our wounds.

Anger, escape or violence are often 'screen feelings' which we place like a screen or shield between us and the other person so as not to hear or recognize what is hurt in us. These 'screen feelings' give rise to a fake behaviour that does not allow any real feeling to be talked about or experienced.

Sadness is the only way out of the pain of resentment, pain which would otherwise get lost in rebellion or silence. Anger is also sometimes a way out of depression because it sets free the rage we held back and turned against ourselves.

'I hold such a tremendous grudge against myself for not having been able to renew our relationship, to keep it alive and full of surprises, that it does me good to accuse him. I even make a list of everything he did and – even more – did not do, so as to hold him responsible for the deterioration. I use dozens of examples that come back to mind to fan the flames of my resentment. I need to be aggressive to force myself out of my nostalgia.'

Explosive anger releases pent-up feelings that are present in silences, submissions or humiliations. And there is also a redeeming anger that sets limits beyond which one should not go. It expresses indignation and reveals injustice.

Resentment, on the other hand, is an accumulation. This is why it is difficult to speak out, to express it through words. It can be related to a vast number of small facts that are insignificant, ridiculous or derisory when considered separately. It is their repetition and the feeling of helplessness and injustice that goes with them that make us resentful.

'I hold a grudge against you because I feel guilty about attacking you so much.'

Humiliations undergone without protest and repeated frustrations that strike distant chords in us create a heavy magna and produce an inner tension that is more and more unbearable. It must be discharged. It must find an outlet or a way of expressing itself. The scapegoat is often the person from whom we expect the most, the person in whom we invest most hope. It is precisely the person who was closest to us, who 'should have' understood, received or helped us, who shies away.

'In my relationship now, as well as in my former ones with my parents, I imagined "missions" they could perform to fulfil my wishes and make my fears go away.'

'I expected from you that I would at last feel loved for what I am and not for the roles that I'm given.'

Parents, companions and children are the main targets of deep resentments. The most intimate relationships are burdened with a resentment that is sometimes close to hate. The more we fasten onto someone our need to be loved and recognized, the more we resent him when he disappoints us.

By being angry with someone else, we avoid confronting ourselves. We avoid seeing our failure, our inadequacy. Anger always reveals our dependence. But it can also be a healthy stage of asserting and claiming, a driving force that pushes us to speak our needs, to make ourselves heard and to separate ourselves from all that is not good for us.

> A man told us: 'I'm seldom angry, but when I am, my anger is as cold and sharp as a scalpel. My anger is like a real surgical operation and, of course, it is on myself that I operate.'

Resentment becomes a poison for ourselves as well as for others when it reaches the stage of brooding and suffering over a long period.

> 'He could have taken me home, but he preferred to stay with his friends to drink and chat.'

'I think it's time I left you, you whose presence for so long helped me enjoy my favourite resentments.'

By thinking only of the last few minutes, this woman has demolished the wonderful day that she and her boyfriend have spent together.

When we brood over a particular relationship, we often grab a single element out of which we build scenarios of blame (which make the other person feel guilty), healing (nursing the wound inflicted on our self-image), or revenge (retaliation, deprivation ...).

We derive so much pleasure from brooding and from continually repeating and modifying an imaginary sequence that we cannot give up resentment. We thus spend a lot of energy nurturing the very thing which makes us suffer so much.

One of the ways of becoming a better friend to ourselves is to give up resentment.

In the past, the notion of forgiveness conveyed by various religions took care of this possibility. Nowadays, the issue is more about recognizing the way we nurture resentment, whatever the element that triggers it off, and whether we use it for submission or for refusal in our essential relationships.

Lucidity concerning our resentment helps us let go, gradually or in one go, of the accumulated violence. We can do this through laughter or sighs, once we have consumed all the poisonous and beneficial effects of resentment. As we feel lighter, we manage to find some distance and we can use the better parts of ourselves to face an unpredictable future.

JEALOUSY

'Jealousy is an awful feeling. It's one of the extraordinary pangs of love,' said Jeanne Moreau to Madeleine Chapsal in *La Jalousie* ('Idées', Gallimard, 1984) and I think this comment is true. For there is no jealousy without love, even though there may be many love relationships without jealousy.

A jealous person might be someone who loves somebody who used to love him. Or it might be someone who doubts the other person's love for him and reduces it to nothing, causing permanent suspicion to pervade everyday encounters and absences.

It would be more accurate to speak of a *state* of jealousy. Jealousy is essentially an emotional and physical state which is supported and fed by the imagination. Few people acknowledge being jealous. Jealousy produces shame in the person who experiences it, for it often brings about violent and destructive fantasies: violence against oneself, violence against the partner or the rival.

We recognize jealousy by its effects: it is powerfully corrosive. It invades and spoils almost any relationships that begin with intense feelings.

Jealousy is the plague of love. Sometimes it has no remedy; it always involves suffering.

We have to face the nature of the love or attachment in which jealousy is rooted. Is this love related to need or to desire? Is this love dreamed, idealized and imagined in such a way that no real relationship can fulfil it?

Jealousy is mainly related to loving out of need. It is made up of uncontrollable and compulsive feelings and sensations that feed upon any real or invented element drawn from a perpetually changing reality and upon impulses of the heart and soul. All those in love know what mixtures of joy and anxiety, of pleasure and pain, expectation and disappointment, bursts of enthusiasm or pits of depression they go through. And if they become jealous, then a specific suffering of great intensity is added.

Roots of jealousy

Some psychologists consider jealousy an acting out of persistent and 'disguised' latent homosexuality. We can sometimes sense this in the fever with which certain men and women imagine and describe the games of seduction and love affairs between their partner and the other person. They imagine these scenes with a luxury of detail and a definite interest in the rival of the same sex.

The origin of jealousy is generally rooted in the inevitable discovery made by each human being in the first years of life. He realizes that he is not unique, and that his mother has already 'betrayed' him. She has already given her love to someone more powerful and more autonomous. This 'betrayal' is one of the origins of the fear of abandonment: the fear of not having one's place, of not being recognized, of being thrown into the emptiness of existence without being connected in any way.

For another person, jealousy can be, later on, a way of fighting against a death-like feeling of non-existence. It is then a stimulant that maintains desire, that keeps alive the attraction the other person exerted. That is why, even if he has no 'real' reason to be jealous, he will unconsciously find new pretexts for still being jealous, because he draws from this feeling all the energy he needs to survive.

Jealousy fed by imagination

The jealous person mainly imagines what the other person, his partner, experiences, feels, does not feel or no longer feels. These imaginary ideas become physical sensations, the violence of which surprises and upsets him as only an inner tornado could.

It is difficult to describe the intensity and power of the jealous person's feelings. Anyway, it is vain to want to reassure or console him; he persistently returns to a detail, a word or behaviour that reactivates his suffering and leaves him in a perpetual state of turmoil. The person who experiences jealousy gets a panicky feeling of being annihilated or ruthlessly rejected.

'I know the taste of nothingness and the tenacious bitterness of non-existence.' (A jealous person)

'When I discover that my lover's feelings have changed or that he feels drawn towards someone else, when I detect the "betrayal", then it is my existence that is at risk rather than our relationship. A flood of chaotic, violent and subtle sensations invades me and brings me back to non-existence. I want to disappear, to flow, to get lost in nothingness. Then, a few moments later, I feel like a volcano that is erupting: I'm trembling, hiccupping, and images of murder overwhelm me.

Oh! how I want to hurt someone! Yes, even to hurt myself: then, at least, in the pain I exist, I feel, I experience something. So I cling to all this self-inflicted pain and, exhausted, I stand up to confront the world and this foolish life that is unaware of all this.

Nobody can understand the secret that dwells in me. Nobody can dispossess me of my suffering. At least, it is mine, my very own!'

Sometimes, jealousy and envy concern more an imagined or simple anticipated relationship than an actual relationship. This is how the imagination can do incredible damage when it feeds jealousy. For the relationship thus envisaged is seen as bearing all future possibilities and wishes, and all that hasn't so far happened.

This is often the case in therapy sessions when a man or a woman imagines and elaborates, in great detail, on 'everything that might be happening' between the partner and his or her rival. This usually reveals more about their wish to control the relationship than about their desire for their partner.

'I want to know everything that is going on between them.'

'It's not possible that she can give to someone else what she didn't give me (her attention, physical love, surrender, commitment). Up to then, I had imagined that if she didn't give me this, it was because she didn't have it, and it had nothing to do with me. But it's unbearable to think that she gives to someone else the same things she gives to me: the same gestures, the same words, the same glances. Our experience becomes derisory, not worth anything anymore. And especially, it confirms that I'm worthless because she had all that and didn't give it to me or gives it to someone else. That means that I wasn't worthy of receiving something unique. This new image of myself is unbearable.'

The state of jealousy goes with the archaic infantile wish of 'living everything' and of 'having everything' that belongs to the other person. This can be accompanied by feelings of envy: 'I want everything that you have'. The never fulfilled wish to control the loved one's feelings is also present. We can recognize here the old and mythical dream of dictating to the other person the feelings he should experience.

- 'I want all your love.'
- 'Love only me.'
- 'Give up all the other people for me.'
- 'Be the same as me and nothing else.'

Sibling jealousy

It has become a banality to talk about sibling jealousy, which is often accompanied by a feeling of injustice. It is true that all maternal or paternal love is unfair in the sense that it is not expressed in the same way to each child in the family.

Children are born at different periods of a couple's history and development. Each child arrives at a different point; he is invested with very different expectations, desires, 'missions' or hopes according to this point. The consequences of sibling jealousy could be alleviated if this feeling were simply recognized and acknowledged.

'I was five years old and I often hit my one-year-old brother's head with my big wooden truck. My mother told me: "You're big; you must love him; he's your brother." She asked me to have feelings I didn't feel. If only she could have stated what my real feelings were: "Yes, you hate him; maybe you think that he's too important, that he shouldn't be here. That's your feeling, I understand that you feel that." This would have helped me overcome my feelings of jealousy.'

'Yes, you too would like to be carried and rocked the way I carry him against my breast. It's true that I had the same gestures and concern for you. When you were sleeping, I came to see you at night and I gave you my breast. Your favourite breast was the left one, where the heart is . . .'

Many pains are soothed and expectations appeased when we express such feelings with words.

Words are only furtive and coarse fragments of reality.

To recognize our current feelings as we experience them, instead of denying them, helps us feel that we exist. 'I exist through what I feel.' Usually, the parental or educational mistake is to deny, minimize or transform someone's feeling of jealousy into a positive feeling . . . which he does not experience.

Parental jealousy

We don't usually recognize and, in particular, it is less common to talk about those vague, shameful or derisory feelings that overwhelm a father looking with envy and jealousy at his tiny son cuddled in his wife's arms. Does he want to be in the son's place (near the mother), in the mother's place (so close to the child) or in his own place, that of the father (whose wife is available, welcoming, and presently unconditionally accepting the demand being made on her). There is so much at stake in the triangular relationship created by the arrival of a child in a couple. Of course we commonly believe that the arrival of a child binds together and consolidates a couple. But very often, the arrival of a third person will throw the relationship off balance and modify the internal dynamics of the couple.

Many men who 'do not want children' should really say: 'I don't feel that I'm able to be a father, for the moment' or 'I don't want to put a rival between us'.

There is an extraordinary scene in the French film *Molière* (by the director Ariane Mnouchkine). The father of the young Jean-Baptiste Poquelin sees his wife killing lice on his son's head. The boy had got the lice on purpose from a friend so as to be able to sit on his mother's lap. The father pushes his son away and offers his own head to his wife's welcoming and receptive hands. He wants to be cherished, welcomed and nursed just like his son. He pushes his son away as if he were a rival.

Feelings of jealousy between mother and daughter, especially at the time of puberty, are more apparent. They are expressed more openly by the mother's aggressive behaviour towards her daughter, who in fact behaves in exactly the same way. Many things are at stake in this jealousy: a conflict of loyalty, the daughter's more obvious seductiveness, her attachment to the father, a too apparent sexual life, the mother's ageing. This daughter starting out in life embodies the resurgence of all possibilities. It is unbearable for the mother when her daughter sabotages these possibilities because it reminds the mother of her own sabotages. It can be equally unbearable when the daughter opens up to these possibilities.

Jealousy within the couple

In love, jealousy is associated with possessing the person loved: to keep him or her for oneself and possibly make him submit to one's own desires and fears. In love arising out of need, this is the price to be paid.

In a loving relationship, it is advisable to assert oneself very early on, to mark out one's territory (time and space), and to frequently clarify one's expectations and needs. We should distinguish better between wishes and requests and recognize the limits of our tolerance and our areas of intolerance. It is important to learn to say: 'This is what is good for me, and this is what is not so good or even unacceptable for me.' This is a difficult task to achieve in a relationship based on long-term plans and expectations, on exchanging and sharing feelings.

If love for another person is rooted in old-fashioned totalitarian and demanding needs, then it is difficult to avoid the relationship being 'polluted' by jealousy. Good and happy moments become contaminated by blaming or claims that are out of proportion with what triggered them off: forgetting something, laughter, a glance, an unfortunate word.

The jealous person's favourite weapons are indirect accusation and guilt. We can make the other feel guilty.

'You don't give me enough.'

'You don't look after me enough.'

'You're selfish. You only think of yourself and of your own interests.'

Another tactic we frequently employ is to disparage ourselves, which also means that we denigrate the other person at the same time.

'I'm not worthy of this anyway.'

'You chose me without really knowing me.'

'I've never been loved.'

When we disparage ourselves we also denigrate the love, attention or marks of interest given by the other person. It is as if we were saying: 'You're really a complete idiot, or you can't be that worthy if you're interested in someone as worthless as me.'

Jealousy is sometimes a desperate attempt to control the other person and forbid him to abandon us. For at the root of jealousy there is the terrifying fear of abandonment, of loss or rejection. Underlying jealousy is the injunction: 'You can't leave me.'

Some people try and express the immensity of their love through jealous preoccupations: 'Look how attached I am to you. Isn't it evidence of my love?'

Jealous people try and convince others they should be jealous.

'If you're not jealous, it's because you don't love me.'

'It's normal to be jealous when you love someone.'

Jealousy does not diminish the love for the other person. It sometimes increases it but mainly it gives it an extraordinary dimension, that of suffering, of pain that can turn into despair

'My jealousy is always there, watchful, and never misses a trick.'

and doubt. But it can also turn into the insane hope of winning back or simple keeping the loved partner. When the partner is lost (separation, divorce), jealousy can then change into hate for him or for the happy rival. It is at this stage that passion might be acted out.

Jealousy in family and social life

What I have to say is that I have nothing to say. But I would like to say something. Wanting to speak and utter words may already be a form of prayer and of resistance to the void.
Eugene Ionesco

In everyday life, numerous situations are used to sustain jealousy and focus tensions. Jealousy is very apparent in family life and leaves deep scars. It can be noticed at mealtimes:

- In glances: who is looking at who? Who is not looked at? Who is looked at too much? Who is not seen?
- In listening: how does language flow? Who is heard, amplified, received, in tune with others? Whose words are not understood or covered by other people's words?
- In the way food is handed around: who is served first? Which bits does he get? Accompanied by what gestures and comments? 'Oh! you eat too much already', or 'You never like anything'.
- In housework: who clears the table, cleans, fetches the dishes? (seldom the father – often the older children or the mother).
- In the place people are given: next to whom? Far from whom?

Clothes and bodily care can be the focus of a lot of jealous behaviour. Everything – colours, shapes or frequency – can be used to nurture suffering.

Because of some parents' unconscious preferences, school, with its good and bad marks at stake, can be food for jealousy. Negative identifications, 'He'll be like his father . . . hopeless at maths' or positive ones, 'He's like me, a literary person', deeply mark children. Comparisons burden some people: 'He does better . . .; not as well as . . .; he fails like . . .' In class, the teacher's pet

'I see, feel and hear only what feeds my jealousy ... and transforms it into suffering.'

is envied up to the age of seven or eight; later on he is rejected and despised.

The position we are given by significant figures in the family (father, mother, elders) can create fierce rivalry that nurtures jealousy.

Injustice of equal parts

'He shouldn't be jealous; I don't make any difference.'

This is no consolation for someone who wants an indivisible and absolute love, who wants to be the only one or at least to feel loved in a special way.

Many parents imagine they are fair and egalitarian when, for example, they do 'the same thing for both children'.

'When I buy clothes for one, I do the same for the other. There's no difference.'

This attitude precisely denies difference. These two children do not have the same needs at the same moment.

'Oh! the injustice of equal parts!' exclaimed this 40-year-old man. 'My mother used to cut the cake into equal portions, believing this to be fair and equitable. But I had huge needs, especially for food. I ate what was left over by my brother who had a small appetite, but I would have liked my needs to be recognized . . . and not through leftovers!'

It is very difficult to introduce in a family or in a community this notion of equal, that is to say different, parts. One can for instance make more portions than there are people, cut them unequally and ask each one to choose his own portion. For some people it is more important to have two small pieces than a big one, for others it is more important to hope for and to get the biggest portion.

We know a grandmother who deliberately prepares unequal chocolate pieces for tea. She answers her grandchildren's protests with: 'Who said life was fair?'

Anyway, some might be less hungry than others or have a more sensitive stomach; some are greedy, others are satisfied with little food . . . or with something other than chocolate.

Handling jealousy

How can we handle our jealousy and that of the other person? We can deal with it by talking about it, over and over again, with the sole condition that we talk only about ourselves. We should definitely not talk about the other person or 'for' him. We should talk about ourselves, as if we were emptying ourselves. Even though it might seem impossible to share this anarchic proliferation of feelings and sensations, we should talk about ourselves as if we were tanning a skin, as if we were scraping off each fold the pieces of painful flesh still stuck to the leather.

To laugh about it might also help.

A young couple were going through a crisis. She was dazzled and attracted by a brilliant colleague who assiduously devoted his attention to her, while he was attracted by another beautiful young woman who made flattering advances to him.

As the couple were going through a painful dialogue, full of anxieties and threats, they suddenly released their feelings with laughter and rage. They started to draw a caricatured and awful portrait of the brilliant colleague and of the beautiful young woman. They fiercely pitted their wits against each other: 'Your blond admirer really fancies himself!' 'Your simpering goose pouts all the time!'

This lasted an hour until they fell into each other's arms, still shaking with laughter, having got rid of, through this healthy catharsis, some of the devils that were upsetting their relationship.

We should never accept the false choices and threats suggested by the jealous person.

'It's either me or the other person.'

'I warn you, you won't get the children.'

We should not let the jealous person dictate the behaviour he expects us to have. But the most difficult thing to do is to avoid feeling guilty when the other person says: 'Look how much I'm suffering because of you'.

For it is true that to say to the other person: 'Your feelings belong to you, your suffering and your anxiety are really yours' can be experienced as aggression. 'You're selfish, you only think of yourself' is the most frequent answer.

We always invite people to differentiate between their feelings and their experience: 'My love seems different from yours; your experience differs from mine.'

The jealous person often uses the words 'mistaken' and 'betrayed':

- 'I was mistaken about you.'
- 'You betrayed me.'
- 'I feel betrayed by you.'

It is fairer to say that the jealous person is betrayed only by himself; this is why it is so difficult for him to get over his jealousy.

Jealousy means wanting to keep the future in the past and to maintain the present forever unchanged.

GUILT

Guilt is present in all relationships. Like a kind of integrated circuit it feeds many components of our behaviour.

Society would probably be a complete monster without the landmarks and warnings marked out by guilt.

Does the strange feeling of being guilty mean that we are cut off from something? Are we cut off from a state of innocence and completeness and is an inner voice trying to tell us that we have to recover it? Sexuality is the privileged domain of guilt and shame, often subjected to the most intense and irrational guilt feelings.

Guilt can proliferate like cancer in some relationships and become like a poisonous link. Many people administer this poison to themselves ('I feel permanently guilty of something'). Others prefer to give it to someone else ('I show him that he's responsible for what is happening to me'). In either case, the relationship is tainted and induces unease and confusion.

> 'I feel guilty of making demands on him, because he feels so guilty when he refuses and he makes me feel so guilty when he reluctantly accepts.'

Guilt develops through entangled networks that are so complex that, when we feel guilty, we sometimes do not know anymore if the guilt is ours or the other person's.

> 'I sometimes wonder if I'm not treating my husband like a child by doing everything he asks!' exclaims a 48-year-old woman, without realizing that she is the one who is treated like a child by her husband's contradictory demands.

Appropriate guilt concerns only ourselves. It has nothing to do with what others think or feel. It is the voice of our conscience that signals to us through a contrite heart that we have broken an inner law. It gives us a feeling of discomfort and maybe remorse, though we rarely fall into such shame that we feel we deserve the death penalty. Guilt is only a signal, a beacon that guides our actions and social behaviour.

> 'I who value truth and honesty so much, well I lied, I cheated. I don't feel happy about that.'

Making ourselves feel guilty

Guilt can also be a mixture of ill-differentiated sensations. It is a blend of fears, denigration, ambivalence and need for power.

Fear of other people's reactions

The fear of the other person's reaction is a large part of what we wrongly call 'guilt'. We fear the negative consequences of our behaviour. We fear our partner's anger. We are afraid of not conforming to his expectations, of disappointing him and, mainly, of being rejected, of losing love, of losing the other person and therefore of losing part of ourselves.

> A young man relates the turmoil he experiences in his love relationship: 'We had had a slight quarrel and hadn't seen each other for ten days. That evening, she phoned me (something she hardly ever does) and suggested that I go to her place. She was tender with me and I understood that she was expecting a reconciliation, which I too wanted. But I was very tired. I had to catch a very early train the following day and I told her so. I postponed our meeting until Saturday.
>
> As soon as I rang off, I felt ill at ease, guilty and anxious. I mainly felt afraid. I thought she'd never phone me again to invite me unexpectedly. I did hear that she was hurt; I should have made an effort, she is so sensitive. I'm always afraid of hurting her and, when I do hurt her, she rejects me. I don't know any more how to distinguish my fear from hers and this is expressed through a vague but overwhelming feeling of guilt.'

Separation means to keep what belongs to me and to lose what belongs to the other.

Guilt and fear of consequences are more often related to what we haven't done than to what we have done.

> 'I haven't phoned, written, given a sign, sent out an invitation.'

Permanent and vague self-blame like 'What did I forget?' and 'What should I do?' hounds those people who are excessively sensitive to duty ('I should') and to other people's supposed expectations.

Some people are particularly prone to thinking 'I should' or 'I should have done'. These thoughts are like instruments of torture that take on extraordinarily twisted forms so as to give no respite to those who persecute themselves in this way.

'I shouldn't torment myself with "I should . . ."!'

'I shouldn't try to respond to what I imagine are his expectations of me. If I give in to all his demands, he will despise me.'

'All the same, I ought to be more firm, to be able to say no, and to not always submit; then, at least, she would respect me.'

The words 'I should', 'I ought to' and 'I have to' are like the lashes of a whip that some people need to spur themselves on in life.

How can we distinguish real guilt from guilt that is related to the reactions of others?

A 40-year-old man wonders: 'For two years I maintained two parallel relationships without either friend's knowledge. I didn't feel guilty, I pretty much understood that I was afraid of making a commitment after having had two painful break-ups. I didn't want to live with either of them, so I let things evolve and gradually I became attached to one of them in particular. One cataclysmic morning, they met each other at my place and both together exposed my omissions, my

'Oh! how happy my partner would be without me!'

silences, my duplicity and my lies. I felt awfully guilty about their pain. I felt like a real bastard.

But am I a bastard? As long as they didn't know anything, I wasn't a bastard. I was in agreement with myself. So what? Maybe I prefer to claim that I am guilty when confronted with them rather than show my weakness, my indecision, my fear and especially my desires.'

We have heard many men say the same thing: for them, monogamy is not an internal law and they only feel guilty because of their partner's reactions. It is only by putting themselves in the other person's shoes that they feel guilty. Their discomfort arises from the fact that their feeling of guilt is linked to the other person's law.

Denigration

Self-denigration is like guilt.

'I'm inadequate, incapable, hopeless and I don't feel equal to the task.'

Those who are greedy for love and care, often have this unchangeable belief: 'I'm not loveable; nobody can ever become interested in me and love me for what I am.'

Children who are not really loved will think that they are not worthy of love rather than think that they have unacceptable parents. This feeling of being bad and worthless is one of the worst psychological tortures that we can inflict on ourselves. It leads to the awful situation of trying not to be what we are, and it induces a very destructive dilemma:

'If I show myself as I am, empty, weak and scared, I won't be loved. But if I pretend, then I'll be loved for what I'm not.'

Comparisons induce denigration and guilt.

'Whenever I notice anything positive in others, I experience it as a shortcoming in myself.'

'I lack self-confidence, therefore I want to fill this lack.'

We need to compare what we think we lack with what other people have or are. Many conformists hide the torments of a deep distrust of their true self behind apparently smooth behaviour.

> It was only when she began therapy at the age of 38 that Anita started to talk about her suffering, which was deeply hidden beneath utterly normal behaviour: 'The slightest thing, word or gesture can hurt me deeply. It's as if I were breaking down, but I know very well how to hide what is happening. Nobody around me suspects this. I manage to smile, even when I am overwhelmed by anxiety and panic.
> It's a real nightmare and nobody can understand the violence of what I feel. It's as if I had no identity. Others invade me. I can only pretend to be a nice little girl.'

When we run ourselves down, we exaggerate any shortcoming or mistake.

> A mother who is irritated with her child will tell herself in despair: 'I'm a bad mother' instead of saying simply: 'I'm angry right now.'

> The pupil who does not understand an explanation will tell himself: 'I'm a complete idiot.'

Self-denigration is the bane of relationships; it offends the person who experiences it as well as the one who tries to love him.

Ambivalence

Ambivalence may be a source of intense guilt. The inner conflict between love and the hate that comes from frustrations, this awful fight between attraction and rejection, creates guilt that tries to contain destructive forces.

But who can promise that the achieved balance will not suddenly be broken? Who can be completely sure that under no circumstance will rage and the most controlled drives get out of hand. Even aggressive desires and fantasies that are well hidden and kept in check concerning the people we are close to create guilt in the person who both loves and hates.

> A man tells us his dreams about the death of the woman he loves: 'I saw myself as a widower, surrounded by my compassionate friends and family. I felt immense sadness regarding all this wasted love. I felt completely at peace, having freed myself of all the blame I had borne these last years.
>
> In these daydreams, I was the ideal husband whom I couldn't be in reality. Then I resented myself for wishing her dead so as to escape my own conflicts.'

Relating as a couple reactivates most of the attachment and conflict that we experience from early childhood on. The experience of becoming autonomous has an aggressive component to it, as if we were abandoning the other person, the parent, child or spouse.

> A 50-year-old single nurse thinks she must devote all her Sundays to her mother who lives in an old people's home. If not, she would feel guilty of letting her down. She feels compulsively drawn to nurse, to give support to her mother and to please her. It is for her an unavoidable duty, a compulsory mark of filial love.
>
> However, during a training course on relationships between nurses and their patients, she suddenly discovered her immense resentment against her mother, which had been hidden since her adolescence, or maybe even earlier. Her assiduous care for her mother, at the expense of all her leisure time, was meant to neutralize her own torrents of blame.
>
> She was as devoted as she was hateful and guilty. After realizing this, which upset her, this woman rediscovered the tender ties that linked her to her mother. She then took far less but far better care of her.

Ambivalence is inevitable in any relationship. Each person is torn between two necessary polarities: the need for independence and distance, and the need for intimacy and closeness. The inner and outer conflict triggered by these opposed tendencies is often accompanied by guilt and moral judgements. Independence will be called selfishness and attachment will be seen as immaturity.

Omnipotent guilt

'My three children are divorced; I know that it's my fault. I haven't been able to prepare them for married life.'

'My parents were always fighting when I was a child and I always thought it was because of me. I felt responsible.'

'I resent myself and I judge myself severely when I have negative thoughts, wishes or feelings. Even my dreams make me feel guilty, I see really incredible things in them; I feel ashamed when I wake up.'

'My father died because of me. If I had made him stop work and take better care of himself, he'd still be here today.'

This form of guilt keeps an illusion going: the illusion of having absolute control and power over the well-being and development of another person – a power over life or death in this last example. Those who cannot give up this omnipotent tie to another person or to themselves prefer to nurture their guilt feeling: it is better to feel guilty than powerless, hopeless and helpless. Omnipotence, however, arouses anxiety. It confers a terrifying power on our desires and fantasies: it makes us think they can become real. If all the persons whose death we wished for died on the spot, we would be surrounded by corpses! Because of this tendency to take charge of others and their suffering we sometimes give out paradoxical messages.

For example, a woman decides to leave her husband because she feels uncomfortable in the relationship, whereas he wants their union to continue. She might say to him: 'I'm leaving you so that you can find and experience another, more harmonious relationship.'

Unconscious guilt

Some people punish themselves severely without knowing why. Accidents, repeated failures, privations and depressions seem to punish them for faults they do not know they have committed – signs that confirm their unworthiness. Strangely enough, these people seem relieved by the torments they inflict on themselves, as if these punishments released them from guilt.

'I suffer, I don't know what I'm atoning for, but it makes me feel more innocent afterwards.'

Others use their sufferings to feel even more guilty.

'What did I do to deserve all this?'

Some even go so far as to commit misdeeds that will at least be ground for their vague and permanent blaming of themselves. They always leave clues that betray them. Somehow, in a way, this eases their conscience.

'At last, I am really guilty of a specific act and I can be judged for it.'

Unconscious guilt can become attached to superficial guilt:

'I blame myself for small, unimportant things as if they were serious mistakes. I am obsessive about order and I must look impeccable. I cannot tolerate any mistake or imperfection. So I make sure I am perfect in small matters so as to get away from an unknown anxiety.'

Beyond the obscure, forbidden and forgotten wishes of our childhood, we all bear a guilt which is linked to facts that took place long before our birth, and in which we have not partaken. Research has shown that the children of persecuted Jews suffer guilt feelings similar to those of the children of Nazis. They bear the weight of the destructiveness or unhappiness of their forbears.

In any transmission from one generation to another, ancient faults and past tragedies are passed on – violent deaths, deaths of children, suicides, sexual transgressions, abortions, abandonments and madness. They weigh on our lives and we feel invested with the obligation to rectify faults committed prior to our life. This also has a positive and dynamic side because it drives us to do things we might otherwise not have done. But sometimes such displaced guilt is so violent that it becomes a death sentence.

> At the age of 50, father of three children accidently caused somebody's death. He was driving at normal speed along a main road when a woman on a motorcycle suddenly appeared and went into his car. She died in hospital a few days later. The man, never got over his guilt and in the following years he became increasingly insomniac and anxious. He repeated constantly: 'She was a mother.' Three years after the accident, he killed himself by crashing into a tree on the same road, alone in his car, shortly before dawn.

Leaving the facts aside, we can ask ourselves what old guilt, linked to his ambivalence towards his mother or his wife, was this man thus expiating.

Our infantile torments are still active in our present relationships, and guilt is based on the traces of imaginary faults in our unconscious memory. Each one of us has to protect himself from bearing the huge responsibility for the whole of human suffering which is unequally but abundantly spread over the whole world.

There are also guilt feelings which are perverted: they refer, in good faith, to a law that is aberrant.

> During the Second World War, the chief of the Treblinka extermination camp wrote desperate letters to his superiors in Berlin complaining of not being able to reach the set death rate. He had not succeeded in exterminating so many thousands per day. He felt guilty about killing only two-thirds of the expected quota. He had turned his orders into an ideology which, like any ideology, pushed him to eradicate evil, and 'evil' in his eyes was represented by the Jews.

At a less horrific level, we also kill, in the name of our beliefs, by stifling creative potential in our children and ourselves.

Making others feel guilty

Certain individuals seem to have some deficiency in their capacity to feel guilt. They relentlessly protect themselves from feeling guilty as if the fact of recognizing their faults meant the end of the world. And they actively make others feel guilty. With virtuous indignation, they know that they are right.

> 'I always said that unfaithfulness could only lead to disaster. You reap what you sow.'

> 'I just couldn't tolerate my children having a mother who was unfaithful to her husband. If she hadn't given in, I would have done anything to take them away from her.'

A story: a fish kept sticking its head out of the water to breathe, but the attempts never resulted in it feeling satisfied. It decided the problem was that there was not enough air. It blamed the outside world for this and became very discontented.

JUDGEMENT

Judgement is a powerful sabotage mechanism in relationships and communication. It undermines self-confidence.

> 'Oh! to be able to express yourself, to show yourself without disguise, without being immediately categorized and defined by a judgement!'

Children receive floods of judgemental comments that any adult would hesitate to say directly to another adult.

> 'You're so lazy!'

> 'Dad, I would like to do photography!'
> 'You'd do better to work at school instead of wasting your time.'

> 'Poor girl, you're so clumsy!'

> 'That's very wicked.'

'You'll never do anything good.'

'You think you're so clever!'

Mockery and derision are even more violent and hurt their sense of self-confidence.

'I would have been very surprised if you had finished the meal without knocking something over.'

'Well, well! Daisy understood the joke; that's unusual!'

We are perpetually passing judgements on ourselves and others: moral, aesthetic, cultural and psychological judgements.

Our first reaction when we listen to someone tends to be an immediate inner appraisal: that's normal, that's strange, that's wrong, that's true, that's good, that's fair, etc. In this way we classify according to our own references other people's opinions and attitudes. But if we give up this normative evaluation of others and allow ourselves to understand them without prejudice, then we risk having to change. We might have to change our point of view. We might have to give up our frame of references and our well-ordered certainties. And we are all afraid of change. We are so afraid of modifying the feeling of identity which we have painstakingly built up and of listening within ourselves to unknown resonances that might call into question our self-image and our way of thinking.

It is terribly difficult to listen to another person and to hear him speak without judging him, yet without losing a critical mind. It can be painful to admit that our children, our parents or spouses have different opinions and reactions to situations that are important or crucial for us.

'Out of religious conviction, I was for a long time a militant in an organization called "Let Them Live" (a French anti-abortion movement). And now my daughter tells me that she has decided to have an abortion. She even expects me to understand and approve of her decision!'

To understand another person is only possible on condition that we put aside our system of values and personal beliefs. We should however remind ourselves that a criticism is not an attack and that criticism expressed benevolently is essential in love and friendship.

COMPARISON

Comparison, the daughter of judgement, is used to back up the process by which we make others feel guilty. We compare what is not comparable, that is to say one individual with another individual.

> 'Your brother doesn't need private lessons, so you can do without them.'

> 'My first husband would never have talked to me like that!'

Differences between people are negated when we want everything to be equal.

> 'Look what I did for you (when you were ill, when your mother came to live with us, when you finished your studies) and look what you're doing (or not doing) for me (when I'm unwell, when my parents are here, when I think of studying again).'

One person's illness does not have the same meaning or effect as another person's illness. Therefore it will trigger off a different or opposite response. To have one of the parents staying in the house is accepted, tolerated and wanted, for a number of reasons, but these are not necessarily to be found when another parent stays in the house.

In relationships, many games are based on the dynamics of 'I ... whereas you ...' and on making the other feel guilty. Our need for justice is offended by the idea that all relationships are asymmetrical. Real communication is based on complementarity and exchange rather than on similarity.

'I so much admired my husband's enterprising nature that I tried very much to be like him. It wasn't my nature, but I found him so wonderful that I felt useless. It was only after our divorce that I understood he was in search of a woman who would be . . . like I was really: trusting and encouraging, but not very enterprising. I thought that I had to be like him so as to please him.'

In a couple, each partner's different needs and wishes may at first be complementary and then become more alike, according to how each of them develops. This can lead to necessary adjustments, conflicts and even separation.

'I heard on the radio that an African country and Germany had traded dinosaur skeletons for Volkswagen cars. Curiously this made me think of my relationship with my first husband. He was older than me and it was as if he were teaching me everything. He taught me life, initiated me, and I felt satisfied. Then I changed. I wanted to learn on my own and also give him what I had learned. It didn't work at all. We separated and he is now living with a woman whom he is teaching about life . . .'
What will happen if this African country begins to need museums too?'

Some comparisons are similar to accusations: they often denigrate the present in the name of 'past times'.

'In the past you used to propose things. You were enthusiastic; you listened to me; you paid attention to me. And now it's different.'

The beginning of a love relationship is often considered like an eternal and nostalgic yardstick. The development of the relationship, compared with this yardstick, is then seen as a loss. If we cannot allow relationships to age, to get a sheen as time goes by, then they deteriorate, like modern objects that get damaged. Wanting to return to the past contributes to this deterioration.

'In the past, you used to take me on your lap. You let me get into your bed, you played at being the elephant that catches the doe . . . and now you say I'm too big . . .'

Comparisons between brothers and sister, often introduced by the parents, sometimes seem to last a whole lifetime. What was at stake during childhood is later turned into guilt, and is often connected to the problem of feeling responsible for ageing parents.

> 'I lived in the same town as my mother and I had her on my back all the time. My sister, who lived 150 miles away, blamed me for not taking enough care of our mother. I saw my mother three times a week, my sister once a month. My sister would say: "You live so near, it's easy for you to drop in." Then my sister came back to our home town but she still only sees our mother once a month.'

When I make comparisons, I sabotage my relationships as well as my self-image.

PROJECTION AND APPROPRIATION

Any intimate relationship is characterized by projections from one person to the other, and by our appropriations of what others project onto us. This two-way movement favours unreal dialogue and crazy communication.

We call *unreal* dialogues those constructed of reactions and screen behaviour that protect us and that prevent us from expressing our deep feelings.

'This man would be able to see far ahead if he didn't always stand in his own way.'

Projection

Projection is similar to the projection of a film. It is as if the other person were the screen. I look at the images I project and really believe that they come from him. I can project many things.

Projection of parental images

I can project onto others and continue to see coming from outside all the messages that marked my childhood.

> 'My overburdened mother expected me, being the eldest, to help her and to expect nothing for myself. It's exactly the same now with my husband. I feel accepted only if I am useful and don't expect anything for myself, especially attention and listening. He needs a wife who is simply at his service and fulfils his wishes and that's all.'

Such is the perception that this woman had elaborated of her place within the couple. To achieve this, she picked out any sign of non-availability in her husband as support for her own belief. She thus puts him, in good faith, in the position of fulfilling her projection.

When we actually met her husband, we did not recognize the person that she had described to us. And as for him, he complained that his wife 'was unable to receive, didn't ask anything for herself, and always believed she had to help and do something for others'.

> A man was idealized by his mother who unconditionally accepted everything he was or did. He is convinced that his girlfriend feels the same about him and does not imagine that she cannot tolerate some of his behaviour. For him, everything is all right; he likes her patience and her receptiveness. She is imprisoned in a projection that flatters her and corresponds with her own ideal of tolerance. She tries to conform to this projection. Therefore she does not express her negative reactions, she hides them from herself and reinforces the projections by trying to appropriate her friend's distorting point of view.

These systems of projection and appropriation work only because the two people involved collaborate. To change this, it is up to the one who is subjected to projections to continually readjust the relationship by stating his own position, by saying who he really is, and by manifesting his true feelings.

Projection of personal feelings

It might be very difficult to imagine that someone very dear to us has different feelings from us. It is through our own feelings that we try and imagine what the other person feels. We interpret his behaviour in terms of what it would mean for us if we behaved the same way. As far as conscious feelings are concerned, we take the measure of the other person by looking at ourselves.

> 'While I was in the maternity ward awaiting the birth of our child, he spent his nights with another woman. So his feelings and love for me have no value because I would never have done that to someone I love.'

We again see that the request for reciprocity or the fear of it is based on projection. According to situations, it might be:

- 'I'm afraid that he'll behave towards me the way I behave towards him.'
- 'He should behave towards me the way I behave towards him.'

We identify the other person with ourselves. We imagine that his way of functioning is similar to ours.

> 'I didn't love my mother; I kept a lot of distance between us. I found it disgusting to touch her body. For years I was convinced that my own daughter couldn't love me because I was her mother, that she must feel only hostility towards me.'

In this case, projection concerns the relationship more than the person: 'a mother–daughter relationship cannot be loving'.

There can be nothing more dangerous than an idea when you have only one.
Paul Claudel.

> 'I am so in love with this girl that it's not possible for her not to feel the same attraction for me. In the group where I meet her, she seems to pay no attention to me but I know that she's pretending. She doesn't want to show her feelings in front of others. Maybe she's

'There is danger everywhere ... even in me!'

afraid of hurting someone or she's just shy. When she turns her back on me, I know for sure that she's thinking only of me.'

People in love can be extremely inventive in interpreting the signs that confirm that their feeling is returned (or not received).

'I have a very critical mind. All the time I tend to judge what I see and hear, so I can't believe that others don't do the same with me.'

'When I love someone, I am not attracted by any other man. So if my man needs other relationships, it just proves that he doesn't love me.'

'Nobody can live with me,' says a man who is unable to live with anyone.

Projection of unknown aspects of ourselves

We are often hardly, or not at all, conscious of numerous aspects of ourselves that try to manifest. Sometimes we imagine that we see these forbidden or underdeveloped aspects of ourselves in others. It might be a 'baby' aspect of me that is still in me or, on the contrary, a responsible adult. Or again, it might be the valorous hero or the malevolent witch, the wise man or the fool in me.

> 'My husband is always right. His judgement is so sound, his opinions are well backed up, and he always has a clear understanding of any situation. I'm not at all like that. I'm always doubtful and I don't understand anything. He said that my training sessions were useless. I don't understand why I enrolled.'

This woman considers herself immature, even stupid, whereas she projects onto her spouse her own unexploited ability to think.

Some children appropriate their parents' more or less conscious projections and give life to hidden aspects of their parents: they become artists or delinquents, debauched people or champions of a great cause. For better or for worse, they live out their parents' aborted or repressed tendencies.

People who use projection most mainly need to attribute to others their 'bad feelings': the greed, anger or hostility that they have repressed so much that they don't recognize it in themselves any more. They always find somewhere to dump these unacceptable aspects of themselves. For example, their political opponents or competitors can fill this function. It is less painful than projecting onto people who are close to them. But as soon as some difficulty arises in the family, then they make use of projection in their thought process.

> 'If there is a problem, it's because of the other person's immaturity, selfishness and insatiability. I remain pure and good, nothing can bring dishonour on me.'

The more someone needs to project his negative side onto another person, the more he is protecting himself and trying to keep his precarious balance by not confronting his own flaws and weaknesses. In this way, people who often accuse others are usually filled with doubt and lacks, and overwhelmed with anxiety. And they are ready to discharge these flaws onto others, onto life, onto the whole world.

Projection of ideals and illusions

Projection that idealizes often occurs during a love relationship or in a significant relationship with a teacher, therapist, etc. It creates a trap for both protagonists. The idealized person does not feel recognized for what he is, even if he self-indulgently cherishes a grandiose vision of himself; and the one who projects is not able to create a real relationship with a real person. He remains ensnared in illusion and in a pseudo-relationship.

> 'In the team of doctors and social workers that I lead, there is a young doctor who persists in seeing me as someone who knows everything and has an answer to everything. Sometimes, I catch myself trying to fit in with this image he creates, and sometimes I tell him about my uncertainties, my ignorance and my helplessness. But there again, he marvels at my modesty and my humility. I once heard him say that I showed myself as helpless only to put other people at ease.'

This idealizing projection is fruitless in the long term. Not being able to confirm and nurture the image the other person has of us, we show ourselves to be disappointing, frustrating and helpless.

Projection of intentions

To attribute intentions, whether positive or negative, to the other person when he has no such intentions is a major cause of misunderstanding. It is a way of projecting our desires and fears onto the other person, of confirming our feelings of persecution or our belief that we are the centre of the world . . . and of his preoccupations. In fact we may give ourselves importance by attributing to this person an intention towards ourselves, even though it might be an intention to hurt us. It makes us feel more important than if we were to realize that he was indifferent, inattentive, forgetful, or concerned about other things that do not involve us.

Sentences such as 'You do it on purpose to annoy me', 'You chose this very day, an anniversary, to be away', 'You want to make me jealous', 'You do everything you can to belittle me', can be understood in this light. The person who is usually saying such things to give vent to her feelings will sometimes be astonished to discover the effect of her unintentional behaviour. For the partner considers these messages to be addressed to him personally. Her justification ('But I had no negative intentions towards you; I did or said that without thinking') will then be another wound, more real this time, for the partner. Deliberate intentions, however, are seldom at the root of difficulties in relationships.

Appropriation

Through appropriation, we make the perception that the other person has of us become ours, as if we have become what the other perceives us to be, without differentiating ourselves, or without distinguishing the things, people and reactions that belong to him.

> 'Since my adolescence', says this 30-year-old woman, 'I have dressed in a unisex style: jeans, shapeless jumpers, short hair. Now I think I'm changing. I sometimes feel like putting some make-up on, wearing a bright dress, having a different hairstyle. When I do that, my husband gives me a contemptuous look. He has said two or three times: "Are you playing cowboys and Indians?" Then my wishes were annihilated, and I felt ridiculous and silly. Instead of feeling pleased with the image in the mirror, I felt as if I was in disguise. The way my

husband looks at me is more important than how I see myself. The femininity that I was really feeling disappears and I quickly put my jeans back on again.'

We don't know what chord is struck in this man when he sees his wife become interested in her appearance. We only see that this woman substitutes her husband's subjective reaction for her own self-perception.

Appropriation is the inner mechanism by which we let other people – their desires, their fears, their needs and their beliefs – determine our identity.

This process is particularly detrimental to children at an age when, in search of their own identity, they are still easily influenced by other people. So much potential is crushed by words which the child appropriates:

- 'You're shy.'
- 'You're just like me.'
- 'You're just like your father.'
- 'You're insufferable.'
- 'You're very generous.'
- 'You're extraordinary.'

Another form of appropriation consists in taking upon ourselves, or in ourselves, what belongs to the other person such as, for example, his anxiety, his suffering or his frustrations. We can appropriate them either by feeling responsible for them or by experiencing them, as if by osmosis.

We seem to absorb other people's unhappiness more easily than their happiness, especially when this happiness is not linked to us. We can also appropriate other people's wishes by transforming them into demands which we take it upon ourselves to satisfy.

'He responded so much to my requests that he actually dispossessed me of them.'

'I want you to look like a real woman … You should always dress like that.'

'My husband wants to give our unborn son the name that my father wanted to give me if I had been a boy. In this way, he wants to please me by pleasing my father. But I don't know anymore what I really want to name my son, in this round of pleasing everyone. Am I going to please my husband by letting him please me by pleasing my father?'

Thinking is like using a pair of secateurs where each one of us cuts the other down to size.
Jules Renard

By appropriating another person's wishes we avoid having to search for, listen to and respect our own wishes. Some people go so far as to live almost vicariously through another person:

parents, spouse, friends and children, or even their boss.

'I don't know exactly what I want, nor what I like. I always get involved with friends who have plenty of wishes and interests. I become involved in their plans and activities. I embrace their passions and their ideas and I do get something out of it … or almost …'

We all know mothers whose conversation is an account of their husband's and children's activities and thoughts.

'What about you?'
'Oh, I live for them.'

But they are the ones who live for her. Many good-willed parents appropriate their children's plans and wishes by anticipating them and taking over their realization.

'My son had gone to the United States, to train in management, and I had prepared everything for him. I set up a small firm just for him to get his hand in on his return. When he came back, he announced to me that he was going to go around the world. Today he's settled in Japan!' exclaims his father nostalgically.

It seems that his son has had to put the right distance between himself and his father, between his own wishes and his father's.

'My son wanted to build a hut at the end of the garden, so I ordered planks made to measure and all that was required to build it. I built it with him three Sundays running. It's superb . . . but I don't understand why he doesn't play in it anymore.'

All the same, there has to be a minimum of projection and appropriation for a relationship to exist. Any link is built on this exchange of subjectivities. These processes only become major sabotage mechanisms when they take on alienating dimensions, remain unnoticed, or never go through any readjustment.

The more separated and differentiated I am as an individual, the more I exist.

In this chapter we have tried to mention some of the most frequent behaviour patterns that imprison us and harm our relationships – with ourselves and with others. By being careful to keep a tight rein on our favourite sabotage mechanism, we can discover the immense field of possibilities that exists when we meet, share and relate.

7 Complaining

I complain, therefore I exist.

We complain a lot in our everyday conversations. Let us listen to ourselves and the people around us. Not a day passes without our hearing personal or general lamentations.

What are we expressing when we complain? We probably express dissatisfaction, pain or grievance. But why do we use complaining, or what is its purpose? When we make a complaint, whether we mumble it or make a point of being heard, we present ourselves as victims of injustice; and we know that victims are always deserving and innocent and therefore should be given compassion and admiration.

Sometimes, the person who complains just feels like complaining; he does not necessarily ask for any reparation. He expresses a feeling of helplessness. He is not in search of a solution. He only wants to consider the negative aspect of a situation.

The person who complains just wants to complain. He doesn't want the reason for his complaint to disappear.

Try and suggest a remedy or solution to him. He will answer: 'Yes, but . . .', especially if you say: 'But you've got everything you need to be happy.'

These words when true are offensive, because they bring the person back to his duties as a privileged person, whereas suffering gives him rights and a sense of worth. This may result, in some relationships or conversations, in an escalation to prove that 'my misfortunes are greater than yours', and especially that 'mine are beyond remedy and permanent, whereas yours are only temporary and relative'.

We can complain about ourselves or we can complain about external circumstances such as other people, society, fate, life or God. So we each tend to blame either what is inside or what is outside ourselves for what we consider to be our misfortune.

COMPLAINING ABOUT OURSELVES

We complain about ourselves, that is to say about what we are and what we are not. Sometimes we keep the complaint to ourselves and brood over it, and sometimes we address it to someone.

'I'm so clumsy.'

'I never manage to keep my resolutions.'

'I'm incapable of saying no.'

'I'm unable to concentrate.'

'I'm terribly shy . . .'

Whether we blacken ourselves fiercely, moan about ourselves in self-pity or criticize ourselves more or less kindly, when we complain we are stating our own powerlessness: 'I can neither accept myself as I am, nor can I change.'

Among the numerous aspects of myself, which aspect is dissatisfied with the others that compete with it? Each human being is made up of a crowd of characters who do not always get on together. Among them we sometimes find an unyielding censor called Ideal or Ego; he despairs when he looks at the discrepancy between his expectations and the useless achievements of the characters over whom he wants to rule. He does not encourage them and say: 'You'll change.' Rather, he declares: 'You're a dead loss.' But, paradoxically, while we denigrate ourselves, we are also enhancing our sense of self-worth in our own eyes or in those of other people, because our complaint really means:

'Don't believe that I'm happy about myself, and that I like myself as I am. My ideal is quite different. It is much grander. I'm not a second-rate person since I have a high conception of what I would like to be. My aspiration to be different is what makes both my despair and my grandeur.'

What will the other person do when faced with a man, woman or child who complains about himself? He may try to reassure and gratify him: 'But you do this very well, you have such and such a quality . . .' This is often not taken kindly, because the person who is complaining does not feel listened to. A woman who was confronted by her therapist in this way exclaimed: 'He doesn't even see how stupid I am.'

'Nobody understands how little I am inside!'

Furthermore, advice on how to change is difficult to accept if the person complaining needs to complain and does not want to be healed. Complaining is not asking for help. It can just be a request that the complaint be listened to. Sentences like 'You're not happy with yourself' and 'You don't love yourself the way you are' bring the person back to his own subjectivity and allow him to hear himself better and be in touch with his real feelings.

Some people derive more pleasure from complaining than from being satisfied. Complaining about oneself often focuses on a specific aspect of the body: 'I'm too fat. I have an irregular nose. I can't do anything with my hair.' A physical feature becomes a sign of deprivation. A human being's essential incompleteness is thus expressed through the complaint.

When we complain about ourselves, it is like the moaning of a soul torn between the different forces that constitute it, go beyond it and elude it.

COMPLAINING ABOUT OTHERS OR FATE

Complaining about others helps to avoid self-denigration and encourages us to be satisfied with ourselves. Complaining is a strategy that has various aims.

Complaining to get attention

**If I had some ham, I would make a ham omelette. Well I would, except that I have no eggs.
(Omelette dynamics)**

A complaint can be an appeal, an indirect request. It tries to win over the other person's feelings and get him to pay attention.

'When I relate my misfortunes and bad luck, the other person can only show me his affection.'

On the mistaken premise that unhappy people are more interesting and profound than those without any problems, suffering can be put forward as our most distinctive feature.

However, it is difficult to handle complaining so as to get attention if we want to provoke the right effect, because people who complain all the time and talk endlessly about their misfortunes make others run away. They induce rejection and a vicious circle sets in: rejected by those around them who are weary of their complaints, unhappy people then rightly complain of being rejected and cause even more rejection.

Complaining is a manoeuvre of seduction, intended to attract others, but it often fails. It might be a relic of childhood memories. Some people reveal that they were only coddled when they were sick or injured, or that they fell ill so that they could at last be tenderly cared for.

Some people who suffered lack of love compensate for their deprivation through greed.

Complaining to blame

Complaining is sometimes an indirect way of blaming the person who is listening. A woman doesn't blame her husband openly but complains continually about her feelings of discomfort, her tiredness, her work, her neighbours, her ageing or society. The people who are close to her correctly hear a vague allegation regarding them, but they do not know when or how they were inadequate. They are unable to fight off a persistent sense of discomfort, for they feel that the underlying blame concerns them.

Such indirect blame creates a state of stagnation in relationships. It avoids making requests and being aggressive. It also helps avoid asserting personal needs or desires. Steering clear of open crisis and conflicts, this type of complaining seems to express a wish for change, but actually helps prevent it.

'If I told her what pleases me and she met my wishes, I couldn't complain anymore, and my hidden claim for complaint – which is that she should spontaneously do what pleases me – would be taken away.'

When blame seems unjustified and impossible to express, we transform it into complaints.

A husband cannot blame his wife for devoting her time to her dying mother, so he will spend a long time complaining about having to do the housework and about the children's behaviour.

A woman cannot blame her husband for having children from his first marriage. She will complain about headaches when his children go on holiday with them.

An adolescent cannot blame his father for his deafness. He will complain mainly about his teachers who don't understand anything.

A man who is too busy and unable to make choices will complain about not having enough time: time escapes him and prevents him from experiencing . . . everything.

'Do you think I'm having fun not being sick!'

An employee cannot blame his boss for being more intelligent and efficient. Instead, will complain a lot about his work conditions.

Impossible complaint is thus diverted onto a third party. Those who engage in counselling others should pay attention to the dynamics of complaints. They should avoid looking for solutions to the apparent topic of the complaint and should ask the question:

'What is he really complaining about and to which significant person of his past or present life is he talking?'

To be effective, blame needs to be unfair!

Complaining to attack

The strategy consists in getting at the other person's flaws and making him responsible for what is wrong in ourselves.

'Look at what I've got myself into because of you! Look at what you made me do!'

'I'm destroying myself for you; see, I'm depressed because of your behaviour.'

'I never have an orgasm with you and this dissatisfaction is making me bulimic. I've put on three kilos again.'

'I don't like our house; I'm very sensitive to aesthetics and these surroundings depress me.'

This form of complaint, which confronts the other person with his own shortcomings, gives us a secure position (of accusing victim) within the relationship because it places the other person in a persecutor's role. It is very difficult to forgive other people the evil we did to them! And the person defined as harmful will accumulate resentment against his accusing victim.

The worst kind of resentment is to be unable to forgive the other person the evil we did to him.

Complaining to justify

By complaining about others, by making them responsible for what is happening to us, we avoid painful feelings of guilt or responsibility.

We can always justify ourselves by complaining endlessly about our parents as well as about society.

'They inhibited me and prevented me from developing my potential. They constrained me too much. They didn't guide me enough. They didn't give me a satisfying image of what a couple is. She didn't teach me how to be a woman. He told me that you shouldn't show your feelings, etc.'

It is an endless litany. Our inadequacies, shortcomings, failures and mediocrity are all our parents' fault. The inadequacies of our childhood created our present state, which is irremediable. We are not responsible for it.

In a process of personal growth and change, instead of abdicating responsibility for ourselves and continuing to nurture accusations, we restore our ability to be responsible for ourselves.

We also blame other people, the local community or 'the age we live in'.

'You cannot be creative or innovative in this town, this country. Everything is so rigid and humdrum. The system stifles me.'

'You can't have spontaneous and lively relationships nowadays. People are suspicious and withdrawn. They are so materialistic, individualistic and selfish.'

'Nothing can be done against them (civil servants, doctors, teachers, police . . . the others).'

This phrase 'nothing can be done' is used as an alibi and a justification for not trying something else and for sinking into irresponsible passivity.

By complaining we also try to make our helplessness be heard and to ward it off, as it were.

'For several weeks an unbalanced person has been setting fire to the neighbouring pine forests. I have cleared and raked all the heather, so I complain about my neighbours who neglect their own gardens. I feel really helpless faced with the unpredictable actions of this man who sets fire to the forests.'

'Oh! if I could at least complain about all the things that are going well in me and around me!'

Complaining to feel important

When we talk about the hardships which have marked our lives and the blows dealt us by fate, the accidents and misfortunes which we have faced, we are really telling about our courage and merit. Our complaint testifies to our worth, since we overcame all this. What would the hero's journey be worth without the ordeals he meets and the obstacles over which he triumphs?

'My husband went away, leaving me with three young children. Nobody helped me. My health wasn't very good. My children didn't enjoy good health either. My parents hadn't been able to pay for a professional training for me . . .'

All this says how brave this woman is to have gone on living. Now she is here with a modest smile on her lips that seems to mean: 'I'm not complaining, but do admire me.'

Self-made men are proud of themselves, but they are complaining if they say 'I started with nothing'.

Elderly people frequently talk about their misfortunes as if they were riches in the bank of importance: 'I have so many things wrong with me. Few people could go on living in the state I'm in.'

The persons closest to these complainers feel guilty because they are happier. It is difficult for adults to listen to their parents' complaints without having to do something about it and remove this reliable asset: a complaint that does not wear out, even with constant use.

'If you knew all the things I put up with – and I don't tell you everything so as not to upset you, but it's hard, you know, all this loneliness.'

Suffering and worth are here once again equated, but under a new disguise. Often advertisements in the 'Lonely Hearts' column include the words 'having suffered a lot'. What message are these words actually meant to convey? Does it mean that the newcomer 'should not make me suffer' or that anyway 'whatever he does, whoever he is, he won't inflict as much suffering'? Whether this be a challenge, an invitation or the negation of suffering to come, it is meant to demonstrate true worth.

In the language of pain, complaining of hurt and suffering is a signal of worth.

Complaining together about others

Complaining to someone about a third, absent party is a common practice. Women gather to talk about their husbands or boyfriends. Pupils complain about their teachers or parents. Men complain about politicians, events or bosses. Complaining together creates complicity, a feeling of belonging to the oppressed group, an illusory sense of solidarity or a real defensive one. A mutual enemy is a powerful link between people. So is the shared criticism addressed to an absent party. Defensive cohesion can sometimes become persecutory.

A woman goes to visit her parents roughly every two months. Each time she has a brief moment alone with her father or mother, he or she takes the chance to complain about his or her spouse.

'She never wants to go out.'

'He still drinks.'

'She's always in a bad mood.'

'He hasn't repaired the chair yet that was broken three months ago.'

'I have to do everything in the house. You wouldn't think he's retired. He's never here.'

Each of them tries to draw the daughter into an alliance against the other. The children's loyalty is put to a hard test on such occasions, because the complaining parent is also asking for approval of his own behaviour, of his good faith. The daughter feels important as a confidante, but this is an illusion because she does not realize that she is never the topic of the conversation and that nobody is really interested in her. All the focus is on the absent spouse.

'After having complained about my mother, my father often left me, saying: "You're here, fortunately!" It warmed my heart.' But did the daughter really exist in the encounter?

Complaining in this way about the other person (she does this, he is like this) disguises the true complaint, which would reveal the real feelings, frustration or disappointment, desires and expectations.

Meaningless complaining

For some people life is a valley of tears; it is painful, boring, hard, disappointing – and, moreover, it is too short!

If I speak, my suffering will not be soothed.
If I am silent, will it decrease?
Job

Complaining as a safety valve

Complaining sometimes merely relieves our feelings. It does us good to exclaim that we have too much work, that our colleagues are impossible, that we are fed up with having headaches or that our children exhaust us.

We would like our complaint to be received simply for what it is: a way of momentarily unburdening ourselves so as to feel relieved. We certainly don't want to hear the retort: 'You got what you wanted' or 'There are people who are unhappier than you' or 'You should organize yourself differently'! Sometimes we need to moan loudly or shout in protest in someone else's presence before getting off to a good start again.

To complain may be a disguised way of unwinding, of yawning, of expressing an ill-chosen remark. By complaining we give ourselves a good time at the expense of the other person's comfort.

To complain about circumstances that obviously cannot be changed by anybody is like a ritual, a social pastime. In fact it often concerns the weather and the passing of time. Conversations about the weather are most appreciated, and the perpetual complaints that accompany them are similar to the choirs of antiquity that announced never-ending unhappiness.

Complaining is a means of discharging and sharing. Stoics who forbid themselves to complain deny their wounds or lick them alone. But sometimes it is as if they themselves have become a silent complaint. They die without a scream! They are too conscious of their own responsibility for what happens to them. They are too proud to unveil their weaknesses, too suspicious of their fellow beings or too convinced of other people's misfortunes. They do not seek relief from the great well of human compassion.

'It's so good to complain!'
'Yes, but keep it in small doses.'

8   When What is Unspoken Touches the Pain

Nothing is ever cut off from anything else. What you do not understand in your own body, you will not understand anywhere else.
Upanishads

We can use numerous languages to talk about ourselves and just as many not to talk about ourselves. There are an infinite number of non-verbal languages. Their vitality is equalled only by their diversity. To illustrate this, let us consider the whole range of conscious or unconscious gestures which we use to try to put outside ourselves what is inside, or the rituals (repetitions, acting out) with which we try to tame the outside world so as to integrate it within us.

It is essentially our body that emits and receives an infinite number of messages. We know today that psychosomatic illnesses are symbolic languages through which we try and tell significant people around us (not necessarily the people we are close to) about our real feelings, when these are censored or forbidden by fears. We will see shortly that these feelings usually express experiences such as loss and separation, unfinished business, 'missions' of loyalty, and interpersonal and intrapersonal conflicts.

Physical ailments constitute a real coded and structured language that sometimes fills the empty space left by a lost or impossible relationship.

The body has an unfailing memory. It stores childhood messages: messages of loyalty to such and such a parent, an obligation to rectify the parents' past faults or to heal their hidden wounds (the child hears these messages very early on and tries to console his parents by setting himself the task of healing them).

Children are extraordinarily skilful at expressing in a symbolic though often clumsy and violent way what is left unspoken by their parents or the people around them. Hurt by this behaviour, the parents fight and denigrate it and even go so far as taking their offspring for treatment – without realizing that the child is expressing precisely what is wrong with or between themselves. As former children, we also use with incredible creativity the language of ailments so as to exist and be recognized.

It seems useless nowadays to pursue or nurture a false quarrel between physiological and psychosomatic ailments. It is more important to move away from classifications, schemes and questions about causes.

Trying to explain everything is a trap. We should give this up and move into new ways of understanding. These may even be contradictory as they have to account for the conflicts (be they existential or related to relationships) through which any individual attempts to remain healthy and well (or to nurture suffering, even violence, in his body against his own will).

Health matters do not just concern medical care, even though today they often end up being treated medically. Most health problems have to do with learning anew how to communicate with ourselves and others. They appear when we have to reframe significant relationships at each crucial stage of our life (birth, early childhood, adolescence, young adulthood, adulthood and old age).

Health matters also concern our ability to become an agent of change in the running of our lives. They concern our power to assert ourselves better in front of others, rather than accepting that others determine our sense of identity and our behaviour and thus remaining ensnared in their wishes, fears or value systems.

Illnesses are symbolic languages with which we sometimes relentlessly, desperately or enjoyably attempt to express what we cannot say with words. They also express what we do not have direct access to, but which nevertheless exists in us.

Though communication with others is vital for each one of us, communication with ourselves remains essential. We must listen

Illnesses are the screams of silence.

to the repercussions of our recent or past history on our bodies and on our imaginary lives. We often have to give up depriving ourselves of relationships and emotions because this ensnares and mutilates us. Unspoken words are as violent for ourselves as for others.

When things cannot be said with words, they will be violently expressed through ailments.

This preliminary statement may seem paradoxical and risks wounding the reader. Because the suffering individual mainly wants to get rid of his pain, he will stifle it with balms and care (if we consider his ailment as a language, this is equivalent to not listening to it).

Any dis/ease must be understood at different levels so that we can recover our health.

Nowadays we notice two apparently opposite but certainly complementary phenomena in relationships.

On the one hand, there is a growing lack of communication between individuals (I am referring here to vital, close and intimate communication and not to mass communication with its excessive information and constant incentive to consume words and images which do not nourish us for all that). Along with this lack of communication and the difficulties we have to express ourselves, to be listened to and to receive, comes an immense suffering. This immense distress is linked to the negation or denigration of ourselves (or of other people who are experienced as bad, inaccessible or forbidden) and leads to solitude. This solitude means that we do not communicate with either ourselves or others. (The worst solitude is not to be alone. It is to be a bad companion to oneself.)

On the other hand, more and more people are switched into some sort of global network, and have an increasingly demanding and personal quest. Individuals want to know themselves better, to live better, and to be better companions to themselves and consequently to others.

This new quest has become urgent for an increasing number of men and women. It is essential and vital, because it is a matter of survival. In fact we have little hold on the social phenomena around us (which condition us). Multinationals plan our future food, our leisure activities, our housing conditions and our way of life. Anonymous, political or bureaucratic entities anticipate our needs and plan answers which already alienate our future. Our real personal power over social issues is almost non-existent; we have little control over all these phenomena outside ourselves.

But we still have potential power: a power over ourselves, over our everyday life, and above all over what makes life interesting – our close relationships. There remains also the fundamental power, which is always threatened and always needs to be defended: to keep in good health.

Human relationships and the discovery of our potential are the only remaining adventures.

Our mental and physical health is linked to our taking responsibility for our lives. Actually, in spite of the astonishing and fabulous progress of medical care and surgery, more and more people are in trouble, in a state of physical and psychological suffering. (Overconsumption of medicine is often linked to a lack of social interaction or communication with ourselves.)

Illness or health does not happen at random. We receive and welcome bacteria, germs, viruses or accidents and very often keep and nurture them with great care! It is actually our body, our organism, that welcomes, nurtures or rejects them. We could even say that what affects us does so to fulfil a function which is beyond our understanding.

As a structuring element of our personality, language plays a part in keeping us healthy, on condition that we remember the rules of live communication. When we are talking, we want to be heard at the level at which we express ourselves (verbal, non-verbal, emotional).

> 'If I tell my husband about my fears, I want him to hear that I'm afraid. I don't want him to minimize what I say. I don't want him to mock me or to try and reassure me, because then I don't feel recognized . . .'

In an intimate and trusting relationship, I should be free to ask, give, receive or refuse. If one of these aspects is missing, the relationship is sick and I suffer.

> 'I don't dare ask what is important for me. I expect her to guess . . . and I often feel disappointed and frustrated.'

> 'I don't dare say no, I feel that others should always come first, that I should please them first.'

> 'It's very difficult for me to receive. I'm not worthy of accepting anything. It is as if I didn't deserve to be loved or to have people interested in me.'

In a conversation, we should have the possibility of talking both about facts and about the experience or resonance, that is to say about what the event recalls in the distant or recent past.

We should also have the possibility of expressing ourselves at the three essential levels of communication:

- the level of reality;
- the level of imagination;
- the level of symbolism.

There are 'blind' areas in many communications. We 'do not hear' the different dimensions which make a relationship healthy.

When words do not find a way to be heard and received, another language comes to life. This is the language of ailments that develop into illnesses, dysfunctions or physical disorders. Members of the caring professions should listen to these different languages so that they can help people to express them in ways other than bodily violence. We call 'relational care' the attitudes, behaviour and words of the caring person that can help a sick person to:

- understand the meaning of his illness in his personal and family history;
- build ties with the people around him;
- clarify his relationship to the treatment and to the main practitioners and specialists who prescribe it;
- reclaim his life choices as best he can.

If we accept that illnesses are symbolic languages, whatever the element that triggers them off, then people in the caring professions should be trained in 'relational care'.

Young children are remarkable specialists in non-verbal languages. Their bodies send out messages to the people around them, who do not understand them as messages but as disturbing or worrying behaviour that should be restrained.

A young paediatric nurse recounts how she was able to talk to 14-month-old Max, who had been in hospital for a few weeks after his mother's fit of dementia. The mother had been put in special care.

Every night, Max woke up distraught and crying, and banged his head against the wooden bed, tearing his hair out.

One night, the nurse took him in her arms and said simply: 'Max, you're not responsible for your mother's suffering.' The baby looked at her for a long time, hiccupped a few times, then stopped crying and fell asleep till morning.

It is indeed true that body language tells not only about our sufferings but also about our aspirations, about all that makes us love life.

Let us illustrate this with some examples gathered and explored in personal growth training sessions. We have no intention of offering an explanatory and all-encompassing model, or to lapse into excessive and therefore blind generalizations. But we want to try and understand certain phenomena of which we are part and parcel, not voluntarily but rather in an interactive and interrelational mode.

Each one of us may have observed and listened to some of the psychological experiences described further on, which have been converted into either stress and external aggression, or into body language.

WHAT DO OUR AILMENTS TELL US?

Ailments (which sometimes become diseases) are symbolic languages through which we try to express:

- personal and interpersonal conflicts;
- unfinished business (and particularly the resentment linked to it) which remains a secret open wound;
- separations and losses which have not been soothed by mourning;
- old messages about being loyal, or about submitting or conforming, which we accept (or oppose with a huge and

usually vain loss of energy) – guilt keeps us linked to the suffering of others and imprisoned in our loyalties.

Crisis is brought forth, one day, by all our unfinished actions, by all the gestures that we didn't carry through, by all the unfinished bits of life with which we weave our days and our nights, by all our aborted meetings with ourselves and others.
Christiane Singer, Histoire d'âme

We will now describe the main roots of psychosomatic illnesses or acting out.

Personal and interpersonal conflicts

Inner conflicts arise each time there is a discrepancy, a contradiction between what I feel and what I do, between what I manifest and what I experience. When I am torn between a wish and a fear, between two wishes or between two constraints, I create an inner state of tension and violence which makes me feel persecuted and unbalanced.

> 'The phone rings and a friend tells me that I'm invited to a party. She accepted for me. On the spur of the moment, I don't say anything. I answer in platitudes and ring off. In the following hour I become feverish and I have a sore throat . . .'

How many sore throats and bouts of flu are only the 'expression' of a refusal that could not be spoken, of a personal utterance that did not find a way of being heard? If I realize fast enough the nature of the link between my sore throat and the phone call, I can cure my sore throat by reclaiming my words. I can call my friend to cancel the engagement she made for me and recover the freedom to make a commitment myself.

> A woman married a highly skilled mountaineer, who liked to take her each summer to the highest alpine summits. She always follows her husband although she is terribly afraid during some ascents. She

would rather he heard her request: she would like to stay at the chalet to read and dream while he climbs. Each summer she has a cold sore that spreads over half her lip. She takes advantage of this to refuse sexual intercourse. On the very day when she feels ready to come into open conflict, that is to say to confront her husband with her real needs and to take the decision to respect her own needs, the cold sore disappears. (Many persistent and painful vaginal infections appear without obvious 'causes' and in spite of negative medical tests: they often express misunderstandings, unspoken refusals and 'violence' in relationships.)

Another woman had breast cancer at the age of 44. She was treated, the cancer was removed and she recovered. Around the age of 50 she tells us how she lived through this experience: 'I hid all this from the people around me, so nobody knew what I had. I took advantage of my holidays to undergo surgery. Even my family didn't know . . .'

We suggested that she had linked her age when the cancer appeared with what might have happened to her mother at the same age. After an initial moment of negation ('Nothing particular happened . . .'), she said: 'Oh! yes! I remember! My mother had my little sister. At the beginning of her pregnancy she felt ashamed and let other people believe that she was suffering from fibroids. As I was studying to become a paediatric nurse, I was the one who looked after the baby.'

Some time later she acknowledged how this birth had 'spoilt her life': 'People took me for the baby's mother and I didn't dare say anything. I let them believe that. I said nothing about my real feelings. As for my brother, when he discovered the baby on returning from his military service, he broke the living room door.'

In both examples we find the same mechanism: to hide, not to express anything, especially about the violence that is felt.

Cordelia is 18. She lives with her parents and she is going out with a male friend who has become her lover. Her parents ask her to be home before midnight. Each time she goes out and meets her lover, she feels sick. 'I had a headache and stomach cramps. During the whole evening I would feel really unwell and off-colour. It became a habit. The feeling of being unwell would stop at around 11.30, then

I would suggest that he bring me back. The last ten minutes always went well. We would make love in the car just before going home.'

It is as if the inner conflict had to be expressed in the language of symptoms.

Unfinished business

The body keeps in its memory everything we have experienced, all the events that have marked us. Some events might have seemed unimportant, but they nevertheless become deeply engraved in us. (This inflexible memory persists, even though the remembrance may have become fainter over the course of the years.) A harmless sentence here, a remark there, is experienced like an attack and remains like a wound.

Unfinished business in childhood has infinite consequences in our body. For a long time it will be 'expressed' through languages which astonish us and often lead us astray.

'I should never have agreed to move with my parents … when Daddy was sent to Paris!.'

When the parents of an eight-year-old boy moved during the school year, he lost his best friend and first love, Clare. Afterwards, each year at the same time, in February, he had an ear infection.

Refusals to hear often produce ear infections in children who feel hurt by the lack of understanding of the people around them. It is as if the children were saying: 'You're deaf there, just where I have an ear infection . . .'

'My mother had never told me about my birth. One day when I was telling her about my wish to have a child with my girlfriend, she told me how I was born: "They put you under an oxygen tent. The doctor vigorously massaged your chest and sucked out a lot of mucus, as if he was emptying a sewer." A few days later I relived all that again at the age of 29: I was suffocating, I had mucus in my throat and sinuses, headaches and a violent allergy to the light which seemed too bright; I had the feeling that I was born too soon, that they had sucked the mucus out too quickly, that I needed more time . . .'

After hearing about the death in a car accident of the boyfriend with whom she had been going out for four years, Paula remained very calm. She put down the phone and continued to apply make-up, as she was going out: 'I felt as if I were anaesthetized. I was surprised to feel no pain.' Paula's story continues 15 years later. She has been married for ten years. Her husband must move to a different workplace. He has been away for ten days. And one evening he phones to say that he has just had a car accident. He is not injured, but the car is smashed. When Paula puts the phone down, she starts trembling. Her teeth are chattering and she has convulsions: 'I felt screams rising up in me. I wanted terribly to scream. I wanted to break things, to hurt someone; my whole body was convulsed. When I was able to phone my husband, without realizing it I called him by my dead boyfriend's name. I think he really understood what was going on. His understanding helped me through a whole period of violence. After that we were able to tell each other things that had remained unspoken for years.'

Unfinished business produces a lot of frustration and brooding. It keeps feelings of worthlessness and of non-existence going. It also nurtures bottled-up anger, desire for revenge, and repressed violence which try to manifest themselves through ailments, and particularly through repetitive symptoms (psoriasis, renal colic, ulcers, etc). They can also be manifested through what we call psychosomatic acting-out, such as accidents, injuries and blows.

> 'I hadn't had a car accident for 15 years. The first car accident happened when I was going to meet the young woman I loved. I still hadn't dared leave the woman I was then going out with. The second car accident happened today on my way to the solicitor for a division of property, so that I could separate from the very woman whom I had been meeting 15 years ago. I now realize that each time, something remained unfinished in these two relationships which are yet so different.'

Separations and losses

Separations are experienced differently according to age and phase of development. Often the real emotion and feelings are not expressed directly and cannot be said. The usual mourning process cannot take place and it leaves a sort of mark in the body, which may then be revealed later, triggered off by some trivial event.

> With intense despair and anger, a 50-year-old man recounts something that happened when he was 7. Coming back from school, he found his friend Naf Naf, the pig, ripped open against the farm wall. His father had killed his best friend and confidant. The boy, feeling terribly guilty, hid all night long: 'I hadn't known how to protect my friend.'
>
> For many years, at Christmas time, he always found a way of hurting himself, of cutting and mutilating himself. His body bears many scars. They reveal his helplessness to save his favourite animal – 'the being I cared most for' – and his guilt which was transformed into punishment.

> A mother of four daughters has suffered from allergies all her life. (By the way, one should always question what people mean by 'all their life'.) She is allergic to certain smells and pollens linked to the loss

of a doll which had been thrown into the rubbish tip because it was 'too old and too dirty'. 'You're not going to keep this filthy doll in your bed,' her mother had said. Every year in October, which was the month when the doll was thrown away, she has a heavy cold. She remembered about the doll on the day when, tidying up the attic, she found her eldest daughter's first doll and broke into tears . . . without understanding why.

Little Louise was 9 years old when her foster mother died at the age of 60. Fifty years later, Louise, by now a grandmother, had a nervous breakdown. Many years later, she told her son: 'You know, I thought that I too would die at the age of 60, like my mother.'

Many adults have this deep-rooted anxiety that they will die at the same age as their parents, or feel guilty of surviving them and of living longer than them.

A 30-year-old woman told her father one day what had happened when she was in the third form, aged 12: 'I felt okay in my class. All my friends were there. One day the headteacher phoned you to say that I was clever and that you should put me in a more selective, stricter school. You put my name down at another school the following year. You abruptly tore me away from my classmates and uprooted me. I was put in a class where there were only "sons of bitches, pretentious and revolting snobs". I didn't feel accepted by them. But you didn't even notice that there might have been a link between this and the infection I had that year! I went to a tuberculosis sanatorium where I found an environment that was good for me . . .

Dad, when you plant a tree, you prepare the soil carefully. You do that for a tree . . . but not for your own children.'

The awareness of children and their requests for quality in relationships should awaken us more often. It was more than 13 years later that this father heard about the link between the infection and the uprooting of his young daughter from her environment.

Thirty-two-year-old Angela, who has been married for five years, tells us in a training group that she has frequent urinary infections.

She adds that it is strange because she had been living with her husband for six years prior to her marriage without ever having any infection. As she listened to another woman talking about the grief of losing her name (her father's name) by marrying, and about her desire to recover the name to which she was so attached, Angela discovered that she had felt the same pain.

A few weeks later she wrote to tell about how she was making progress health-wise. Her infections had completely disappeared. She had renewed her relationship with her father, and felt in a much greater state of harmony. It seems that Angela had experienced her marriage as an amputation of her name. This had left an unhealed and still purulent scar which manifested itself as a urinary infection.

One of the mysteries of the body is its ability to express things in unpredictable ways. We are always very astonished, each time we can recall a significant event, to discover that words might have expressed it.

If we express things with words, we don't have to express them through ailments.

A new-born boy was abandoned at birth by a young, distraught and panic-stricken mother. She also was threatened with abandonment. The boy was adopted at a very young age by a farming couple who had already, after many miscarriages, adopted a girl who had died suddenly at a very young age. The boy arrived in the family some time later. For the first six months, he yelled all night long. His foster mother and father would alternately get up and rock him to stop him crying. He would go to sleep while they were with him, but he would wake up again half an hour later and would resume his anguished and worrying screams.

Forty years later, he mentions the fear of abandonment that still dwells in him and his outbursts of anger triggered off by a hurtful word or gesture. He wonders: did the baby scream to be sure of his parents' presence and have confirmation that he wouldn't be abandoned again? Did he scream to prove to his traumatized parents that he wouldn't also suddenly die in the night, like the little girl?

The screams were a language. By silencing them with the rocking, the parents prevented the baby from expressing his anxiety. By letting him scream without going to see him, they would have let his anxiety overwhelm him. But a true word could have been spoken. 'Yes, your mother let you down on the very day of your birth and you're afraid of being abandoned again. But we're here and we certainly won't let you down. The little girl who was here before you suddenly forgot to breathe. But you are not responsible, you didn't take her place; you're here, sturdy and alive. You don't have to burden yourself with her death and our grief.'

Old messages about loyalty

Children, as well as the former children that all adults are, often want to heal their parents' hidden wounds. It is as if they have to embody their parents' wounds, disappointments and short-comings. These loyalties and attempts at healing can take on a bodily expression (illnesses, accidents, various injuries).

Children may also be given 'missions': they must be successful, happy, unhappy, fail, prove, belong . . . But this often implies submission, identification, debt or opposition.

> Thirty-seven-year-old John had sinus trouble and bad colds several times a year. This lasted for a long time, until 30 years later when he was able to tell his mother the 'truth' about a childhood event. He had concealed from his parents that he had nearly drowned at the age of seven. The very day when at last his mother listened to him, she opened her arms and said: 'Poor little boy'. He was then able to cry for a long time. He 'let go' of all the frightening water he had silently retained for so many years; and so he was able to let go of his chronic sinus trouble.

This is an example of faithfulness to an old message and to old commitments.

> An adult daughter wanted to offer her mother the little baby her mother had lost in a miscarriage. A little boy would have filled his grandmother with joy. But the daughter had no son, 'only' three girls. A few years later, she had a cyst on her left ovary which she spontaneously associated with the little boy she hadn't been able to

*'If I listened to my sinus trouble or sore throats, I would discover my fears
and particularly the silence that enshrouds them.'*

give her mother. (Around the family dinner table, her mother was
always placed on her left.)

When we listen to the signs manifested by the body and associate
these signs, we hear wonderful – and not necessarily tragic –
stories: stories about links and attachments, stories about filiation
when, through a specific symptom, a child for instance tries to say
that he is also a Smith because he bears a symptom that he
associates with the Smith side of the family (when the Jones line
attempts to appropriate him).

Body memory is extraordinarily rich. No wonder it needs to be
expressed. Sometimes the body seems to scream in the silence of
words.

The body tries to express itself, to let go of conflicts, burdensome feelings and repressed demands. It attempts to get rid of feelings of debt. It is, at times, like an extraordinarily stormy battlefield where contradictory 'demands' clash.

Counsellors and people in the caring professions are confronted with the following dilemma: if they heal the patient, then they destroy the symptom and stifle what is trying to express itself through this medium. This is why classical medicine, which tries to restore the functioning of the body and abolish the consequences of infections, risks missing what is essential: to listen to what is struggling to be expressed even if it is through the body.

Of course it is necessary to treat all of these aspects. Some kind of 'relational care' should support and back up the usual therapeutic and medical treatments.

Very often the relationship with the person who is providing care is in itself a kind of symbolic process of reparation, though this is not necessarily a conscious process. A gesture, a word or an association restores a link (that escapes the understanding of both the person giving care and the one receiving it) between a bodily symptom and its meaning. Some therapists have this ability to introduce into the relationship equivalent symbolic links and thus restore the meaning that was missing. The power of an attitude, a gesture or a way of listening is proportional to its symbolic dimension.

THE CAUSE OR MEANING OF ILLNESS

'Relational care' must enable the sick person to relate to the meaning and symbolic function of his illness. The search for a cause (to explain and justify the illness) too often takes priority over the attempt to understand the meaning.

A 40-year-old man has resumed his studies to become a social counsellor. A few days before his assessment, violent pains assail him.

His doctor diagnoses ulcerous anal fissures and advises him to undergo surgery immediately. He feels downcast and links with this what happened at various times of his life, each time he had to confront a test or face an ordeal: he had appendicitis at the time of his fourth year exam, hepatitis at the time of his high school graduation and a nervous breakdown before another important exam.

By linking all these facts together he gives himself the means to face the situation positively. The repetition enabled him to recall the message he had received at a very early stage in life: 'Oh! you'll never succeed. You shouldn't even bother preparing yourself for an examination!' Any possible success was like a transgression. The risk of being unfaithful to this message was expressed in his physical symptoms.

Too often, in fact, when we want to give an explanation for an illness, we find either a physiological cause or a psychological cause.

'I've had insomnia ever since my husband left me.'

This attempt to explain away an illness or a dysfunction is an illusory trap. We should not only search for the cause of an illness or a trauma. We should also look for its meaning, and consider the illness as a language, as something that signifies something else in a chain of associations and meanings that are beyond our conscious grasp.

The woman's insomnia might therefore mean self-deprivation. It might be a punishment she is inflicting on herself for having disobeyed her father who had advised her not to marry her husband. Is she trying to make up with her father again? Is she trying to show him her allegiance: 'You were right, Dad. Look how I'm being punished.' We do not know, but by searching for meaning instead of cause, we often achieve a change. A symptom is relinquished and an essential relationship restructured.

What do a baby's ear infections mean? Could it be: 'Mummy, you don't hear me; you don't hear anything.' The meaning is usually about blocked ears – but whose?

How many persistent psoriasis cases which have been treated for years by competent but sometimes deaf dermatologists will literally dissolve once the violence they contain is expressed in words? A 30-

year-old woman who expressed her terrible anger against her sister who had stolen her doll's name at the age of five was able to 'let go' of tenacious psoriasis that only needed to be understood!

When repressed memories come back to our consciousness, then the symptoms linked with them can be relinquished. This helps to loosen our grip on events and messages that have been recorded inside us and that might create future conflicts and tensions.

Of course the mother of this 13-year-old adolescent does not know that she is recording in her daughter's body, as it were, her own judgement against 'people who don't know how to love only one person at a time'. (Maybe she is talking about her own boyfriend who has several parallel relationships.) And when the girl is 15 and feels attracted to two boys at the same time, she has a violent attack (diagnosed as appendicitis). She expresses her conflict ('I'm fond of both') and her attachment to her mother ('I don't want to disappoint her'). She also experiences an inner conflict because of the self-image she has internalized ('I don't want to be considered a loose girl or a whore . . .').

At the third attack (a few minutes before leaving for hospital to have her appendix removed) a conversation with a friend throws light on her inner conflict and uncovers her contradictions. It enables her to accept her many attractions . . . without having to undergo the mutilation of surgery. 'The appendix went down like a balloon.'

Stephen is eight years old. His mother, who is single, has invited his grandparents and an aunt to celebrate his birthday. The evening looks promising. The child is joyful and relaxed. His mother's boyfriend phones to tell her that he would like to spend a few days with her. She invites him that very evening. A short time after the boyfriend's arrival, Stephen suddenly develops a high temperature. He is examined and his temperature is taken: it is 104°F. He goes to bed and the birthday party goes on without him. It is as if Stephen were punishing himself and punishing his mother for not having been able to make a choice between him and her boyfriend.

A ten-and-a-half-year-old girl, on returning from a skiing holiday, suddenly started to have violent stomach aches, to vomit and feel dizzy. This lasted over two months until she was able to tell her grandmother that she had kissed a boy on the mouth. She was afraid, because she had heard on the radio that Aids could be caught by kissing.

Most paediatricians know how anxiety can be expressed through the body. And yet they too often tend to treat the symptoms!

Paula had been married for 12 years. Already a mother of two, she was pregnant for the third time. But her husband didn't accept her pregnancy. He had told her that he would divorce her if she kept this third child. So Paula had resigned herself to having an abortion. Since then, she has had serious, sudden and irregular haemorrhages. Everything 'is all right' on a physical level. But who can help her find out about her wound? Which aspect of her is bleeding in her? Who can listen to her so that she can hear the wounded part of her which is revealed through her haemorrhages?

It took her six years to find out (thanks to a trivial event) and recognize that her relationship with her husband had been hurt and severed. His ultimatum ('It's either me or the child') had broken something in their relationship. The blood of her haemorrhages revealed this rift between them, the bleeding open wound in their relationship.

His name is John. It is the name of his mother's brother who died very young. A wound has been inflicted on him through this name. It is the mark of his mother's wound at the death of her beloved older brother. How can John experience pleasure and be sensuous? His loyalty tells him to punish himself, to anaesthetize himself and not to nurture the life within him. John has had a steady relationship with a woman for six years, but he doesn't feel 'any pleasure with her'. His erections only let him penetrate her and wait – but nothing happens. His 'impotence', his inability to have pleasure, makes him consult a sex therapist.

Gradually John accepts the need to give back to his mother the suffering that belonged to her. He accepts the need to give up his name which is too related to death and instead gives himself a life-bringing name. The whole dynamics of his behaviour change. Sometime later he writes tell us to about 'his way out of impotence and his access to pleasure'.

Peter is an Israeli studying in France. He is living with a young woman. In a few months he will get his engineering degree. His parents decide to come and see him. They intend to remind him of his duty towards his country: he will have to go home after getting his degree. Peter is torn: he loves his girlfriend. He has become attached to France and does not envisage returning 'straight away' to his own country.

When his parents decide to cut short their stay and go back, Peter offers to drive them to the airport. On the motorway, just a few miles from the airport, he stops at a layby to relieve himself and, just by stepping out of his car, breaks his leg (double fracture, hospitalization, metal pins).

Peter does not think that the 'accident' has any link whatsoever with his conflict and his relationship to his parents or to his girlfriend. If we add that the first part of his engineering examination was to take place the following week – do we need to convince anyone? Meanwhile, he treats his fracture as a fracture, and no more.

Joan had decided to get married, whatever happened, before the end of the year. During a New Year's Eve party she suddenly but formally became engaged to a friend. The whole family was present. On the following morning she woke up very sick. For three months she was sick every day and presented the same symptoms (stomachache, heartburn, headache). After three months she went to Morocco with her friend and decided to take the pill. On her return her symptoms increased but they only appeared during the eight days preceding her period. 'Each time I was sick to death for a week.'

She got married in the autumn. For 16 years she was chronically ill, suffering for several days a month . . . except during her two pregnancies: 'I've never experienced nausea while pregnant.' During all these years there were no fights, no blame or protests in her relationship: 'We were always even spoken. We were seen as an ideal couple,' she added.

One day a fight broke out between Joan and her husband. It was a liberating outburst and she was the first to be astonished by it: 'I couldn't believe my ears to hear what I was saying; rebellion overwhelmed me. I screamed "I have been sick ever since I've known you, I never had anything before . . . You present yourself as a victim, but I'm the one who is trapped in our relationship."' After this wild and vehement outburst, her symptoms disappeared and she recovered the health she had had as a young girl, but her relationship with her husband became difficult, that is to say real.

She had started to change and particularly to recognize how much her 'New Year's Eve engagement' had been more an acting out than a real desire. She had paid the price for it with so many years of psychosomatic illness. Later on she was able to tell her husband that the anger she had expressed towards him really concerned her, because she had been deceiving herself.

When Mary was 9, her father died at the age of 39. She remembers his death very well. She was doing her homework at the end of the day, at nightfall, when her father stood up, took a few steps, then fell in a heap by the fireplace. For years, she experienced this precise moment, 'nightfall', with agitation and irritation, 'a feeling of unease'. It is precisely on her own 39th birthday that she manages to link her behaviour with the memory of her father's death.

Associations between dates remain engraved in us, leaving a trace which can be reactivated at crucial times. They may also help us unveil difficult or unfinished business. We suggest that we should resort to a kind of archaeological research within the family to uncover hidden links that do not connect two individuals together, as we would believe, but rather their life histories. When faced with an illness or an accident, we should question what happened to our father or mother when they were the age we are at the time of these events. It is a difficult search, because it may concern two or three generations and even our children.

A man discovers that the heart attack he had at the age of 42 can be compared with a similar event in his father's life: at the age of 42, his father had nearly lost his life in a serious car accident.

A woman whose mother had been ill since her birth suddenly had to act like a nurse at the age of 17. She became responsible for her family (seven brothers and sisters) when her father was taken to hospital for cancer while her mother had to stay in bed because of sciatica. She handled the situation with devotion and competence while taking her high school diploma. For years she carried on a busy life in a caring profession.

At the age of 39 she discovered that she had breast cancer. By searching for the meaning (and not the cause) of this, she realized that her eldest daughter was exactly the age she had been when she was obliged to look after her parents. It is as if she had been waiting for her daughter to reach the right age to take over the role she had been given – to be her parent's mother – so that she could at last be taken care of and nursed, and stop being hyperactive.

Repetitions and recurring life patterns can mark a whole life in this way . . . if we allow them to do so!

'Each time I put myself in a conflictual situation, without being able to express my position, without being able to be heard, I have a car accident. It's never serious, but expensive (the body of the car, the lights, the doors, the wheels are damaged). That's why I've got into the habit of taking a taxi after any unspoken conflict.'

SYMBOLIC PRESCRIPTIONS

If we accept the idea that bodily ailments (which sometimes become diseases and real somatic problems) are symbolic languages, it means that it is possible to heal them by not only curing their symptoms, but also by uncovering their meaning, the hidden words in which they are rooted. This implies that we can treat them with symbolic responses.

So sometimes we suggest 'symbolic responses' which can be heard and can play an active role in recovery and help clear up the symptoms.

Six-year-old Thomas has been suffering from asthma for two and a half years. His father left his mother when he was three and a half (this is the element that triggered things off). Thomas plays alone. He refuses to play with his brother and sister and refuses the social life offered by his mother. He cuts himself off from everything. Thomas often says: 'I don't like the air in this house, I prefer Daddy's.'

We suggest to his mother that she should use a large bottle on which she should glue a label with 'Daddy's air' written on it, and to which she should attach a small pipe for breathing the air in.

On the day that the mother brings home the bottle of air, Thomas is playing in the bath. He calls her and says: 'Look, I'm a fish. I'm breathing under water.' She told us later: 'From that day on, he never had another asthma attack. I was very moved by this symbolic reconciliation.'

We also suggest what we call 'games', symbolic prescriptions concerning some aspect of the patient's discourse or of the symptom which we feel has an intense symbolic resonance. Occasionally, we have suggested to someone that he play Mozart music to his kidneys or his liver, or that he imagine the nape of his neck like a dried-up sponge slowly swelling with water as it sinks down in the sea . . .

Four-and-a-half-year-old Edward goes to nursery school for the first time. From the third day on, he defecates in his underpants. His father gets angry, threatens him, and promises a good hiding if he continues. 'You're a big boy now.' Edward tells his mother: 'I can't hold it in. It comes out by itself, it pushes and comes out.'

We suggest that his mother should tell him about his birth. She bursts into tears and says: 'I never told him about that so as not to upset him; he was born by Caesarean.' However, she accepts the need to tell him about her own experience and about the decision taken by the obstetrician . . . She told us later that Edward's anal troubles disappeared the following day.

A child was 12 when his father committed suicide by hanging himself. The silence around the event, in the family as well as in his own life, caused him often to have a pain in his throat (suffocations, sensations of strain and tightness). During the next 30 years of his life, he underwent numerous surgical operations for tonsillitis, cysts, ganglions in the throat and neck. We suggest that he should talk to his father in a symbolic game and tell him about his anger . . . and his love and faithfulness, manifested by all his scars. These denote the existence of his father who had disappeared too soon and to whom he had not been able to say 'I love you and I resent you.'

A surgeon friend agrees that some symbolic reference to 'what he has removed from his patient can be beneficial.'

> 'My relationship with them is completely changed. I have also noticed a decrease in post-operative complications.'

For example, we suggested that a videotape of a Caesarean could be made and the sealed tape offered to the mother. She can decide for herself if she wants to see how her child was born.

In this creative field we can introduce the fantasy and magic of the symbolic world. We can invent tales for our children by letting our imagination freely and actively associate on the basis of a symptom. We thus link different aspects of their inner world to everyday life. We give them images and fables which take into account reality as well as the vast field of the unconscious.

Let us experience the power of words beyond their meaning.
Let us get in touch with meanings beyond the pain they create.
Dominique Meunier

When we listen to what is expressed by the body we should be careful not to confuse cause and meaning. Too often, we tend to search for causes and explanations. We too easily substitute explanation, which is a search for knowledge and control, for understanding, which is a search for meaning.

Too often, we talk *about* our body. We talk *for* it instead of letting it express itself. We can also relate to our body through many symbolic languages. The body needs to be heard rather than controlled.

All illnesses and ailments are not as negative as they might seem at first. They have meaning. In a sense, they represent a way of restoring balance in a threatened internal system. They reveal the unspoken.

Each individual organism is in itself an ecosystem that cannot exist without being linked to a larger ecosystem made up of the people around us and our close relationships. Each illness, each attack, has one or several hidden meanings, which must be disclosed if we want to stop having medical treatment and recover.

If only we would listen to our body and build a better relationship with ourselves.

If only we would listen to ourselves when we are with others, so as to remain alive and healthy.
Let us try . . .

9 Terrorism in Relationships

'If you really loved me'

Without imagination, love has no chance.
Romain Gary

Terrorism in politics uses violence to provoke a change in others by upsetting them and creating a climate of insecurity. This is also true of terrorism in relationships. It is a perverse form of terrorism in so far as it does not put forward hate or war, but exerts violence in the name of family love or of love. Generous feelings, loyalty and the fear of losing love are misused to make the other person conform.

Terrorism in relationships occurs every day around family tables, under the soft light of house lamps, in beds, be they marital or not, in cars going towards the holiday sun. In the family, in a couple, in close relationships, in all those places of intense commitment and emotional expectation, we exert as much violence on others as we have projected desires and fears onto them and been disappointed in our expectations.

Victims of emotional terrorism make use of violent words: possession, suffocation, feeling crushed, imprisonment, tyranny, paralysis, mummification, death.

'It's as if I were dead'.

'I don't exist any more in front of him.'

'When she talks like that *for* me, I disintegrate. I lose the feeling of wholeness.'

Terrorism is an attempt to substitute one thing for another.

- We substitute our wishes for the other person's.
- We put our needs first, before the other person's.
- We replace the other person's ideology with our own.

'I can't bear it anymore to hear people talk for me. It destroys me.'

Terrorism in relationships can take the gentle form of benevolence – 'It would be better for you to . . .' – or of paternalism – 'I thought it would be better for you not to go on holiday on your own, so I asked John to go with you'. But it can also take a form that is more obviously violent (criticism, blackmail and blame): 'If you don't get married in church, it's because you don't love us any more. You're not my son anymore', 'If you see this person again, I won't talk to you anymore'.

It can also take the terrible form of paradoxical injunctions (contradictory messages) or of denial (behaving as if the other person had not said anything, as if his opinions and desires did not exist). One subtle form of denial involves taking over another person's words by answering:

'Yes, I know.'

'I knew that you would tell me about that.'

The we thought is thus deprived of its value because I already possessed it before it was expressed.

A VARIED ARSENAL

Terrorism can be subtle and involve neither fight nor apparent tragedy. Its weapons include sullen silences, sarcasm, such signs of intolerance as sighs and harsh looks, caustic remarks, provocative glances, exhortations, calls to altruism, to feelings of pity, guilt or shame. It can also bring into play refusals of sexual intercourse (or other things), heavy silences, irritated gestures, tears, inquisition, denigration and many other tactics. Some people are true artists and jugglers in their relationships: they act like extraordinarily skilled tightrope walkers on the tightrope of manipulation.

When we can stand back or when we are not directly involved, we can even laugh at and admire these acrobatics that aim at provoking unease, imbalance or even madness in the other person.

But why do we use this infinitely varied arsenal? Our purpose seems to be either to change the other person or to prevent him from changing. Anyway, we want to use him (as a dumping ground, as a foil, as an auxiliary, as a source of gratification, etc), to keep him in dependence, to link him to a situation, to a person.

When we cannot give ourselves enough love, attention and care, the people who are close to us have to provide them. If they do not do that spontaneously, in a way that suits us, we exert pressure on them so that they respond to our expectations. We try to obtain through guilt, seduction or force what is not given freely.

An so terrorist-like dynamics set in when we depend too much on others for our needs. We also use them when we cannot tolerate that those who are dear to us do not live up to our hopes, or are different from our image of them. Relational terrorism is rooted in all the intentions, desires and fears which we express, project onto others and pin on them under the pretext of love.

When we were babies, we only had to cry or pull a face for someone to guess our needs and satisfy them. We find it difficult to let go of such power.

'I need you and I'll do my best to make this need become yours.'

Of course, in any relationship we want the other person to think, act or feel differently from the way he does. We want to make sure that the other person is aware of our love and of the relationship that we are offering.

'I would like him to talk to me more.'

'I would like my children to love the high mountains like I do.'

'I would like her to be more joyful and welcoming when I come home.'

'You can't do that to me'

Wishes pinned on others become terrorist-like only when they are transformed into demands and when various means of exerting pressure are used to infringe on others and do violence to them.

A 15-year-old adolescent shouted down the phone when his mother announced that she wouldn't be back for lunch as planned but would only be back for the evening meal: 'You must come back. You can't do that to me. You must drive back immediately. Do you hear me? I want you to come back as arranged . . .'

Neither our feelings nor our wishes do violence to others. But our defence mechanisms (denial, etc), our fears and tensions do:

'I'm so afraid of losing my self-esteem that I need to denigrate someone else.'

'I'm so afraid of being abandoned that I jealously keep a watchful eye over my partner.'

'I never take any initiative so as not to risk making mistakes.'

'I am so convinced that my relationship and my life are a failure that I oblige my daughter to be successful in everything. She must live and be happy for me.'

How can we get rid of something we lack?
For instance, how can we get rid of our lack of confidence?

When we are afraid of being abandoned and continually anxious that we will be rejected, we exert ruthless and pathetic – in fact pitiful – pressure on people around us. Nothing reassures us. We interpret everything as a confirmation of our deep feeling of being devalued.

'You don't ask me anything anymore, that means that you don't count on me. I don't interest you anymore. I have very little place in your life . . .' And a few days later the same person will say: 'You always ask me to do things for you and afterwards you don't even tell me if I did it right. You don't thank me, as if you were taking everything for granted. I exist for you only if I'm useful for your work and even that . . .!'

Blaming and complaining are used to keep a hold on the other person and at the same time to reject him so that he in turn rejects us. This confirms the intimate belief of those who are afraid of being abandoned:

'I can only be rejected, particularly if I show myself as I am. But if I put up a pretence, then I won't be loved for what I am. So I show myself to be insufferable and I ask the other person to accept me in this way without condition, and to reject me.'

These contradictory messages addressed to ourselves and to

others trigger off anxiety. They give the impression that there is no way out other than rejection or alienation. The person who is afraid of being abandoned – as we all are, more or less – desperately and relentlessly tries, at the same time, both to avoid and to bring about the tragedy (or its repetition) which obsesses him. Everything is used – especially when things are going well – to endanger the relationship and bring the protagonists to the brink of discouragement and despair.

> A weekend planned with enthusiasm presents itself under favourable auspices. But on the day before, it turns into a disaster because of a detail which is used to systematically sabotage the project.
> 'I was expecting your phone call to know if it was still on.'
> 'Remember, I called you three days ago and we discussed our plans again; I'm to pick you up at ten . . .'
> 'Yes, but if this week-end were really important for you, you'd have called me this morning. It's an ordinary, trivial thing for you. You don't care about it. If if doesn't work, you've got other opportunities.'
> 'There's no question of other opportunities. I'm talking about this weekend with you.'
> 'I don't feel like coming anymore. I feel that you don't care about our relationship . . .'
> And so follow hours of reassurance, promises and little attentions. Even before it has begun, the weekend was costing dear . . .

Good intentions

> 'If you loved me, you wouldn't be away so often.'

> 'If you loved me, you would want me just when I want you.'

'If you loved me' means 'you don't love me'. The one who loves is trapped by these words which dictate how he is to provide evidence of his love while at the same time denying it.

> 'I love you and I want to continue living in my two-room flat', a girl said to her boyfriend having recently left her parents' house. 'If you really love me,' answered the boyfriend, 'if you loved me as I love you, you would want us to live together.'

In this example, love is equated with resemblance, similarity of tastes, desires and feelings. It is confused with the relationship. The person who hears that could say:

'I acknowledge that I love you, and my love is different from yours. But I'm talking about our relationship when I say that I want to live alone for a while.'

To differentiate between relationship and feelings is one of the most difficult things to do. It is all the more arduous to disentangle these two levels when one or the other of the partners wants to maintain the confusion.

'I'm fed up with your studies: you're often away, you're never here. The children are complaining too. You have to choose: it's either me or your studies . . .'

'For years I had migraines nearly every weekend', tells a woman. 'My husband was wonderfully patient and caring. He took care of the children and coddled me. Now, after a process of personal growth and homoeopathic treatment, I have no more headaches. But my husband continues to ask me persistently, especially on Saturdays, if I'm well, if I've no pain, if I'm not tired. His solicitude has become unbearable. I feel stressed. Does he need me to be unwell?'

Another woman rebelled one day and screamed that she didn't want to be treated like a sick person, like a fragile and irresponsible woman. In the face of this outburst, her husband remained calm. Then he said to her compassionately: 'I can see that you're very tired, you can't control your nerves anymore. You should take a rest. Don't worry. I'll take care of everything.'

And so with good intentions, his behaviour denies what she had been saying. Denial is a way of not taking into account what the other person says. Without meaning to, he continued his repressive work. He repressed the change that might have threatened his own balance. This example enables us to differentiate between rebellion, a spontaneous and reactional impulse, and repression, which appears structured and organized, like implacable terrorist tactics.

The history of this couple and the progress of the woman towards autonomy continued with them going through an awful divorce case. The repression exerted by the husband was even supported by the judge. Descriptions of the steps taken by this woman, such as undergoing rebirth or primal scream therapy, and passages from the books she had read, such as books about naturopathy and *Talking with Angels* by Gitta Mallaz, were used as evidence of her mental disorder. Her children were taken away from her, and the judge said: 'You are far too independent to be a good mother.'

The effort made to maintain the other person's weakness or sickness betrays the immense helplessness of the person who, in this way, attempts to cling to a dominant position. But the helplessness is never expressed. It is denied and fought against by using violence towards others, in the name of beautiful principles and finer feelings. Such violence does lasting damage and may separate forever two individuals . . . especially when they stay together.

In the name of our interest in others, we try to impose on them a way of life which we think is good for them.

A young woman exhorts her mother to go out more, now that her children have left home: 'You should go and see exhibitions. You should buy yourself clothes, travel, make plans.' On each visit, she insists: 'Have you done anything new?'

The mother feels guilty of wanting to stay quiet, of letting go. Her daughter pesters her because she can hardly conceive that her mother is in a totally different stage of life. She cannot imagine that she has less energy and different wishes.

Intolerance is usually based on a lack of imagination which prevents us from realizing that others have different reactions and needs. There is no distance in our identification with the other person.

Moodiness

The relationship terrorist may pull a provocative or ravaged face to exert pressure. In this way the frustration he has not been able to handle is projected onto others.

> 'You enjoyed yourself without me. Well, I'm going to sabotage even the memory of your pleasure!'

> A woman and her daughter spent a weekend in Paris. They went to the Picasso Museum, to the Opéra and to various restaurants. On their return, they are still amused about their discoveries. On the landing, the mother imitates the tenor and the daughter the heroine of the opera. The door opens. The 'father/husband' pulls a long face: 'I thought you were coming back by the 7.30 train.'
> They fall silent and say: 'We're exhausted. Let's go to bed straightaway.'

When we are moody, we obstinately refuse to express through words what our pride finds unspeakable: 'I feel hurt. I'm jealous. I feel excluded.'

> Back from a good weekend in the mountains with friends, a man feels his joy disappear when he sees the long, sad face of his companion who welcomes him with these words: 'So, it all went well for you then . . .!'
> And yet she had said: 'Go on, have fun. Don't worry about me ...'

The need to talk and the fear of saying.
M Benin

A painful experience borne in silence, which we try to forget by looking for compensations, is often at the root of this terrorism. The wound is often beyond words.

> 'I feel hurt without being able to say why. I can only say that I suffer pain because my integrity is wounded.'

When we are sulky, we display anger and suffering but our wound remains hidden. Many sufferings overshadow and conceal the

*'I've been waiting for you for hours, sad and desperate ... at the thought of
how you were enjoying yourself without me!'*

real wound, which they conceal, even from the consciousness of
the person experiencing them.

**It is characteristic of an unbearable suffering to reveal the secret
wound and hide it at the same time.**

Some people, whether children or adults, play the silent game
called 'being in a bad mood'. It consists of not talking to the other
person while respecting a certain code. So as not to go back on
their position, they wait for the other person to take the first step.
This requires great concentration and a lot of attention . . .
directed at the other person. Nevertheless, some apparent
formality is kept up and both parties go on talking emphatically
about daily concerns.

'My wife is never as pretty nor pays as much attention to me as when she's in a bad mood with me. She talks to some outer me, but the "I" that I know as me does not exist for her.'

Some groups of children can cause misery and despair by sending a child to Coventry.

'Come on girls, let's not talk to her anymore. She's capable of telling the teacher everything.'

'I was eight years old when one of the big shots of the class spread a rumour that I was bedwetting. "He stinks, can't you smell it? If only he washed!"

I tried to explain that we ate garlic at home. For two years I was rejected by nearly all the school. I hated my parents for eating garlic.'

'You're the bad one'

Terrorism consists of trying to shift all the blame on to others when there is a conflict, a difficulty, a separation or a painful disagreement in a relationship. To keep a morally perfect image of ourselves and to feel on the good side, we have to prove to others that everything is their fault.

'I can't bear to see "bad" feelings, shortcomings or deficiencies in myself. I have to reject all the negative things outside. Therefore I desperately try to convince the other person that he is at the root of the problem and that I am the innocent victim, in spite of all the goodwill I showed.'

We are all convinced that our inner demons only appear as a reaction to the other person and would not exist with another partner. Some depressions after the loss of a spouse who has been seen as 'bad' are linked to the fact that negative aspects can no longer be projected onto someone else and now have to be acknowledged.

'The worst thing he could do to me was to be stupidly killed by a reckless driver . . .'

A woman got married at the age of 18 to escape her family. All her life she has blamed her husband for not being the way she wants him to be. 'You haven't been able to take on your role of man and father. Look, it's my father who lent you money to start your own business. I'm always the one who takes decisions: to move to another flat, to take steps to buy a house, to organize the children's holidays. I even pushed you to go and see my father for the proposal. He urged me not to get married to soon . . .' The woman is trying to saddle her husband with her own difficulty in putting some distance between her father and herself. Her deep loyalty to her father prevents her from truly accepting another man.

A tired father slapped his son who did not obey him quickly enough. He is overwhelmed by a feeling of guilt, and he becomes a 'terrorist'. He tries to convince his son of the legitimacy of his action and to fob off his guilt on him: 'You irritate me on purpose when I come home. You never listen to what I tell you, you . . . you . . .'

The father's need to justify and reassure himself by transferring his own aggression on to his son will be more burdensome and detrimental than the slap.

Children are often generous as well as dependent. They easily take on themselves all that is wrong in the family. They readily become willing and cooperative scapegoats. But this is not acknowledged, so strong is the adults' belief that 'a good father is always right' and that anyway 'they will thank us later'.

We often confuse upbringing with loving. And this confusion persists in our adult loves.

'If I don't conform, I won't be loved.'

'Though I was always disappointed, I still continued to hope that I would be loved better if I acted the way I imagined they wanted . . . It was an impossible and endless task. I was constantly depriving myself, hoping to be satisfied by my parents. I was always prepared to receive what they "should" have given me, and never received it.'

The need to transform the other person into the 'bad one' may result from a wound.

A woman who was left by her husband cannot tolerate the implied denigration. In her despair she screams: 'You can destroy everything, except the children: I won't let you do that.' She thus goes so far as attributing to the father the intention of destroying his own children. This attempt to turn him into a persecutor enables her to lift her spirits She perpetually reframes things to her own advantage and burdens her husband with her feelings so as to avoid the truth about herself.

The best way not to confront the negative part of ourselves is to attribute to others the bad role, the role of the 'nasty one'. We justify our own intrinsic violence by their behaviour. Very early on children learn how to explain any conflict with the sentence 'He started it' in a tone of outraged innocence. In this way they clear themselves of the pleasure they took in attacking. They also resort to irresponsibility, which is one of the most frequent and current strategies ('It's not my fault').

At certain times of the year, the roads and motorways seem only to be frequented by irresponsible people. I call them 'The Just'. They never realize that the manoeuvre they executed so skilfully startled the driver opposite so much that his car drifted into the ditch. The Just Person is already far away evaluating the opportunity for his next skilled manoeuvre. Some drivers also want to teach others: they will take any risk to provoke a salutary fear, or even better, to bring awareness to the absent-minded or awkward driver who may have disturbed them . . . even if he wasn't aware of it.

Not speaking

When we do not say anything and impose nothing, we in fact behave like a terrorist in the most subtle way. We want to obtain affection and attention without having to ask for it or show our need. We compel those who love us to be always guessing, calculating and watching our reactions.

Sentences like 'Do what you want', 'I don't care' or 'As you like' can be like poisons in the relationship. When we say this, we do not define our own position. We delegate this responsibility to the other person. In family or marital life it may trigger off rejection and contained violence which is then expressed through acting-out and displacements.

> 'What would you like for your birthday?'
> 'Anything you want.'
> 'I was thinking about that sailor jumper that you like?'
> 'If you want.'

But we do not always try to receive when we do not ask. We may be indicating in this way our own 'right distance'. And we may experience other people's attention and responses as an intrusion and impingement on our privacy.

> A father who lets his children do as they want in the name of freedom and autonomy is, in his own way, exerting violence on them. He lets his own need to be approved and to avoid confrontation come first, before his children's needs, which might be to receive clear orders and reactions. He does not lay down any rules but his attitude implores: 'Don't do anything that would make me unhappy.'

This form of indulgence combined with silent emotional pressure is a real aggression against children. And this is all the more so since children need their parents to define their positions clearly. They need to see and feel where their parents stand regarding such a problem or such a question.

Some silences are noisy enough to be heard.

PSYCHOSOMATIC ILLNESS

The body needs to express itself to become aware of itself. It needs to be listened to.

Psychosomatic illness can play a dual role in the dynamics of terrorism in relationships. It can be a weapon and also a means of strategic defence. Its mention can be very powerful in producing guilt, for instance during a phone call:

'You know, I'm not at all well. I'm getting old, but don't worry. Go on holiday all the same . . .'

'I don't know what happened, but the other day when you left for your training course, I suddenly felt sick in the kitchen. What if the children had been left alone! Everything is all right now, I called the emergency medical service, but they could not come. After that I felt better. I must go and have a medical checkup. Don't worry . . .'

Illness can also be a defensive measure against the terrorism of others: it gives us the possibility of refusing a request without having to confront the other person.

'You know very well that with my painful back I can't travel for a long time! How on earth can I accompany you to your mother's?'

'My cystitis and sciatica are very useful. My husband doesn't even ask me to make love any more. He never stopped harassing me before. His demands were really too much for me.'

'Since I've had trouble with my spine, Dad doesn't oblige me to weed the garden anymore.'

Illnesses can be a form of terrorism against ourselves to counter the terrorism of others. When the balance of power is too unequal in a relationship, illnesses can be a lesser evil.

COLLABORATION

Terrorism can be exerted only with the collaboration of its victim. Indeed there are often two victims, because terrorism can be mutual. Weakness can have a tremendous power. When we submit to someone, we attribute a fantasized omnipotence to them, or at least lend them or even give them an exaggerated power.

Nancy came for a consultation. Let's listen to her and concentrate on her behaviour rather than her husband's, as her words would tend to induce us to do.

'I'd like to take a break and review my life before taking the decision to start work again or separate.' [She dissociates these two options without realizing that they go together.] 'I feel stifled. I can't stand this life where I exist only for the comfort of my children and my husband and even of my in-laws who interfere with everything. My husband thinks that being together is an obligation. It shouldn't be something that we wish for.

On Saturday mornings, Francis asks: "So what shall we do today and tomorrow?" I don't even have time to suggest an idea; he already has a ready-made suggestion. He catches me unawares. I would like to answer: "Nothing, we'll stay here together."

But I feel I'm in the wrong and that I'm mean not to be enthusiastic about a project which doesn't suit me. I can't stand it anymore. He stifles me. He's getting me down. And money! Oh, money! It started a few years ago with the birth of our third child, whom he didn't want. I have to be at one and the same time elegant, careful to vary the meals, and I must make no mistakes in the management of the household money, that is to say his money. In addition to that I have to save money. Sometimes, I've the impression that he would be pleased if I gave him money back. I did it once: I paid a cheque into his account. He told me: "That's good. I'll be able to give you less!" Which one of us is completely crazy? He usually says: "But what do you do with all the money I earn?" He confuses the money he earns with the money I spend to run the family.

What hurts me most is when I at last suggest going out and he answers: "But what's the matter with you? At what time shall we get back? Don't you know tl ɪ ˈ have to work?" I work too, and I work hard without earning anything! I earn the humiliation of being supported, of always being in debt, and the despair of thinking that it is an endless situation. I hold my tongue so as not to aggravate the situation. I constantly feel at fault and inadequate. I'm convinced he's better than me and especially that he must be right.'

Today, after a long and shared reflection, Nancy realized how mistreated, neglected and alienated she had become by seeing her husband as omnipotent. 'At the beginning, I mistook his rigidity and his demands for strength of character. He knew what he wanted; I was so often indecisive!'

She slowly realized that she could be different. She could give herself a sense of self-worth without searching for it by rebelling in reaction. She could assert her point of view through ways other than refusal or sabotage. The relationship made her feel stifled, so she started to do yoga. But she realized that this wasn't sufficient, and that she had to find her own space. She discovered that she had her own desires, which differed from those of Francis. Her lungs, blocked by the power attributed to others, started to expand. She listened to herself and respected her own wishes. Now Francis is the one who is unsettled by the change, and new adjustments will be necessary.

Let us speak out for ourselves instead of accusing the other person.

Our collaboration with the terrorism of others becomes a form of terrorism against ourselves, through self-repression and self-censure. When we take tranquillizers, we contribute to this abdication. Most consumers of tranquillizers (66 to 70 per cent) are women. Women depressed by marital violence are prescribed psychotropic drugs more often than men are. It calms them down and helps them to endure their victimization. Tranquillizers are like Bandaids applied to conceal the trouble in the relationship – the loneliness and the helplessness.

This enforced silence is akin to the pressure exerted in many families to be sure that certain topics are never mentioned.

> 'Mummy, why is Auntie Kate pregnant when she doesn't have a husband? Is it like the Virgin Mary?'
> 'There's no comparison. Don't talk nonsense. Finish your meal and go and play outside.'
> 'At school, they said that there are fathers who do things to their daughters and that one should talk about it. Do you think that Dad would do things like that?'
> 'Do you want a clout? You're mad to imagine such things! The things they teach you at school nowadays!'

After several hurtful answers, open repression becomes useless. Children carefully censor themselves. They will continue to do so in their relationships as adults. Unable to say their real feelings or opinions, they will express themselves through acting-out, accidents, psychosomatic illnesses, or adhering to commonly held opinions.

Most adults that we meet complain about the terrorism of silence in the family in which they were brought up.

> 'There were no words. There were no words to say anything. There was silence at the family table, everywhere.'

> 'My mother cooked. She didn't say anything.'

> 'My mother talked all the time, but she didn't say anything.'

Most of them also complain of having perpetuated this silence by a kind of inner repression, ruled by imagination.

> 'If I tell him, he won't understand anyway and he'll get angry.'

> 'If I showed how I really feel, other people would make fun of me and despise me. I would resent myself.'

> 'There's no point in talking, it doesn't change reality. I don't want to risk hurting someone.'

> 'Why talk about my sadness at finding myself alone, it's normal, isn't it?' (It is as if what is normal was not worth mentioning.)

Children very early on sense that expressing things through words, however vital and necessary it may be, risks triggering off even more threats, violence or rejection. So they keep silent.

BEYOND RELATIONSHIP TERRORISM

Terrorism feeds on fear. The power of terrorism lies in the combination of two fears: our own and that of other people. We have many fears that build a fabric in which are woven the past, the present, the future, the unpredictable, the unknown and the known.

When we exert pressure or violence, it is always because of our fears:

'Don't dress like that.'

'I think that you're letting yourself go a bit too much, with your mates.'

'I don't see what good it will do you to study, to go 150 miles away from here for your training. You're alright as you are, you'll only create trouble for yourself . . .'

'Don't you think you should stop . . .'

The worst kind of terrorism is to let the other person believe that you're expressing his point of view, when in fact you are expressing yours.

'Don't tell the others about our relationship.'

I am afraid that he is talking about me, that he gives a distorted image of me and reveals my intimate life. I do not trust him; I enjoin him to keep quiet. I want to control his speech, even in my absence. I exert even more pressure with judgements, even threats.

'Your need to talk about us to your mother is childish. It might separate us.'

'If you tell others about what is happening between us, I can't let myself go.'

Beyond the fear, there may of course be the wish to preserve some intimacy, to protect a relationship, and to keep it privileged. The other person, afraid of judgement and separation, will obey and restrict his own words and freedom. He will not dare stand up for himself, and say for instance:

'I'll say what I want to whom I want, but I am taking you into account.'

Or he talks all the same and, in turn, exerts pressure on his confidant.

'Don't tell him that I told you . . .'

Fear will induce him to obey or secretly disobey.

Obedience and conformity

What makes us obey other people's messages and injunctions, giving their terrorist-like behaviour a hold and power over us? It is certainly our fears. But it may also be our difficulty in knowing clearly what we want, think, feel and are at this moment. We first have to know these things, and then dare to assert ourselves and stand firm. Our feeling of debt or our sense of duty makes us, and sometimes even obliges us, to let other people determine what we should do.

'I must agree to get my hair cut, otherwise he'll be unhappy.'

'I must go and see my mother (even though I don't want to) because she'll say that I neglect her, that she's too lonely . . .'

Mothers often burden their children with demands which are in fact ruthless injunctions. The child's behaviour and sense of identity is determined by the mother so that he or she will conform to her expectations. In adulthood, some people cannot exist or live their own life because their life has always been determined by someone else. In therapy, we frequently hear about this kind of submission and repressed rebellion.

'I can't behave in any other way. I resist; I flee; I struggle. I throw a tantrum and then I do what she expects of me.'

Some drug addicts understand their addiction as a sort of safety curtain which helps to put an insurmountable screen between themselves and their mothers. The drug acts like a separating third party even though it invades and devours them with such violence that sometimes there is no way out.

In many relationships, there is an alternative: a choice between determining our own sense of identity and letting others determine it.

The most alienating parental messages are those which define what the child is. Expressions such as 'You are' leave a stronger impression than 'You should'. 'You should' leaves some room for free will, for the possibility of not conforming. 'You should' deals with actions and behaviour and not with the person, as do the 'You are' expressions. 'You are' imposes a self-image which becomes an unavoidable definition of a personality that has not yet been structured.

'You are like my elder sister who never thought of others.'

'You're not clever enough to study.'

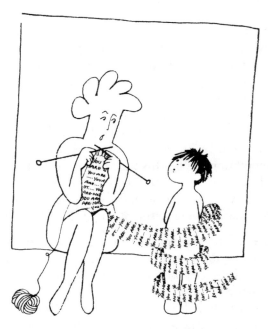

'If I let you define who I am, Mummy, how will I grow up?'

'You have an artist's disposition.'

The more flattering images imprison nonetheless, because they oblige us not to disappoint others. They create a permanent challenge, an obligation to conform to the suggested model.

'You're more intelligent and reasonable than your brothers.'

'I know that I can always rely on your help.'

Sensitive children organize their potential according to the model that is attributed to them. They respond and submit to other people's expectations and definitions.

It is also difficult for adults to have a clear sense of their own identity. We all have a thousand facets and so many contradictory desires and potentials. The kaleidoscope or our fears, desires and ideas forms ever-changing images. We are caught up in a whirl of aspirations which also make up our inner richness and explain our life's trials and errors.

If someone turns our kaleidoscope one notch further and tells us: 'This is what you are or what you should be', we will recognize ourselves or certain parts of ourselves in the reflection he offers, in the definition he gives of us. We are then drawn onto his ground, into his perception, and we may feel at home there. We can agree: 'Yes, I'm like you', or 'Yes, I'm the way you see me', even though we saw ourselves differently a while ago. It is not a question of changeability or dissipation. In us, there are a thousand temptations to be this way and as many to be another way, which intertwine, are amplified or paralysed.

To make my own position clear, the crucial question might be: 'What predominates in me at the moment, in this situation?'

- Does the need to be approved, to agree and to be on good terms predominate? Is it likely to silence my judgement, my criticisms and my opposition? Or do I really agree and am I really convinced?
- Is it the wish to hurt him by telling him about my aggressive reactions to his betrayal? Is it the wish to understand and

accept him? Is it the need to keep silent, and to go away and forget?

- Which aspect of myself shall I listen to?

In this inner conflict between numerous forces, it is sometimes easier to let others and their real or presumed demands determine who we are. When we do so, we turn away from our own choices, which are too difficult to make, and from our ambivalence; we evade the sense of identity we have given ourselves, and which anyway cannot contain the whole of us.

The aggression we felt towards another person during a too long absence vanishes the moment we see him, smiling and warm, confident, and sure of our unconditional welcome. Which of these two facets are we going to show? The one which was mulling over our frustration and aggression? Or the one which feels satisfied and appeased?

By repressing one or the other we are anyway going to betray ourselves. Therefore we let ourselves be overwhelmed by the feeling that is wanted and expected by the other person and that was also in us. But repressed anger will surge again, usually in a different place and in a different manner.

Every relationship is an interaction. We feel touched, modified and sometimes reconciled by the encounter. When we were alone, our diverging feelings conflicted with each other. Different aspects of us were fighting in our heads and hearts and, to fight them more easily, we projected one of them onto the other person.

We can also assert our position by expressing both facets:

- our vengeful brooding;
- our joy and our pleasure.

'This is what I went through while waiting. This is what I feel on seeing you.'

We learn to say yes by daring to say no.

Holding your own

> A father is worried. His adolescent daughter is going through a crisis. She is hostile, uncommunicative and rebellious. He is convinced that she needs to talk to a third party because he is not well positioned to talk to her. One day, he gives her the address of a centre he has heard about, where she would be listened to and helped. 'Why are you giving me this?' she exclaims, 'you know very well that I won't go!' The father takes back the note and goes away feeling bitter. 'She doesn't want to receive anything from me', he broods, 'she refuses everything I want to give her . . .'

He let himself be stopped by his daughter's reaction ('You know very well'). He did not hold to his own position. However, it would have been enough to say:

> 'Here's the address, it's up to you what you do with it. It's true that by doing this I show that I'm worried about you. I'm doing something for my worries concerning you. If you recognize them, maybe you will do something for yours.'

The daughter is then faced with a choice of action:

- She can recognize herself in her father's perception and accept the sign offered.
- She can choose not to recognize herself and therefore not pick up the message offered.
- Or she can listen to her father's concern without conforming to it, thus making her father feel that he is being listened to.

Not taking on other people's games

Dialogues between relatives and close friends are often mutual attempts to determine the other person's behaviour, generally by attributing to him the negative role. It is a way of reinforcing our own position of victim or of being 'the good one'.

An elderly and lonely mother asks her daughter to phone her every Sunday evening. She therefore defines the frequency and time when her daughter must 'take the initiative' to call her. Is she in this way holding on to the illusion that her daughter wants to phone her regularly?

The daughter hasn't been able to assert her own position. She agreed and now she often forgets to phone. She phones on Monday and the first words she hears are of course a complaint and a blame: 'You didn't phone me yesterday.' She justifies herself, explains that she had gone out, etc. They debate a long time without realizing that the whole system is fraught, and that the daughter doesn't adhere to what her mother wants. The daughter could for instance set things up in this way: 'I'll be home on Friday night. If you want, you can call me between eight and nine-thirty.' Or she could explain: 'I don't want it to be so regular. I'll call you depending on when I am available.'

KNOWING OURSELVES

We should confirm to the other person that we recognize his desire so as not to be trapped.

If we do not want to be alienated by terrorism in relationships, we have to define our own sense of identity and assert our own position continually while recognizing the demands or feelings of others.

'I understand how important it is for you that I get married in church, but at present it doesn't mean anything to me.'

We can also protect ourselves against 'sadism' by maintaining some inner distance, and by handling our emotions better without identifying with them. 'That too will pass.' We are not obliged to put our nose under someone else's 'exhaust pipe', and then moan about the 'pollution'. Neither are we obliged to let the fears of others resonate too strongly with our own, and then accuse them of being tyrants.

The opponent

The opponent often collaborates with the terrorism he is subjected to. In spite of appearances, the person who opposes and fights the other person's point of view and systematically declares that he doesn't agree, actually lets the other person determine his stand instead of asserting it himself. He asserts himself in opposition to someone or something, but he often does not present his own project or desire. He is unable to leave aside his reactions.

> 'My friend wants us to build a house together; she has a lot of ideas. I don't agree. I don't know what I want, but at least I do know that I oppose her project.'

Protestants gave themselves a name which made their stand clear. They were protesting against the practices of the established Church.

The illusion of a fake consistency grounded in opposition and rebellion is a necessary step for adolescents before they are able to build their own system of references. Some people remain stuck in a position of protest throughout their whole life and thus avoid having to affirm their own positions.

RESISTING TERRORISM

Be it acted out or undergone, terrorism reflects our fears and weaknesses. However, terrorism in politics and terrorism in relationships are fundamentally different. The former is intentional, devised, premeditated and conscious. The latter is acted out in a generally compulsive way: it is non-intentional and usually subconscious. It penetrates relationships with incredible skill, subtlety and constancy. It disappoints expectations, frustrates intentions and sabotages the best resolutions.

Terrorism in past or present relationships is at the root of many physical and psychological ailments which become chronic so as to enable us – and this is a paradox – to survive in a chaos that would otherwise be intolerable.

How can we become immune to those who, in the name of our mutual love and of their interest in us, try to influence our emotions, behaviour, thoughts and way of life?

- If I submit, I take care of his needs, but I reassure him to my own detriment.
- If I rebel, I declare war on him and risk a separation.
- If I ignore the pressure, he or she will make it stronger.
- If I say that he does not leave me any room to breath, he will deny it.

How should we act, so as not to be invaded by our partner's fears, shortcomings or fanatical convictions?

> 'She's so clever at demonstrating to me through tiny everyday details that I'm not a satisfactory husband.'

> 'My father makes me feel all the time that he doesn't trust me and that I disappoint him when I do this or that. It undermines my self-esteem and reinforces my doubts.'

Many of us cannot shut out the anxieties of others, specially if they resonate with our own. How can we protect ourselves? Some people prefer to escape and play a similar game with someone else (if they have not been able to get rid of the mechanisms which push them into such games). Others, after painful experiences, prefer to go it alone.

As for these two authors, we shall try to offer some signposts in the coming chapters. We hope they will show the way to greater differentiation and responsibility, so that we can all become better companions to ourselves and to others.

There must be limits, even for those who want to go beyond them.

10 Responsibilities

Often in a relationship we tend to deny responsibility for what we feel by displacing it elsewhere.

'YOU'RE RESPONSIBLE FOR WHAT I FEEL'

'If I feel something, it's because of someone or because of some event. So they are responsible for what I feel!'

This is, in short, one of the most tenacious myths in relationships.

'I'm angry, disappointed or sad because he forgot our appointment . . . or because she didn't understand . . . because she tells me that she loves me and turns her back on me as soon as we're in bed . . . because he did not answer my letter . . .'

The accused person is generally a parent, a lover, someone with whom we have a close relationship. He therefore becomes disappointing because he frustrated our expectations. Sometimes we burden him with our resentment and accuse him of every inadequacy. We make him responsible for whatever happens, be it good or bad, for our successes as well as our failures, for our laughter as well as our tears.

The omnipotence we attribute to others makes us give up our responsibility for ourselves. It is as if we were irresponsible and helpless.

'I feel lost, panic-stricken and I'm suffering . . . so how can I be the one to do anything about it'.

And in many other forms we face the familiar vicious circles.

'I'm moody because she's moody when she sees me moody.'

'If I'm complaining, it's because you're so often away.'
'If I'm often away, it's because I am fleeing from your recriminations, your bad moods and your complaints.'

We can find an infinite number of reasons for not feeling responsible for what happens. We always evoke external causes. In this way we often avoid making choices or taking decisions. He said to me . . . she wanted . . . he behaved in such a way that I could only attack him, leave him, help him, do such and such for him, take charge of him . . .

In the spring, Gerald tells Elisabeth that he wants to spend two weeks of the next summer holiday alone. She has nothing against it (but is she for it?) and plans to go on her own to a nudist camp. But Gerald reacts violently: 'I don't agree at all!'

Elisabeth gives up the idea. The couple make a few plans for a holiday together, but in June, Gerald again talks of going away without her. He is ready to take their son with him. And he adds: 'If you really care for this nudist experience, then go ahead.' Elisabeth tries to enrol at a camp, but everything is booked up; she enquires elsewhere, but there is no room either. She is furious: 'What sabotage! He prevented me from carrying out my project. He forbade me to go, then let me when it was no longer possible. He spoilt everything, he manipulated me.'

Elisabeth questions Gerald's changes of mind but she does not question her own submission or her way of letting herself be manipulated, of letting someone else decide for her. She does not ask herself: 'Why do I obey him?' The spoilt holidays are a shock. Later on she will learn to stop accusing Gerald. She will have to look at both (conflicting) tendencies – independence and submission – in herself and to find a balance between them.

'I've the impression that I'm living like a savage and I risk serious consequences if I go on my own way without taking the reactions of others into consideration. I don't feel that I'm myself when I'm influenced by another person's desires and fears.'

In relationships any strategy based on the conviction that others are responsible for what we feel risks leading us to a state of helplessness, stagnation or even madness. Such strategies exist because they provide justifications and alibis, especially when they are associated with childhood experiences.

'I was never allowed to express myself, so I can't show what I feel now.'

'I was forced to control myself, so I can't let myself go now.'

'I was told that sex was something bad, so I'll always be frigid.'

The child's emotional and psychological dependence certainly does create some kind of conditioning, but what is odd is how we cling to it all our lives.

We should differentiate between what has been done to us at a certain period of our life, and what we perpetuate for years or decades.

Must we implicitly pledge lifelong loyalty to parental messages, often questionable ones, particularly when we project them onto our significant relationships? But there are other ways of making others responsible for what we feel. In couples, each partner often represents an unacceptable part of the other's personality, and we all too often make our partner responsible for any change in our feelings.

'If you hadn't forced me to have an abortion, I would still love you.'

'If you hadn't continually called and pursued me, I would be free of you and not have to suffer in this way.'

'If you weren't so dependent, I'd feel a lot more free.'

Others are considered to be the cause of our feelings and resentments; consequently we expect them to take charge of them and put up with their effects.

'I'm like that because of him; therefore he must stop behaving like that and everything will be better.'

This last example illustrates a paradox. An unbounded omnipotence is attributed to the partner. Yet at the same time the speaker thinks she is powerful enough to oblige her partner to change by the sheer weight of her unhappiness, the pressure of guilt and the violence of her victimization. Fantastic (phantasmagoric or real) wrestling matches start in this way in some close (marital or parental) relationships and can last for years. Based on informal and totally crazy laws, these wars can last several generations. It is like saying 'I claim irresponsibility for what I feel and experience.'

As for wanting to change others, is it for their sake or for our own?

WANTING TO CHANGE OTHERS

The idea that others are responsible (for what we feel and what happens to us) will lead us into a common trap in relationships:

the attempt to change others. It seems so logical and obvious that it is the others who have to change.

> 'I can't bear my colleague's nervousness; I end up feeling nervous as well. It's obvious that he's the one who should become less nervous. Anyway it would do him good.'

> 'I would like my friend to resist me, so that I can assert myself. He always agrees with me and I don't know where I stand with him.'

> 'I never know what she expects from me because her plans and intentions concerning me are always vague and confused.'

> 'I always feel frustrated with my father because he never expresses his feelings. I've been waiting for a more authentic communication with him for many years. He must have some feelings, but he never lets them out. That means I can never really talk with him, so I attack or oppose him. Then he gets angry and breaks off the conversation.'

> 'I feel swamped by my mother's desires and fears. I wish she would learn to control herself and not pour it all out on me.'

We think that it is quite legitimate to want to change others to make ourselves feel better and put a stop to our discomfort. The temptation to change others, or to initiate our change by first changing them, dies hard. This keeps our relationships in a static state, on familiar and known ground.

> 'I know in advance how things will go. I'll say this and he'll answer that. He's always like that . . .'

> 'I'll never be able to tell my mother that I live with a divorced man or that I've had an abortion. She'll reject me as if I weren't her daughter anymore.'

When we pay attention to the reactions with which other people protect themselves, we miss what has been touched off in them.

In relationships I might be incredibly skilled at ignoring some aspects of both myself and the other person:

• What does a relationship with a man who has already been married represent for me?

- What is hurt in my mother when she discovers my relationship with a man who has already been married?

My attitude might enable me to remain blind to my own shortcomings, but it is often reciprocal.

'Don't force me to choose.'

'Don't push this sharing idea on me.'

'Don't expect me to hide the fact that it hurts.'

We all try to solve dilemmas by asking the other person to modify his or her expectations and desires. Both sides assert their own position by asking the other partner to suppress his or her own demands. Unfortunately, one of our oldest aspirations of the human race has been the influence to what others want – perhaps to find proof of their love and to test their attachment.

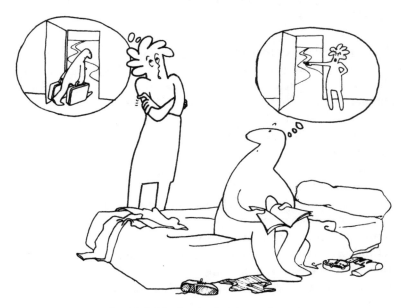

'I wish he'd take the decision to leave.'
'I wish she'd throw me out.'

'If you loved me, you might let what you want come second for a change; you wouldn't hurt me by being so inflexible.'

This mother, who can no longer bear her 24-year-old son's presence at home, enjoins him to act instead of her: 'You should have a job, earn your living, be independent. You should feel like wanting to have your own flat.'

He answers: 'I've got all the time in the world, but if you want to throw me out, just say so clearly.'

She wants him to have the energy to leave, and he wishes she had the courage to throw him out!

The effort to change others in the way we want is doomed to failure; it leads to repetitive phrases and is filled with veiled violence and repressed hatred.

'I WANT TO BE RESPONSIBLE FOR WHAT OTHERS FEEL'

Some people tend to feel responsible for what others around them feel. Many parents see themselves as the source of their children's failures, successes and positive or negative characteristics. They view their offspring as extensions of themselves. The children repay them later when they accuse them of being the cause of all their problems (rarely of their well-being).

Children too are very clever at taking on false responsibilities and carrying the burden of their parents' pain. They try to heal their secret wounds, or to relieve them of their disappointments and anxieties. They feel that they are the cause of their parents' fights or divorce, of their sorrows as well as their joys. Their natural self-centredness does not enable them to imagine that they might have no responsibility in what is happening. It is too hurtful to have no responsibility in what such important people are going through.

Guilt, a widespread and damaging feeling, is often rooted in an illusory feeling of omnipotence. A good deal of upbringing is based on threats, denigration and aggression. Guilt gives a feeling of existence, which compensates for the self-negation engendered over many years of our upbringing. Children who grew up with a depressed parent often retain a diffuse guilt feeling based on a false belief.

'I could have given him joy in life, completeness, health. I could have avoided disappointing him:

- if I had done . . .
- If I had been . . .
- if I had stayed . . .
- if I had known . . .
- if I had believed him . . .'

Some people want to introduce a healing quality into their relationships. They want to put right and repair damage for which they imagine they are responsible. Others (parents or loved ones) feel their children's or partners sensitivity to guilt and illusory power and take advantage of them. They sometimes even exploit them.

'My husband had a serious accident just after we quarrelled, and I feel responsible and guilty; it's all because of me.'

We wonder whether this spouse would be relieved or disappointed to discover that she does not have the power to determine her husband's behaviour. If he destroys himself, believing that it is because of her, it can only be a personal decision and his own choice.

'My mother never recovered from knowing that I'm married to a divorcee. She would rather see me dead, she told me. Sometimes I feel like committing suicide . . . but I don't even know if that would please her.'

We do so many things supposedly to protect others! 'I don't let my husband see that I can manage perfectly well without him; he needs so much to feel strong and protective.'

'I had headaches for more than 20 years. After a process of personal growth, my headaches disappeared. But the most astonishing thing was that my husband continued to persuade me that I should rest, that I still had headaches. He wanted to take charge of them at all costs, even when they didn't exist anymore!'

'I hide my doubts and my vulnerability from my son; he wouldn't be able to stand having a helpless father.'

'I never talk about money matters with him, it makes him ill at ease.'

Couples, families, or professional and friendly relationships often have stable and reassuring systems of mutual protection. These set us limits and moreover they suggest roles and behaviour which enable us to know 'where we are going'.

To feel responsible for the reactions of others sometimes gives us a convenient alibi and helps us to avoid the torments of our ambivalence.

A woman can no longer bear her husband's dependence on her, his watchfulness, his constant demands and his need to experience everything through her. After many years of hesitation, she tells him about her decision to divorce. He then becomes very depressed and she gives up. She decides to stay with him. 'If I leave, I'll be responsible for his despair and destruction.'

In this way, she is able to solve her own dilemma (to stay or leave) by not believing in her husband's ability to evolve, and by taking upon herself complete responsibility for his psychological state.

When we remain caught in the desire or absence of desire of others, we avoid making any effort to differentiate ourselves, to tear ourselves away from this alienating game and to discover a more dynamic attitude, even though it may sometimes appear selfish or even cruel. Moreover, we feel that people around us would accuse us of being selfish. This enables us to feel even more victimized and to go on accusing or denigrating ourselves.

The impression that we are responsible for what others feel brings us back to early childhood, a time of omnipotence when we did not yet feel differentiated from the people around us.

A married woman has had a lover for eight years. She states that she is unhappy about the situation. She would like to make a choice, but she cannot leave her husband because he would have a nervous breakdown, and she cannot leave her lover because he threatens to commit suicide. At no time in the course of a long conversation is she able to express her true desires and feelings. Her whole life is based on her impression that she is responsible for the future and happiness of one or the other.

Later on, evoking her childhood, she recounts her mother's depression at her sister's birth, when she was six. She had felt responsible for her mother's state for two reasons: she might have caused it by her aggressive behaviour and desires, and she had to make amends by taking care of the baby and the whole household.

When she became aware that she had not caused her mother's depression, she exclaimed: 'All that power I thought I had did not exist at all; it was an illusion of omnipotence!'

I'm a woman, a wife, a mother, a lover, a little girl, even a baby!'

When we feel responsible for what others feel, we also nurture a sense of power which is difficult to give up. We try and keep control over the relationship to maintain at all costs an illusion of omnipotence over others, over their feelings and experience. Too often we confuse omnipotence with the strength of attachment. The other person will recognize the strength of our love if we take to heart the slightest vibration of his sensitivity, or the slightest blaze of anger.

I AM NOT RESPONSIBLE FOR WHAT OTHERS FEEL

Culture and upbringing collaborate in making people feel guilty and responsible for what others feel.

'Your sister is suffering because of you.'

'You are upsetting your brother.'

'Your father is unhappy about your behaviour. Your mother even told me that she regretted being alive after hearing what you'd done!'

But which child could tell his father: 'You're disappointed because of my bad marks at school. But it's your disappointment, Daddy. I think you should do something about it. I don't want to take care of it, either by working better or by feeling guilty for being a bad pupil.'

In a way, our feeling of guilt is a distortion of the compassion that we experience for others from childhood on. Our ability to identify with others makes us distressed when we see the people we love, or who love us, suffer. When we say to someone who claims that he is unhappy because of us that we don't feel responsible for his suffering, that person will be shocked and of course become indignant. He will accuse us of being unaware, perverse or sadistic.

Shouldn't the man who leaves his wife be responsible for her distress? Won't the woman who leaves her husband, or her children, because she feels unable to take care of them alone, feel guilty when she imagines their loneliness? (Of course she will not think of her own loneliness, which others will call 'freedom' or 'thoughtlessness'.) Aren't we always responsible for the person we have conquered? (See the fox in Saint-Exupéry's *The Little Prince*.) No, we're not . . . and yet, in a way, we are a little. Conflicting loyalties, whose roots are often much older than our own lives, reappear.

It is difficult to act in accordance with our innermost being. We want to please, to help and to conciliate others. We don't want to disappoint them. But if we feel responsible for how others deal with their feelings, then we are trapped.

> After many years of struggle and exhortations, a devoted daughter gives up. 'If my father's choice is to destroy himself with alcohol, then I'll stop ruining my life by trying to prevent him from drinking and trying to save him. He can have his alcoholism back, it's really his. Besides, this third party (the alcohol) that he has introduced into his life between him and me, between him and others, is really his favourite companion. It belongs to him. I now consider myself free to do what concerns me, and to follow my own priorities.'

> Another father took away a lot of destructive power from his anorexic daughter when he told her: 'I don't feel responsible for your eating or not eating. My responsibility is to give you the possibility of eating.'

When we give up being responsible for others, we also have to refuse to help them escape the consequences of their own decisions.

> A Jewish father had told his son that if he got married to his non-Jewish girlfriend, he would refuse to see his grandchildren. When the son became a father, he did not leave his father to deal with his own ultimatum. He invited him regularly in spite of repeated refusals, and presented himself with his child on his father's doorstep, forcing him each time to restate his decision, thus asserting clearly to the father and his own child that the rejection was unilateral.

'That's Dad, acting like he's the child!'

When we avoid collaborating in the games suggested or imposed by others, we regain our ability to define ourselves or assert our position better. So intense and imperious is our need for approval that it is most difficult to assert ourselves and to take a stand in front of others.

We are fully aware, as we write this, and especially as we encourage those who take part in our training sessions to take responsibility for themselves, that we trigger off powerful and passionate reactions. We provoke upheaval, create disorder and encourage people to give up their usual games in relationships. Personal growth brings to light the most subtle and permanent form of terrorism. It blooms in intimate relationships and it is exerted in the name of love. Any revolution in relationships heralds both more difficult and happier days and certainly proceeds along the tumultuous paths we have described.

I AM RESPONSIBLE FOR WHAT I FEEL

We find it fairly difficult to admit that we are responsible for what we feel in a relationship, whether we experience it through our body (sensations) or our sensitivity (feelings).

Very often an event, an action, a word or an attitude awakens and triggers off emotional charges that dwell in us. But they only trigger them off. They do not create them. They are there. They reactivate and reveal real feelings, sensations or perceptions that are already embedded in us.

However, the assertion – 'Everyone is responsible for the feelings he feels' – may appear like real aggression to some people and give rise to vehement protests.

'My mother is depressed. I'm not responsible for the burden of anxiety that I feel. It is hers, but then I feel it for a whole week after I see her . . .'

'My son is dead. I don't know how much the despair that overwhelms me comes from that or from me?'

'My boss is despotic and unfair. It is that which makes me feel rebellious and discouraged.'

We feel a real shock when we begin to accept our responsibility for our own feelings, so natural is our tendency to want to treat in others the cause of our problems. Indeed Adam must acknowledge that he willingly ate the apple, or Eve that she decided to obey the snake.

As for me who was born millennia after them, I had to acknowledge (after a lot of effort) that I was madly in love with a woman. But the intensity and beauty of my feelings had no hold on hers, which were dedicated to someone else. I am indeed responsible (but the word is not really adequate), I am co-responsible for what I feel. It does not help to scream, to be heartbroken or to attack the woman who does not return my love. When we begin to respect our own feelings, we acquire a new dignity, precisely because we acknowledge them as ours.

What are we cultivating?

Just as a gardener is responsible for his garden, we are responsible for the feelings we cultivate. Of course, the gardener cannot ignore the climate and soil, natural happenings, thunderstorms, the amount of rain or sun. But this does not do away with his responsibility, that is to say his watchfulness and actions.

First of all we are responsible for the way we infect or worsen our wounds.

> Someone left the window open. A mosquito flew in and bit me. The careless person is not responsible if I scratch the bite and transform it into a wound. But I can still accuse him of having inflicted this large wound that makes me suffer so much . . . by leaving the window open.

Curiously, many people attribute to the attitudes of others the interpretation that is most detrimental to their own self-esteem.

'*Let's cultivate ... ourselves!*'

'If he doesn't take my opinion into account, it means that I'm wrong.'

'If she doesn't love me as I want, that's because I'm not lovable. I'm not worthy of being loved.'

'I know that when he sighs deeply, it means that I'm boring him. I talk too much. He doesn't want to be here with me . . .'

'I know that I'm involved when he alludes to spoilt holidays.'

We call this mechanism 'appropriation', that is to say the ability to appropriate a word, a feeling, an action or behaviour that belongs to another person and to make it ours by becoming what the other person says that we are. I become ungrateful, stupid or nasty when someone perceives me like that as well as when I rebel against that perception. It does not occur to me to accept that it is only someone else's point of view. 'Yes, you see me like that, ungrateful, stupid or bad. What makes you see me like that . . .?' Can I differentiate myself from others sufficiently and not appropriate their experiences and perceptions? Can I integrate them? In that case I must then try to handle what others triggered off in me (because I haven't been able to differentiate myself!).

Someone hurts and frustrates me. I find him insufferable. But the wound, the frustration, the intolerance or, in a word, the suffering, is to be found in me. So I have to deal with my suffering. This process seems hurtful when, in training groups or counselling sessions, we suggest it to people who have been wounded by suffering, distress or depression.

'But I'm suffering because of him; how can I, in addition, take care of my own suffering?'

It seems unfair and simply impossible. How many children could tell their mother and father: 'Mummy, Daddy, I beg you, try and do something for yourself, for your fears, your worries, your anger and your suffering.'

How many men and women would similarly dare tell their

partner: 'Well, you feel helpless about your suffering. So you want me to do something to diminish it. You would like me to change my behaviour or my feelings to suppress your pain. But I'm simply asking you to listen to your pain. It's yours . . .'

There is a widespread belief that feelings cannot be controlled.

'That's the way I am. I can't help it. I can't change.'

'I'm often compelled to do things I don't want to do, that harm me or make me unhappy; I can't help it.'

It is as if feelings were imposed on us by external or internal forces that we cannot control.

'I've fallen in love.'

'I don't love you anymore.'

'I've lost the trust I had in him.'

We give up responsibility for this other aspect of us which we sometimes call our unconscious. Since its 'invention' by Freud, the concept is often used to denote an uncontrollable part of us which acts in spite of us. 'If I did it, it was unconsciously.' We make abundant use of the unconscious as an alibi or an excuse to justify some or our limits or inabilities in relationships. We need so much vigilance, attention, openness and acceptance to reclaim our behaviour and feelings and to get rid of the influences that marked us.

'I hate him. This is my responsibility. This is my way of struggling and confronting what he said or did, what he is.'

'I'm disappointed by her, but I'm the author of my own disappointment. I deluded myself in my expectations; I attributed to her the qualities I wanted to find. Maybe these were the qualities which I haven't yet managed to develop in myself.'

'I'm jealous. I'll take care of my jealousy and I'll see whether I or my jealousy will win!'

'My father was too important for me. I loved him too much. So, for a long time I didn't dare confront him. Today, I take the risk of contesting and criticizing him, of telling him about his shortcomings and about my expectations, my disappointed hopes, my wounded reality . . .'

The only war we can put an end to is the inner war that takes place in us. The only transformation which we can achieve is our own transformation. It may also trigger off change in others as well as in relationships.

Instead of waiting for my father to tell me about his feelings, I am going to tell him about mine. My freedom is to decide what I want to do with the situation that is imposed on me. If I think that my boss has arbitrary, unfair and contradictory attitudes, I can react in many ways.

- I can be satisfied with the pleasure of relentlessly speaking ill of him with my colleagues.
- Bitter and hurt, I can withdraw.
- I can try to act and speak to him.
- I can try and understand his distress and helplessness.
- I can try and overcome my reactivity and thus put to good use for my own personal growth his sudden changes of mood; I can also develop many other inner or outward attitudes and question their sterility or fruitfulness.

In the end, I might thank my boss for having been in my path and for having put me through an ordeal that helped me grow. We call this reframing situations and feelings.

The awareness of our own responsibility for what we experience can give us an extraordinary feeling of freedom, even though we will at first feel imprisoned by ourselves rather than by others. Since every relationship involves two people, I have to take charge of myself and of my side of the relationship, and only mine.

*'I'm only responsible for my side ... but I wouldn't mind controlling the
other one as well!'*

My side of the relationship

In a relationship, I tend to either feel responsible for both sides
('If the other person has no pleasure from making love, it's
because I'm inadequate, unattractive, and don't know how to
manage') or I feel no responsibility at all ('The party was boring;
they didn't know how to create an interesting and stimulating
discussion').

We are not responsible for the whole relationship, but only for
what occurs on our side, for what we bring and for the way we
receive what the other person brings. This sometimes obliges us
to apply to ourselves the very criticism we make about the other
person.

A woman said: 'I'm anxious about the idea of a stable relationship. I've already found three men who are afraid of making a commitment, and I am beginning to think I use this to avoid finding stability. Then I can carry on wanting it, and I can blame men for avoiding commitment.'

'For years I let others judge me and pigeon-hole me. I let them talk about me. I let myself be trapped in an image, a way of functioning . . . in which I didn't recognize myself at all. Today, I don't let others determine who I am anymore and I have become more mature.'

'You're not entitled to a reduction.'
'Well, you think I'm not entitled to it, so you can't give it to me. But I'm not going to let you decide for me!'
'But I'm telling you! You're not entitled to this reduction, this seat.'
'Yes, you're telling me that you cannot give it to me. Could someone in management review the decision?'

The conversation can last for months, but after getting to the general manager's office it might lead to a positive answer (if it was worth all that).

'If my practitioner tells me, after having examined me: "Oh dear! I'm worried about this. I'll get you to have an X-ray", today I prefer to answer: "Do something about your worry and I'll come back and see you . . ." I don't want to be treated according to the other person's worry, but according to my needs.'

We can transform and reverse the dynamics of a relationship by asserting ourselves. This will force us to discover how we create our own suffering.

On a personal growth course, a man talks about his distress at not finding 'simple, direct and immediate' relationships: 'I had a new relationship with a young woman. It was a smashing, light and very creative relationship. Our mutual suggestions stimulated us and gave spice and flavour to our lives. One evening she asked me: "I'd like to know what I am to you. What are your feelings and your intentions? I love you and I'm fond of you." I answered: "I don't love you, but I care for you. I derive a lot of pleasure from our encounters, from your presence and from the way you are."

It was only a few weeks later that I understood how the words "I don't love you" had been unbearable for her. She had received them violently. I had however expressed my feelings, my pleasure and my attachment to the relationship. But this wasn't enough; I had to feel something when I wasn't with her. She had to dwell in my heart. Having pleasure and being happy with her, meeting her, wasn't enough.

The relationship was unbalanced. On her side, there were feelings and a desire for something more. On my side, there was a feeling of completeness when we met but no love feeling. I didn't love her. So I couldn't after all tell her that I loved her, even though this was the most important thing she expected from me. We lost sight of each other and I am still nostalgic for our meetings. They were so lively.'

This man wants to talk about *his* difficulties with 'simple' relationships. But in describing the situation, he evokes and calls into question his partner's difficulties. He hasn't yet perceived his own participation in his friend's or rather his many friends' difficulties, since he reveals that his relationships take on a repetitive pattern. (As soon as there is repetition, we should question ourselves rather than others.)

Later on, he will discover how his choice of partners and his behaviour set up and reinforce the kind of love relationship that he denounces and deplores.

Asked whether he has ever been in love with a woman who does not love him, he exclaims with a heartfelt cry: 'Oh no! I would be too hurt! It's always the other person who loves me and asks too much. I don't want to but I suppose I do tend to encourage and then refuse people.'

The kind of answers (aggression, caresses, protection, etc) that we usually receive can give us some information about the messages we send. Our body expresses all the sides of our personality, from the most physical to the most metaphysical ones. It also perceives the personality of others, even though this is not always a conscious process. Complementarities work well in the ring of attractions and repulsions. And so we often tend to look for the same kind of people.

When two people meet, in a flash each unconscious

recognizes the other and they interact, for better or worse. They enter the ring almost automatically, and behave in a set way, which is often linked more to the past than to the present. (This dual vision of individuals who are, on the one hand, modelled by the environment and lost in endless mirroring games and, on the other hand, isolated, responsible, masters of themselves and trapped in their own conflicts, can make us feel dizzy. The difficulties of encompassing these two aspects in the same glance are seen in the heated debates that pit family therapists against psychoanalysts. The former deal mainly with the powerful interactions at work in the family, institutions and social movements. The latter consider that the intrapsychic individual apparatus and its inner conflicts come first.)

The power of conscious and unconscious interdependence and even unconscious collaboration between individuals, especially in couples and between parents and children, may lead some people to start therapy. They try to discover their role in this complex chain of interactions in which they are, at one and the same time, part of the mechanics, the movement and the result. They try to find their own desires under a mass of conditionings and reflections.

Some patients make progress and deep within themselves discover a mysterious, complete and original space which cannot be spoilt by anything or anyone. They feel the need to make and maintain contact with this inner core. They have to be in touch with it if they are to engage the very substance of their lives into relationships and actions without becoming corrupt, lost or damaged and without having to protect themselves like a seed in its shell. Such people are looking for who they really are, beyond other people's perceptions of them, beyond the demands of the present and the future.

But this attempt to distinguish between what is self and what is other always remains an arduous and unexpected task. It can create confusion and requires repeated attempts at defining their own sense of identity. Scientists increasingly demonstrate that

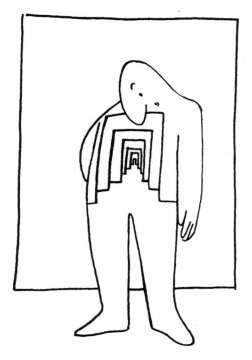

'It is a long way to the inner core!'

there is no clear boundary between a living organism and the ecosystem of which it is a part.

INTRA- AND INTERRELATIONSHIPS

We should coin a word that would describe both constitutes our relationship both to others (stimulations, answers, reactions, interactions, responsibility, complementarity, mutuality) and to ourselves (programming, memory, repetition, amplification, differentiation, self-image, conscious or unconscious inner conflicts, perception of our body, responsibility for our own life, resources and shortcomings, intrapsychic economy). We suggest we distinguish these two poles by the words 'intrarelationship' and 'interrelationship'.

Intrarelationship (our relationship to ourselves) evokes the image of inner links which derive their meaning from our innermost being. Our relationship to ourselves could be described as a vast network of linked and programmed circuits, which can open up some routes and close others, reinforcing certain types of behaviour and inhibiting others.

We could have an image of integrated electronic systems that 'process' information from outside according to a certain code, and even for a certain purpose.

By confronting these two notions of intrarelationship and interrelationship, we want to bring out their apparent contradiction.

> 'I am entirely and solely responsible for everything that happens to me, and we are all interdependent.'

> 'I can play an active part in what doesn't suit me. Everything that others do can touch me, either by expanding or diminishing me . . . I can't abstain from communicating. I'm part and parcel of a system of exchanges whose forces and stakes are sometimes beyond my understanding and of which I'm also the driving force.'

To become a sensation, every perception goes through a system of filters and channels already marked by significant childhood experiences. Many circuits lead to the same dead ends and crossroads and become like a very sophisticated radar system which picks up the target and then directs the whole apparatus towards it.

> A 38-year-old man says that he cannot bear to eat off someone else's plate. He systematically refuses his partner's tender and loving offers in a restaurant or at home ('Come on, try this'), for instance when she holds out her fork to him. He adds: 'In a ten-year marriage, I have never been able to tell my wife that this brought back to me very painful memories of meals. I was the oldest child and I was obliged

to finish my sister Fiona's meal. It smelt bad. I've never been able to disobey my mother. I felt nauseated, yet all the same I had to eat . . . it was hell.'

We fully understand that any experience closely akin to the past will connect with it. It will inevitably evoke the association of 'finishing up the little sister's meal'. It will lead to a refusal, to an unsaid but unsurmountable refusal, whatever the actual stimulus.

Another man relates the rows he had with his wife about his attitude towards drink at the family table.

'I couldn't help filling my glass to the brim, with water or wine, anywhere, at home or elsewhere. It was uncontrollable. I emptied the glass in one good, greedy gulp. This small thing gave rise to many conflicts and unpleasant remarks, but my behaviour didn't change. That's just how I was. Later, I remembered that, as a very young child, I had never been able to help myself to drink on my own. My mother always told me: "Wait, wait, you'll break something, leave that." She helped me to drink, but the glass was always only half-full, because a whole glass of water would have hurt my stomach and spoilt my appetite. I still drink with the same violence and pleasure the half-glass that was given and the half that was refused. The full glass, emptied in a gulp, represents my autonomy, my freedom, my pleasure. It is the sign of my independence.'

Another man noticed that he always stops a bit ahead of the stop line at red traffic lights. 'I can't help driving just a little forward so I can't see the actual red anymore; I then have to tie myself in knots to see the change to green. It's only very recently that I associated this behaviour with transgression. It is as if I always had to go a bit further than permitted. It is as if I were the one to make the decision and not someone else. Therefore the frustration seems smaller and less aggressive to me. This also pushes me to "betray" in relationships, to steal something from my best friends, to deceive their trust in one area or another. It gives me an illusory feeling of being stronger, of dominating the situation, of taking my revenge for some refusal or lack of recognition. Traffic lights act on me like spurs that trigger things off without my realizing it.'

If we listen carefully to all these things, we can discover them inside ourselves. Even though we cannot change our attitudes, we can express ourselves through them and talk about them.

Our relationship to ourselves is the basis from which we communicate with others. This is why it is so important to uncover some of our unconscious attitudes, to unveil them when they play too many tricks on us. It is not a matter of controlling our unconscious life but of perceiving its influence and the tricks and pranks it plays on us.

The unconscious is a maniac curator! Alas, it often chooses to preserve all that is bad, too difficult, too painful and too dangerous, all the things that we relegated there because we were not able to confront them. Deep in ourselves, these hidden sentries become unyielding censors of renewal and change. If we were able to conquer some of their power, we could use more of their inexhaustible strength to increase our potential for joy and vitality.

Most people tend to believe in one of the following statements.

- We are the sole authors of our own suffering and joy. No other person can create our own feelings of pleasure and sadness.
- Simultaneously, we are intrinsically dependent on our environment, which stretches from our biological, social and cultural background and from our close relationships to far beyond the stars. Somehow, the position, radiance and movement of the stars also exert an influence on what we are and what we are doing.

However we can give ourselves some landmarks to enable us to distinguish our real responsibilities more clearly. In the following chapter, we shall explore a few directions which could help us become better companions to ourselves and, therefore, to others.

To gain freedom, you don't have to reach anything outside yourself, but you have to give something up inside.

11 Becoming a Better Friend to Ourselves

It is difficult to accept that inwardly we are neither man nor woman at birth; we grow into being men and women.

Not only do we have to deal with the development of our own feelings, but also, if at all possible, we have to welcome the feelings and development of others.

If we agree to be responsible for what we feel, we will have to change many of our attitudes and ways of thinking. Our perception of others and of ourselves will be transformed. It is a painstaking and lifelong task to become our own best friend.

To be a good friend to ourselves means:

- discovering that solitude can be fruitful, complete and a source of encounters;
- finding that it is possible not to be bored in our own company;
- not dwelling on first impressions of others and being able to look at ourselves in a benevolent and stimulating way;
- letting go of self-depriving dynamics produced by our inability to recognize our own needs and desires: we often behave like critical, demanding parents, not rewarding or encouraging ourselves enough.

To become a good friend to ourselves we have to become more complete, not by suppressing or remedying our lacks, but by not keeping our wounds open. For too often we take the risk of feeding our suffering – which is related to our shortcomings – by looking for completeness outside of ourselves. In this way we attribute to others the power to repair damage inflicted on us. It is a remnant of the childhood dependence we experienced for many years, at the beginning of our life, when we were just out of the womb. At the time, we expected satisfaction and comfort

Let's not hesitate to hold out a hand to the best … in ourselves.

from other people's actions, gestures and words. Later it is as if we were implicitly or explicitly trying to use others for our desires and fears. We spend a large part of our life trying to pursue the dependence impressed on us in early years, so we do not hesitate to shape our attachments according to these outmoded dynamics. This dependence is at the root of terrorism in parental or marital relationships.

To become a good friend to ourselves, we should respect four essential principles.

- We should aim at managing better the inevitable 'pollution' produced by any relationship.
- We should deal with the impact and resonance of other people's messages on us.

- We should learn to reframe everyday events, problems or aggressions.
- We should take charge of some of our own needs.

MANAGING INEVITABLE 'POLLUTION' IN RELATIONSHIPS

Any living body exudes waste. This means that it is alive and, paradoxically, the production of waste attests to its vitality and dynamism. In a state of hibernation, far less waste is produced. Some people live as if they were mummified: they seem to live slowly, inching their way through a restricted life. A relationship that is alive also produces waste. It exudes ashes and parasites, which, if not taken care of and evacuated, may poison, in the strongest sense of the word, communications and sometimes personal, professional and social life.

Where does the waste come from? What is it made of? It comes in particular from the misunderstandings inherent in any attempt at a relationship.

- What we say is not what others hear.
- We do not answer what others say but what we understood.
- We decipher and associate through our own filters and with our sensitivity . . . without always recognizing other people's sensitivity, codes or system of values.
- We forget to negotiate with ourselves (with our fears, desires, resources and limits) before negotiating with others.
- We try to induce others to adopt our beliefs.
- We want to convince them of the soundness of our point of view . . . for their own good.
- We want to change them.

Waste also comes from the poisons represented by judgements, projections, comparisons, expectations of reciprocity and discrepancies (*see* chapter 6). In brief, each time we try and communicate, we take the risk of being influenced, disappointed, made to feel insecure, or gratified by others.

As for us, we have to arrange our expectations according to priorities so as to manage 'pollution' in relationships better. When we expect too much from others or from our environment, we become vulnerable to any frustration when answers are inadequate, insufficient or different from what we had planned.

'I expect others to satisfy my desires without having to claim for more. I experience any discrepancy between my expectations and the answer given as a personal attack. It arouses anger in me and I reject anything that frustrates me. In this way, I live in a permanent state of dissatisfaction with everybody, including myself.'

We imagine too easily how others ought to behave, and we imprison them (often without their knowing) in the type of behaviour which we think they should adopt. A lot of energy is needed to overcome the infinite disappointments, frustrations and discomforts this causes.

'I'm in love with him', acknowledges a young South American girl, 'but I don't show it. A woman must never say that. I would like to know if it's something serious for him or if he sometimes invites me just for fun. I conceal my feelings. I'm afraid he'll guess, but really I would like him to guess . . .'

After many months of waiting ('It's up to him to take the initiative!'), one day the young girl dares to talk about her feelings. 'Me too!' answers the young man.

The first cry the young woman utters at the beginning of this relationship is therefore a complaint: 'Why didn't you tell me then?'

We can try to be more selective, lucid and realistic in our expectations. We should also try to be more flexible because having set expectations prevents us from receiving and sometimes even seeing what is offered. It might not coincide with our expectations, but it nevertheless exists.

To cope with and try to reduce the 'pollution', we mainly have to pay attention to the way we communicate (the form of our demands, the clarity of our messages) and listen. We should also gain some understanding of ourselves. As transmitters, we are also responsible for the quality of listening that we want to receive.

MANAGING THE IMPACT OF WHAT OTHER PEOPLE SAY

We have to deal with the impact, the resonance and the emotions aroused by the actions or words of others. Actually we are not immune to the negative charge of some messages. An unobtrusive sentence, a word whose emotional connotation strikes a chord in us will literally 'poison' us. We all know that experience: after a discussion, a phone call or a letter, we feel a diffuse sense of discomfort, tension or even anxiety. Like an acid or a persistent poison it upsets our organism and thoughts for several hours or even days.

In this field, the rule could be: the harder it is to communicate, the more alive we have to keep the relationship. That is to say: we have to go on listening, paying attention and being open instead of going away and breaking off the relationship.

We can ask the person who hurt us to repeat his message and express it in other words. In this way we may enable him to be clearer and to find words that are closer to his thoughts. We can reformulate what we heard and understood, to be sure it is what the other person wanted to say. For it is so easy to misinterpret according to our degree of vulnerability and intolerance or because what was said was unclear.

'When he told me that our relationship would certainly not last very long, I understood that he already felt like going away and rejecting me. Many years later, I realized that in this way he was expressing his own fear and insecurity and his wish for stability in our relationship.'

We have a formidable power, which we seldom use: we can

acknowledge what others have said by formulating aloud to them what we have heard.

> A nurse tried several times to suggest a modification in the way patients were visited at their bedsides. The consultant, a clinician, reprimanded her: 'You're not going to teach me my job? Who do you think is in charge here?' For several days she was distraught, not knowing 'what to answer to this attack'. By discovering a way of confronting the consultant, by not letting herself be upset by his 'reaction', she can continue to assert herself and confirm that she heard him: 'I know you are the consultant in charge, but this is not the issue. I'm talking about the possibility of modifying the visiting procedure so that we can tend to the patients better . . .'

Some simple measures might help us keep in touch with the other person and examine both points of view, side by side as it were, instead of opposing them. They are nonetheless difficult to apply in the emotional context of a dialogue.

- We can listen to what the other person's reaction, behaviour and attitude touch in us and recognize it: 'Yes, that's how I feel, inside of me. But what about him, what is he saying?'
- We can ask for another formulation of the message, if it is incomplete or ambiguous.
- We can ask for the specific intention and meaning given by the other person.
- We can try and understand what the other person says and to whom he is saying it. (A woman flings at her son: 'I wonder who you'll be like if you go on like that!' What is she saying and to whom?)

We can reread the letter we received. We can ask about the meaning of words and actions. We can dare to go back over a past situation and, particularly, over the differing experience and perception of each person concerned in this situation. We should remember that communication is only made possible because of difference. These attempts can help us to be less trapped by the initial attacking or denigrating meaning attributed to the message. It is always the one who receives the message who gives it meaning.

When we have been affected or hurt by the attitudes or words of others, we can relieve ourselves of our discomfort, our suffering or brooding by means of a symbolic action.

- For example, we can write, in an unrestrained and even exaggerated way about our anger, despair and accusations. We can write it all down and throw it away later, when the turmoil has subsided. We can symbolize the situation by enacting it with objects. We can immediately reward ourselves by treating ourselves to chocolate (the Russian poetess Marina Svetaia considered chocolate the ideal remedy against sadness . . . when consumed in small doses), or with a bath (water absorbs negative things and cleans them), so as to heal the wound. We can draw or paint what is happening inside us.
- We can introduce a slight distance that enables us not to identify completely with the feeling of anger, rejection or sorrow, or the sense of being bad or worthless. We can find out which part of us is hurt, and which image of ourselves has been bruised.
- We can listen to the chord that has been struck and to what the experience recalls in our personal history. For instance, I might find out that mockery and comments about my body remind me of my father's mockery when I blushed or turned pale under his gaze or under the impact of his gestures.

REFRAMING EVENTS AND FEELINGS

By looking at ourselves, at others and at the situation from a different perspective, by reframing them, we can reverse the polarity of our feelings. By seeing the positive side of an event, we modify its influence. We can then assert ourselves differently. We can become more mature or overcome a sense of failure. We

can initiate a more authentic communication after a confrontation.

'When things do not work well between us, we talk a lot with each
other. This helps us understand each other more fully.'

'I dreamed of a teacher who would accept my own answers and not only
the good answer he was expecting (his own or the one in the book!). I
dreamed of a teacher who would tell me one day: "James, in an essay of
453 words, you wrote 445 words correctly." I got so many bad marks
that confirmed my mistakes without acknowledging my successes!'

'I once wrote to a prominent civil servant to obtain a specific
authorization. My letter stated: "My grandmother said there were
two kinds of civil servants: those who tried to find an article in
regulations that would allow them never to fulfil your request, and
those who found the article in the regulations that would permit
them to answer your request . . ." '

It is possible to keep and accumulate good things and good
experiences. They can be placed side by side with bad ones, but
they do not necessarily neutralize them. Therefore we should
accept that neither a relationship nor an individual is
completely good or completely bad. How many people believe
that they have to be flawless and devoid of weaknesses to be
loved and to love!

For example, a separation can be reframed and seen as a dynamic
process and not as a disaster. It is possible to go from 'He left me'
to 'We helped each other to grow till he could leave me, till I could
live without him'.

Some loves are similar to 'nurseries' which enable one of the
protagonists to grow, to develop, to become self-confident so as
to be able to go elsewere. How many couples have experienced
the adventure of loving each other so as to be able to separate
and leave each other!

**He wanted to leave someone so as not to deprive himself of other
opportunities. In fact he was the prisoner of his own freedom!**

This more dynamic view of life's circumstances favours imagination and creativity.

> A man told us how the refusals he had met had pushed him to surpass himself. He had been compelled to look for solutions and to find in himself resources of which he had known absolutely nothing: 'Today I can thank those who said no to me.'

There are many different ways of understanding an event.

> 'This child is insufferable. Each time my wife and I start talking, he gets into mischief over and over again and I have to take harsh measures . . .'

> 'This child gets his parents frightfully angry with him to prevent them from quarrelling. He knows very well how so many previous discussions have turned out. He sacrifices himself so that they can live in harmony.'

Reframing also means reclaiming and sometimes reconciling different and antagonistic aspects of ourselves.

> 'I had a bad dream. There was a man who treated me with the utmost contempt.'

Everything I dream of is an aspect of myself. What part of me despises another part of me? How many utterances like 'I hate' mean 'I hate myself'?

When we reframe events, we simply look for the positive side of what happens to us. We look at situations from the perspective of our 'growth', of the meaning of our life, of our rebirth through pain or pleasure. The positive trend in American psychology, so-called New Age psychology, makes us sensitive to this.

- How did this unhappy love help me to grow, and to recognize myself through numerous discoveries?
- How did my son's rebellious adolescence energize the family?
- How did this bankruptcy open me up to values other than material success?
- What potential did my parents' weaknesses and shortcomings enable me to develop?

• What courage did this woman need to 'abandon' her family, confront her guilt and follow her own path?

Whatever the circumstances might be, events in our lives bear meaning and are signs to which we can try and listen, beyond their effects and immediate consequences. For only our perception and our way of listening help us confer real meaning on the outside reality.

Being a better friend to ourselves makes us develop this too often ignored sixth sense, which enables us to be astonished and filled with wonder. It makes us venture further into the unpredictable, to accept the risk of the unknown.

Each gesture can be a creation.
Each encounter may become a work of art.

CARING FOR OUR OWN NEEDS

We can take direct care of some of our needs instead of making others responsible for their satisfaction. Expecting the other person to satisfy our needs constitutes one of the most deadly sources of mutual frustration in a couple.

'I make you responsible for the satisfaction of my needs and expectations, for my state of fulfilment or unfulfilment. I also make you responsible for my frustrations, my suffering, my sadness or my love for life.'

If we want to assert our position more clearly in a relationship, we must accept the necessity to say no. This will enable us to say yes, which will then be a real yes.

'Dis-agreements'

When you say no!

It awakens
Old anxieties

Unexplored fears
Fleeting shadows of unexplained calls
Abysses of unvoiced anxieties

When you say no!

The sky closes
And my life stops
Hope is ripped apart
Death is unveiled
And I find again
The fascinating face
Of vertiginous moments

Yet
When you say no!
You reveal
Your existence
You remind me of it
By refusing yourself

You affirm
You offer me
YOUR desire
Where hope looms
Beyond fear

When you say no
When I listen to your no
And accept it
Without feeling negated
Without feeling torn apart

Then we can begin TO BE
YOU and I

Precarious
But oh so fruitful moment
Of a TRUE MEETING.

                                              Sarah Charlier

With a better understanding of the limits of our tolerance, we can
discover more quickly what is good or bad for us in a situation.

We can thus avoid continuing to do something that is not good for us. We are so skilled at keeping going in others what is not good for us.

> 'It is so important for me to claim that I am my father's son. Yet I spend my time running him down, criticizing him and not acknowledging him.'

We can learn to be more present in the here-and-now rather than frozen or lost in a past that pursues us, or imprisoned in the dependence of an always uncertain or threatening future. When we put our pleasure or the satisfaction of our needs in the hands of others, we run the risk of many frustrations.

It is difficult to grasp the idea of being responsible for the satisfaction of our own needs. For we stick to an infantile myth: 'There are other people for that, aren't there? If they love us, they must take care of us!' Deeply engraved in us is the messianic belief that salvation, happiness and reward come from above, from elsewhere.

We can also define our own rhythm, mark out our own space, and give ourselves time when we take on a project. We should not have to account for what we think or feel, do or do not do. Some people constantly need to justify their actions, words or way of life and exist only to be acknowledged or approved by others. This emotional dependence deprives them of creativity and resourcefulness.

We can transform a wish into a project and make our dreams come true, by turning them into something that is possible. Many people, when they wish for something, stay in the world of dreams or imagination. To make a wish come true, it is crucial that we turn it into a project. To leave the state of mere wishing means to step into reality by concretizing the wish into an action (this doesn't mean acting out), by confronting it with reality. This is the first step towards implementation. With the project starts the search for means, the encounter with limits and constraints. It can sometimes even become associated with other projects. Decision-making means making choices and this also implies making renouncements: a necessary step on the path towards realization is confirmed.

Freedom means being able to choose, and therefore to renounce.

To be a good friend to ourselves we have to be tender, benevolent and kind to our body. This also means taking care of our vital needs (food, sleep, living conditions). For example, do we pay enough attention to our meals? If we eat alone, we can make an effort and set the table, switch on music and welcome ourselves as we would welcome a distinguished visitor. We can take care of our dress and well-being.

We can determine to enjoy our own company. We can also laugh kindly about ourselves, look at our lives with humour and tenderness. We can change our appearance and the way we look at ourselves in the mirror each morning. Our gestures can be done with a sense of fullness. We can enjoy the pleasure of not having to consider anyone else for a while. We can go out, read, unwind in a bath, take our time.

The time we take for ourselves is so precious that sometimes we find it difficult to make room for it. People who devour time are often ruthless with themselves.

People who cannot bear to be alone continually try to run away from themselves by creating all kinds of diversions (meetings, phone calls, parties, celebrations). People who cannot bear to be alone at night impose their presence and body on a partner. As if in a relay race, they pass on their own dissatisfaction, disparagement or anxiety to others.

When we acknowledge the dissatisfaction or discomfort as our own, when we recognize our real needs or feelings, we can begin to look in ourselves for what we need. We may be able to do something to confront or reduce a need or a wish (but we should do something clear and avoid indirect, compulsive or inaudible appeals which cannot be received). Or we can accept our solitude as a sequence in our life, part of our life and not the whole of it. If we cannot satisfy a wish immediately, at least we can recognize, name and welcome it instead of letting it develop into a vague form of fear of solitude.

To be a good friend to ourselves does not mean that we should live in a state of self-sufficiency, in a closed universe, barred from relationships. To become a better friend to ourselves, we should start a dialogue and begin a relationship with the different aspects of ourselves: this will enable us to know ourselves better and to get a clearer view of ourselves. Our understanding of ourselves will improve. We shall indeed become more open, more sensitive, more in agreement with ourselves and therefore more attractive – in a word more full of life.

There are only two ways of dealing with life: either you
dream it or you do it.
René Char

BEING A GOOD FATHER OR A GOOD MOTHER TO OURSELVES

So as not to suffer from thirst, we must become a spring.

We can become good friends to ourselves by giving up dependence. Can we become a good father and a good mother to ourselves, and stop looking for father and mother substitutes in the outside world?

In this relationship with ourselves, we can assume and differentiate paternal and maternal roles: tenderness, warmth, understanding, motherly benevolence and unconditional love. Criticizing ourselves for what we do or what we are does not mean that we deprive ourselves of love.

If, in a relationship now over, we experienced something good and vital, we do not have to destroy and reject it. By learning to recognize and keep the memory of goodness and happiness, without transforming it into regrets, bitterness or actual suffering, we strengthen this nourishing function that we need.

> A woman writes: 'Today, each time I want to have another helping of a dish and to eat more than I need, I ask myself: "What am I really hungry for? What do I want, deep down . . .?" The mere recognition of my true hunger (behind my apparent hunger) and of my deep need (behind this escape into bulimia) prevents me from stuffing myself, and filling myself up with junk food as I have done for years.
>
> I got rid of – I mean I gave away – a stock of several pounds of chocolate and biscuits that I had stored away for my emotional famine.'

Paternal attention functions as a landmark. It gives us a direction, a scale of values to which we can refer. We mark out our path; we insist on a few requirements; we delay satisfaction with the prospect of a greater good.

To be a good parent to our feelings, we have to recognize them and listen to them. We have to learn something about them, and also to set them limits. We should not let them have unlimited power. In this way we learn to look for what is good for us, beyond our immediate satisfaction, the satisfaction provided for instance by alcohol, cigarettes, tranquillizers and sleeping tablets. There are plenty of inner 'tricks' that can help guide us.

> A woman said: 'When I realize that I have started denigrating and comparing (the other person is so much more this or that), I stop myself. I don't know why, but I speak to myself in French: "Arrête de comparer!" (Drop the comparison). And I answer: "OK!" My inner dialogue has a sense of humour.'

> 'I have painstakingly learned to identify people and situations which do me good, inspire and structure me. I avoid or set limits on those that leave me anxious, with butterflies in my stomach, and unhappy. I recognize what is not good for me, whatever others might say. I can leave and drop what isn't good for me.'

Here we have in mind the numerous psychosomatic illnesses produced by guilt, contained anger and prohibitions. We can authorize ourselves (in the sense of becoming the author) to be attractive or sensuous women, vulnerable or impetuous men.

'I've been feeling lighter for some time, having lost 20 pounds after the last training session . . .

Twenty . . .! It's a lot, but I don't want to stay like that. I want to lose more, maybe a bit more slowly.

Twenty pounds! I could define this gradual letting go of a burden in this way: I suppose at first I lost several pounds of fear, fear of gossip, of talking about myself, of asserting myself, of daring to say yes, daring to say no . . .

Then the pounds that used to conceal my woman's body partially vanished. I had an extraordinarily tender conversation with my father and mother. I was at last able to behave as a woman who had lived a woman's life, with her female body, with the man she loved. The three of us knew it before but we had all kept silent about it.

The moment I was able to kiss my father, I certainly lost a few pounds mingled with tears. I also noticed that this year I haven't had an ear infection as usual at the beginning of summer. Then I bought myself a skirt. I'm being good to myself.

Eventually the pounds which were a mixture of regret, bitterness, betrayed trust and bullied tenderness well and truly disappeared . . . I think that I have been able at last to mourn a love. After five years a wound has healed.

I think this is what those 20 pounds were made up of. Now I have to get rid of the anxieties which still seem firmly rooted deep down in myself. At times my "favourite saboteur" reminds me that she is still around, especially when I'm at a very low ebb.

I'll take all the time I need to gradually get rid of all this. I'll learn to enjoy my own company better.'

An obese man suffered from the burden of his weight, the terrible heaviness of all the 'I have to' that punctuated every single moment of his existence. 'I have to leave, I have to get up, I have to be here, I have to do this, I have to . . .' He could not disobey all these injunctions which were like terrible orders. He led his life submitting to the most ruthless of tyrants: *himself.*

When he decided to drop all these 'I have to's, and to disobey his own dictates, his weight went down too. He regained his real body weight, exactly 140 pounds.

A young woman wrote about her discoveries: the links that connect her daughter and her mother through herself. 'At last I am aware of the long silence which my mother imposed on me when my body had been violated. I kept silent . . . for a long time, without daring to tell.' [She refers to a rape in her childhood, at the age of 11.]

I remember that I attacked her, at the age of 15, with murderous and fierce words. My mother said: "You spit out venom, you're like a snake. What have I done to God to deserve such a daughter?" Words can indeed be murderous, and so can our repressed words, the words we were denied or that remained unspoken . . .

After the last training session I realized that I have never trusted my mother and also that I didn't trust my own ability to be a mother. Was it precisely that, this inability to be a mother (alone with a daughter), which I had projected over and over again onto my daughter? Maybe my daughter has suffered from that, as much as from her parents' divorce.

Julia, who is now six, has had hives on her face for three years now. She scratches herself, hurts herself even more and gets marks on her face. Today I see them as the marks of my own fear, and of my long-denied anxieties which she has heard. I accept it and can let go of all the guilt that sticks to me:

- the guilt of having confronted my father, of "having disappointed him";
- the guilt of having made my mother cry very often and of having derived pleasure from it;
- the guilt about my body, which became an object of desire too early;
- the guilt of having said to my former husband: "I don't love you anymore";
- the guilt of separating a baby from her father and of breaking up my family and marital life;
- the guilt of breaking up another family, the family of the friend I live with, a family of three.

What a burden of guilt!

Many people told me: "You'll regret it. You'll have a rough time. You'll be unhappy sooner or later." These curses frightened me for a long time. I had the impression that I would have to pay dearly for all these debts, that they would hit me out of the blue when I least expected it . . . So I've been expecting them all the time. This is how I've been living until recently.

Today I'm beginning to love myself again and to love the people around me (it was about time, after so many years). So I thought I would write to tell you about this reconciliation with myself.'

To be a good father to ourselves can involve doing the work we have to do today so as to be really free another day. It can also mean feeling and containing our sexual desire instead of getting rid of it irresponsibly, carrying out our desires and dreams without annihilating them through disappointing gratification. It is not a question of our will but of relationship: of building a respectful and benevolent relationship with the warmest part of ourselves. This action of reunification brings together different aspects and facets of our personality. We often let antagonistic aspects of ourselves fight and battle against each other. Meditative experiences can help us recover a sense of unity by bringing together our oppositions and antagonisms. We should imitate the art of the Epicureans who knew how to limit and delay pleasure, and how to savour it instead of consuming it.

We can become more demanding about the quality of the relationships that are good for us. We can recognize our limits, and not let ourselves be tormented or persecuted anymore by an unreachable ideal of ourselves.

To be a better friend to ourselves, we have to identify more quickly our major sabotage mechanisms, especially comparison, with which we disparage ourselves, and appropriation, through which other people's judgements of us become ours, and we become what they perceive of us.

By manoeuvring between benevolence and demands, we should not lose sight of the direction which is most significant for us. We discover that growth is endless, and this gives us a stimulating feeling of insecurity because nothing is ever won or achieved.

Tomorrow is the first day or our life yet to come. We are different and the consciousness we have of ourselves makes us separate from everything around us. We are alone with a unique life. Only in ourselves can we find true unity, and only from inside can we find and draw life.

Every gesture can become a work of art, a creation.

BEING A BETTER FRIEND TO OURSELVES

We are at the heart of all our relationships, which does not mean at the centre. Therefore we are responsible for the esteem, love and respect which we feel towards ourselves.

We are also responsible for any possible improvement in our relationships. This does not mean that we are responsible for the whole relationship.

We have the responsibility or the pleasure of our own blossoming and happiness.

Let us not count on others to take charge of us, to take care of us and satisfy our needs, appease or protect our fears.

Let us not expect answers from others. Let us examine our questions, extend our perceptions, listen to our experience and thus trust the unpredictable that dwells in us.

Let us dare to assert our difference when others attempt to define our identity ... through their own point of view.

Let us experiment and create real things that carry us beyond what we believe. We will not produce anything that we cannot handle.

Let us take good care of ourselves, every day. We are unique and extraordinary ... even if we have forgotten it. Let us live as if were were alone and relate to others whenever it seems possible.

Let us see other people as gifts and, even better, as gifts that enrich our life.

The worst solitude is not to be alone, but to be an awful friend to ourselves ... by being bored in our own company.

So, let us not hesitate any longer. Let us be a good friend to ourselves. Life will repay us a hundredfold.

We reach the point where individual experience meets the experience of former generations, the infinite sequence of living beings, profoudly rooted in the primeval and unfathomable depths.

Lou Andreas-Salomé

12   Differentiation

At birth, we leave a state of cosmic autonomy for one of human dependence.[2] We begin our lives by experiencing a parental, physiological and emotional dependence which later becomes an emotional and psychological dependence on relationships. These early significant relationships act as a model and an outline for the scenarios which we throughout life play.

From then on, any development towards growth, expansion, creativity, change and the overcoming of repetition will be based on the necessity to know and differentiate ourselves.

WHEN OTHERS DETERMINE OUR IDENTITY

Most difficulties in our adult relationships arise because we allow others to determine our sense of identity or our behaviour, or we attempt to imprison others in our images of them. We easily imagine how other people should behave towards us. They do the same with us.

> 'When I come home, she could leave the kitchen and welcome me in the corridor. She could at least say hello!' he says to himself, switching on the television.
> 'When he comes home, he could come to the kitchen and ask how I am before watching the news on the telly!'

> 'At work I expect my colleague to see me as an attractive woman, even though I don't want to pursue our relationship further. But he addresses all his enthusiastic remarks and commentaries to passers-by whom he always notices from his window: "Did you see that woman? What elegance! I like her style very much." '

Unspoken expectations are the most desperate ones.

These silent expectations and requests remain unspoken because we take them for granted. We think it is up to others 'to respond spontaneously'. Maybe we hold on to the childhood belief that others know better than us what is good for us. Anyway, others often don't seem to hesitate to say what they think.

'You should go less often to this study group on Hinduism and keep your feet firmly on the ground. You should have other friendships.'

'If you don't make love, you can't be a whole person.'

'You shouldn't leave your wife; she still loves you and furthermore you love her, too.'

We also let ourselves be influenced by the reactions of others, sometimes by one simple reaction (reacting is not acting from ourselves) or by their attitudes, refusals or lack of desire. A reaction is behaviour that hides a real emotion.

'When I started psychotherapy, my husband talked with a mocking tone about what he called "being wrapped up in oneself". So I avoided telling him about my progress and discoveries. Many years

'*What your mother says is correct!*'
'*What your father says is true …!*'

later he was able to tell me that he had felt jealous. He had been afraid of what I was going to say about him and had regretted my not telling him about what happened during therapy.'

We begin our sentences by anticipating what the other person's point of view or behaviour might be, and we confuse his point of view with ours.

- 'Don't you think that . . .'
- 'You agree that . . .'
- 'Wouldn't you like to . . .'

We try to make sure of having the approval of others even before expressing our own opinion or desire. Our need for recognition and approval is so great that we frequently sacrifice our own standpoint and our own view of the situation.

'I'm offering you this book, but I hope that you'll always keep it and not give it to your children.'

She should refuse such a gift. A book or an object that is given escapes the control of the giver.

Obviously, in giving such a gift, the giver wants to be reassured ('Keep it always') that the relationship is perennial. For the person who accepts a gift under such conditions, it means implicit commitment. The person who accepts the gift could take his own stand by saying: 'I accept your gift without, for all that, feeling committed. I accept it as something that will liven up our relationship.'

Gifts and offerings are like the vivifying and sparkling bubbles of air that enliven the water of a fountain. I built a fountain in my house to make the silence vibrate. It runs from east to west to follow the course of the sun and it functions all year round to link the seasons together.

DIFFERENTIATING OURSELVES FROM OTHERS

To progress means to separate, which does not mean leaving or losing each other. We see life as a succession of births. First we leave our mother's womb, then we have to abandon our mother's and our father's image of us. We also have to leave behind their fears, their desires, their disappointments and their personal myths. We have to pursue the same effort elsewhere: the people who love us want us to enter into *their* fears, desires and personal myths.

So, going from birth to birth, fed by the sap of life, we exist more fully.

Existence is this movement, this attempt to recognize ourselves as different, as fundamentally distinct from others.

Life is only a succession of births.

Any process of personal growth enables us gradually to assert ourselves, to confront others and thus to move out of a position of submission or opposition. In fact, we notice that most human interactions lead to both these positions in relationships. There are many ways of submitting, be they explicit or implicit. They can range from pseudo-agreement ('Well, it doesn't cost me anything to accept!'; 'It gives him so much pleasure!') or fake support (which does not really commit me) to alienation.

Opposition covers an equally wide and subtle range, from conscious to unconscious sabotage.

> 'I realized that I was refusing this trip abroad when I discovered at the border that I had forgotten my passport.'

> 'He had told me that he didn't want a baby, and I obeyed him by using contraception. And then, I don't know what happened, I found I was pregnant in spite of my IUD . . .'

Opposition can be expressed through open or latent refusal, evasion, conflict, or even through the desire to destroy and suppress the other person.

We need to be very tenacious to take our stand and resist other people's attempts to determine our sense of identity, so as not to let them put us where they want us, and not be trapped by their perceptions.

For instance, in a couple, one person's clear stand often triggers off opposition from the partner, who attempts to make him change his position so as to make it appear like a reaction of opposition. We wonder whether preferring *opposition* to *apposition* is not a Western cultural trait. In fact we have noticed that any suggestion that both partners express their opinions and examine them side by side in a dialogue (apposition) is unbearable for the second person. It again stimulates opposition so as to 'suppress' the first person's quiet point of view.

Do we feel more comfortable when we fight than when we give up? Two main attitudes seem to underlie these dynamics: certainty and doubt. Certainty closes the door to dialogue and communication; doubt or uncertainty invites reassurance and calls for an answer. Between certainty and uncertainty, there is room for confidence, that is to say for risk.

I take the risk of taking a stand, as I am, where I feel I am.

'I'd like a second child,' he says.
'But you don't realize, we already find life difficult. It would make it even more difficult . . .'
She does not take her own stand, but attacks his point of view. She tries to change his desire. Having learned to keep his own stand, he repeats: 'It is my wish to have a second child.'
She will then try to define him by telling him what his intentions are: 'You don't think of me, of my wish to have a job again, of my fear of the delivery. You're selfish . . .'
And he goes on, like a record that is scratched: 'I only said that I wanted to have a second child.'

What prevented the woman:

- from acknowledging his desire?
- from taking her own stand about not wanting a second child?

She could have listened to what this wish meant for her husband. She could also have explained how much she would have had to give up for a second child and talk about her own priorities. They could have communicated about their different opinions. They could have communicated about a wish they did not share.

Sharing makes us see how intolerant or impatient we are. The splits between our desires and fears become apparent to us. Even though communication is a pleasure, it is a difficult task to share our differences in addition to the points of view we hold in common.

THE DIFFERENCE BETWEEN 'HEARING' AND 'AGREEING'

Ordinary language tends to confuse hearing (I heard your wish, your demand, your need) and agreeing (I agree to fulfil it, to answer it, to satisfy it). It takes us a long time to discover and accept that communicating does not mean agreeing.

'I hear very well that you want to make love, but tonight I am preoccupied and tired. I'm not in the mood. That's how I feel, it has nothing to do with you.'

Such words are less hurtful than a turned back or a refusal.

A request can be received, but not necessarily satisfied.

We all have mythic expectations as far as communication goes and in particular we all desire the confirmation or approval of others.

'Tell me that you agree with me.'

'Tell me that I'm right to think that, that I was right in doing that.'

For some people, to communicate well means to agree and hear each other, to understand each other without conflict, opposition or even differentiation.

We often hear people say 'I can't communicate with him (with her)'. And when we ask them to be more specific about what is going on, we discover that they mean: 'We don't agree. We don't have the same opinion.'

'I can't talk to him about this movie. He didn't enjoy it and I found it wonderful.'

'I don't understand his liking for horror movies. Sometimes he stays awake till one o'clock in the morning to watch these stupid movies. They're completely crazy!'

She asks in an attacking way: 'But why do you watch that? What does it bring you?' She won't be able to talk to him about what he sees and feels. Yet, the important thing is not what he looks at (what is outside him) but what he sees and feels, inside.

THE DIFFERENCE BETWEEN ACTIONS, INTENTIONS AND REACTIONS

'One morning, I took a tray and ate my breakfast in the other room because the news deafened me. My husband asked me what was going on. I answered good-humouredly that I needed calm on waking in the morning and that it was useless to stay where I felt disturbed. If you had only seen his face! Afterwards he managed to have the news on as little as possible or else he would apologize by saying: "There are important events happening in the world." I wouldn't like him to deprive himself of the news he's interested in, but I'd like him to listen to it without my being present and without feeling attacked.'

In this example, the woman respects her own pace and her wish to have a quiet breakfast. But her husband attributes to her a rejecting, critical or demanding intention. Many misunderstandings arise from attributing intentions to others or from feeling hurt by their behaviour. The intentions that we impute to

'*I feel like travelling on my own ...*'

others reflect our fears. They are usually linked to doubts and feelings of denigration or persecution.

'I want to go on holiday on my own,' said an adolescent.
'Well, what's wrong with us?' retorted his parents.
If the adolescent does not let himself be trapped by the discrepancy between what he says and what he hears, he will persist in his endeavour and turn it into a plan. 'I didn't say that there was anything wrong with you, I said that I wanted to go on holiday alone. I'm thinking of going to Corsica around the 20th of July.'

'It took me years', said a young woman, 'to understand that when my boyfriend told me "I want to be alone", it was neither a criticism nor an attack against me.'

FIGHTING OR CONFRONTING

Paradoxically, it is our wish for agreement and our need for consensus that drive us to fight. We attack other people's opinions or wishes in the hope of destroying them and replacing them with a point of view similar to ours: 'You shouldn't wish for that.'

In confrontation, two points of view are placed side by side, in apposition instead of opposition. Confrontation means facing up to others without expecting them to agree with our own stand or conviction. The great fear of confronting different points of view is certainly linked with the difficulties which we have all experienced in attempting to become separate from others. We are afraid of discovering what we have in common if we are so different. What will bring us together and keep us together? But maybe that is precisely the pleasure of being together, the feeling of well-being that comes with being able to be ourselves, and accepted in our uniqueness.

How much suffering and waste of energy could be avoided through this simple process: recognizing the other person's belief and acknowledging his point of view before trying to define ours.

'For years I had been in conflict with my mother about my daughters. She was scandalized to know that they lived with someone or changed boyfriends. She was bewildered, mainly because she could not put the label "fiancé" or a social reference like "He's in business" onto these young men who were identified only by a first name, or even worse by a nickname. They had not yet found their professional path or were looking for a job.

I felt attacked and criticized for being too permissive a mother. I did my best to convince my mother: "You know, times have changed, nowadays . . ." For years, our meetings were spoilt by these confrontations, until I told her: "Yes, you are shocked because of your belief that to live with someone is not right. It's a sin, that's what you believe, I know." I stopped trying to convince her of the fact that nowadays young people, morals, or the idea of a couple have evolved.

I refused to feel guilty and our fight stopped. In a word, I accepted that my mother had different beliefs from mine. I mainly understood that these beliefs were important for her. She cared about them, and she could keep them without my attempting to dispossess her of them.'

Many people ask their parents to recognize their own values, their different way of like, while refusing to recognize their parents' values.

Paradoxically, we ask for tolerance while displaying our own intolerance.

'Your religious beliefs trap you and are narrowing your life down, Daddy. I always suffered from your intolerance. I need you to recognize how much it cost me to conquer my freedom of thought.

You stayed with Mummy even though you couldn't stand her any more. I could see it. You should have divorced, as I did. It's less hypocritical.'

To be recognized, it is necessary to recognize others first.

Children and adults who all their life were subjected to numerous demands to change ('Be different, be the way I want you to be') in turn make excessive demands on their parents.

'Mummy, I would so much like you to take care of yourself, to take care of your body, to pay more attention to the way you dress . . .'

'Daddy, I would like you to drink less, to work less, I would like you and Mummy to go out more often together. I want you to be different, Daddy . . .'

The search for agreement, even though it is sometimes essential, should not be the purpose of communication. Meeting, sharing, confronting ideas, points of view and wishes are what is essentially at stake in a lively relationship.

Of course, when opinions diverge about a shared project or issue (to have a baby, to buy a house, to reorganize a firm, to establish a certain way of relating), confrontation does not solve the problem. It clarifies it and helps to identify each person's point of view.

We can take four possible stands on a proposition or a project involving us.

- We can unreservedly agree with it.
- We can agree but with reservations about certain points.
- We can disagree with it ('Don't count on my collaboration or on my resources').
- We can oppose it ('I'll do everything I can to prevent that').

When we mention the last proposition in company training sessions or in professional areas, it raises waves of protest, ruthless criticism and massive rejection.

If we take the time and trouble to experiment with it, to propose it as a real mode of collaboration – a way of collaborating that implies differentiation, which is valid in a specific context and should be recognized as such – then we will see a complete change in the climate of relationships. There will be more enthusiasm and creativity, and skills will become more efficient. It also helps to constantly energize relationships that might otherwise become frozen and fixed in everyday routine. Any living relationship can come to an end, depending on whether we and others grow or not, whether we make the necessary and liberating changes.

To clarify irreconcilable points of view may lead to renouncements. We then have to deal with our frustrations.

- 'I give up going on holiday with you.'
- 'I give up this relationship in which I don't feel well.'
- 'I give up this collaboration.'

We are more powerful when we maintain and reassert our stand by resisting other people's attempts to define us than when we oppose others and attack them in contradictory debate.

If we give so little importance to others that their 'otherness' disappears or is destroyed, we have no one to talk to. Communication therefore becomes impossible.

DEFINING OUR SENSE OF IDENTITY

When we stop letting others define who we are, it becomes more difficult to know what we want.

- What are our priorities among our numerous wishes?
- What are our fears, needs, limits, resources and refusals?

We have to discover the limits of our tolerance as well as our vulnerability. We all have weaknesses and immature areas. Hearing certain words or facing certain kinds of behaviour makes us feel 'poisoned' or so wounded that we become lifeless. These areas resonate on past lacks; they touch and feed on unfinished business which has left us with a more or less conscious wish for completeness. How many failures, humiliations or frustrations continue to intrude into our behaviour in search of reparation, justification or realization! Years later, they may burst into a relationship and seem completely incongruous in that situation.

> 'I don't know what came over me, during the meal when I aggressively took my friend to task. I attributed to her, behaviour or an image in which she didn't recognize herself at all and which hurt her for the rest of the evening . . .'

> 'Why, in a family meeting, do I need to allude to an intimate topic so that it triggers off drama and damages several close relationships for many months?'

Our need to define who we are will indeed meet various obstacles: these are related to our dark side, to conflict and repeated behaviour, to false beliefs which burden us and make us feel alienated in spite of ourselves.

All the same, despite these obstacles or risks, let us try and define who we are and take a stand.

> 'I used to always let others choose for me; now I choose. This gives me an incredible creative potential but it also scares me to death.
> It's something new. I find it difficult to assert myself; at times, I

would still like others to suggest everything, to tell me how I should be, what I should feel, appreciate or refuse.'

When we stop making others responsible for what is wrong with us, we realize that what we considered to be an external conflict is in fact an inner conflict, an ambivalence.

In a couple, both partners generally have similar needs concerning distance and closeness before getting to know each other. Then a pattern develops and divides up needs between them in a such a way that one person mainly seems to wish for closeness while the other wants more distance. In this way each partner's inner conflict is repeatedly experienced outside.

It is a never-ending task to know ourselves, together with our mutations and permanent features.

To keep an eye open inside ourselves enables us to see a step ahead.

By recognizing our feelings more and more quickly in the sequence of our sensations, we can try and handle better what they trigger off. We can confront our emotions directly and therefore do something about them.

Feelings are like delicate and powerful children in need of constant care. By listening to them carefully, we hear more clearly the feelings that we give birth to or the resentment that stifles us.

Instead of incriminating others, questioning them and wasting our energy on them, we could take better care of ourselves. It is not easy to recognize our real feelings. To survive, we often hide them behind false beliefs and self-images or rigid defences.

'Hidden behind the intelligent and competent adult that I am is a violent and desperate child who can only express himself through irony.'

Change means accepting the feelings that hide behind defences or fears. Pain may be concealed by anger or resentment just as sadness may hide aggressiveness. Under the guise of good feelings

'I learned never to reveal the little boy who lives and cries within me ...'

we banish emotions that we consider undesirable, and particularly those which were considered undesirable in our original background.

> 'I wasn't going to talk to her about money at such a time and remind her of her promise to give me the same amount of money as she had given my brother to help him set himself up. Now that she's dead, nobody talks about it. I would feel ashamed of asking for it, as when I was a child. I was thought to be selfish each time I asked for my share or the same share as my brothers . . .'

Very often, hatred in fact reveals the depth of our attachments and our expectations. We hesitate to recognize our real feelings even to ourselves, because they seem false. The opposite feelings would also seem true. We could say that everything is true, the most contradictory as well as the most incoherent. For we can also understand contradictory feelings in apposition instead of in opposition.

'I love you *and* I hate you.'

'I understand you *and* I feel anger.'

'I accept your requests *and* I rebel against having to give in so completely to them'

We let other people's desires and demands determine our behaviour for a specific purpose. This solves inner conflict and ambivalence by making our wishes swing over to one side (the side specified by others).

But we can state who we are and attempt to clarify the chaos of our own wishes. It forces us into choosing, that is to say into renouncing other possible choices.

Fairly often we do not really choose. For instance, let us say that we have two contradictory wishes for the evening. We feel like being alone, and we are also tempted to visit a friend who has invited us over. Whatever our decision, if we do not clearly give up the other wish, a nostalgia will remain and disturb either our solitude or our meeting. So, when an unexpected proposition occurs, we tend to hurriedly adhere to it, thus evading our own contradictions.

In fact it often seems easier to let other people's desires, needs and expectations determine our behaviour. But a 'poison' will then remain in the relationship: our own wish which we were not able to identify or even express to ourselves. This pseudo-acceptance is unwittingly expressed by a more or less discreet and generally passive sabotage of what we are going to experience with others.

Before we negotiate with others, we must first negotiate with ourselves, with our fears, desires, resources and limits. Otherwise, we risk handing the choice over to others and presenting them with false choices.

'It's either me or your studies.'

'Either you stop drinking or I leave.'

'If you don't behave better, you'll go to boarding school.'

'You're old enough to have your own place. After all, you ought to be able to take the decision to go and live elsewhere, to have a more stable job, instead of living here like a parasite.'

We induce others to take in our place the decision we cannot take . . . for example to throw him out, to stop this dependent life that burdens us. How many times do we attempt to get others to make a decision for us, to express our own choice? We may even drive them to realize our own wish.

OTHER PEOPLE'S RESISTANCE TO CHANGE

When we try to say who we are and to differentiate ourselves from others, we meet with incredible resistance in the people around us, especially at the beginning. It is as if our close relationships were at risk and their values challenged.

'I started rebelling in my relationship', a woman who had been married for 12 years told us, 'when my husband at the family table made the remark: "There's no salt or pepper." I answered. "Yes indeed, you've seen that there is no salt or pepper." I continued to eat. He was astounded and flabbergasted. He had seen me so often stand up hurriedly, apologizing for my forgetfulness. He experienced that as an injustice. He mumbled: "I work all day long, I don't want to take charge of everything . . ." A while later, he yelled: "I don't ask you to check the oil level in the car, do I!"'

The feeling of injustice is sometimes so strong that the whole relationship seems to be questioned by a little sentence like this one, which can cause reprisals and guilt because it does not belong to the usual game. The differentiation suggested by one partner is understood by the other as a rejection, or an unbearable attack on what he values or on his frame of reference.

'Two years after our wedding, he started to attend this institute for personal growth, which I categorized as a sect. He straight away wanted me to enrol. He became interested in morphopsychology and instinctual therapy. He made me read books and articles. He warned me that those who criticized the ideas of the founder (who died in 1912) were infantile, "not enlightened and therefore not to be associated with".

I was shocked by the preface of the beginners' book, which I perceived as racist. It developed elitist views in opposition to my own views. Therefore I refused to go further and reasserted my own choices.

A month later, he attacked me again, saying that the analysts of the institute had told him, after having seen my photograph, that I wasn't the right wife for him, that I had made a mistake in getting married to him and that I had to leave him for his own good and his future growth. I was astounded that he accepted their "diagnosis". He was the one to leave after four months.'

This example illustrates, in an almost caricatured way, another phenomenon, the corollary of change: the acute proselytism of some people who, having discovered or had a revelation of a path, change into preachers, if not inquisitors. They impose their new faith, belief or way of life with a sectarianism that leaves no room for communication or sharing. It aims at unconditional membership . . . and therefore induces dependence.

Newcomers of all ages and backgrounds who are initiated into 'sects' go through the same process. For instance, some participants in our training sessions are sometimes tempted to present their discoveries and enthusiasm with a violence that blocks the people around them and makes them react for years. These people put us into the category of dangerous gurus, of whom one should beware, and against whom one should protect oneself. So this book risks being thrown in the fire. Why not?

People who assert themselves in this way also experience inner conflicts, which they must confront in solitude and sometimes despair. They want to maintain their stand but they also need approval.

'I need to assert myself and I need the approval of the person I'm bothering: it's incompatible. Therefore I'm tempted to give up my point of view.'

'I'm not going to make a fuss about it, it doesn't really disturb me ...'

'I can assert myself in other areas; it doesn't matter ...'

There is also the hope for reciprocity.

'I let my behaviour be determined by him in these areas, but I determine his in others.'

'I accept this today; tomorrow, she'll accept my point of view.'

When we examine everyday behaviour in marital and professional life, or even in a friendship, we notice that some people dominate others. It is always the same person who determines the other person's behaviour; there is always a leading character whose personality is partially built on the control of others.

When these positions are accepted and observed by both sides, there are no problems or tensions; everything is all right for both parties. Trouble begins when one side changes his stand and does not want to be controlled anymore. At first this new position looks like opposition and starts a conflict.

In family relationships, crucial issues are expressed through tiny everyday things: food, hygiene, order, the dividing up of tasks, social contacts.

'Mary and Peter have invited us for lunch on Sunday, and I accepted; you told me that you were free,' she says.

'I already asked you not to make a commitment for me without my agreement.'

'I couldn't reach you and I know that you like to see them.'

He hesitates. It's true, he's free, he likes to see them . . . Is he going to make a fuss? Will he feel alienated for so little? 'Well, you made a commitment on my behalf. I won't go.'

'But what will they think? You're doing this on purpose to annoy me; you're spoiling my possibility of enjoying myself, and yours too!'

He too feels uncomfortable. He had to do something to be heard.

He doesn't like to hurt anyone. The weekend is spoilt. He wants to protect the couple's harmony; he cares for the relationship. He will stick to his stand and keep on listening to her struggling under the impact of the change he initiated and in a way imposed on the relationship.

When differentiation leads us to readjust our behaviour, we think that the relationship should change. We also suggest that things be expressed in words, because the other person will also be compelled to readjust his own attitude. He or she will in turn experience an inner conflict. He will be forced into a differentiation which he does not necessarily want. Some relationships then reveal themselves as dead and meaningless.

'When I asked him not to think and act on my behalf, my husband exclaimed half-seriously, half-jokingly: "But how can I be useful then!"'

Another woman exclaimed: 'But what shall we talk about if I can't talk about you?' She obviously confused talking about . . . with talking to . . . the other person.

Some relationships do not last, while others go through difficult phases. They may be threatened by a crisis and may find a new direction and different dynamics.

There are two basic accusations in any long-term emotional relationship: 'You've changed when I needed you to remain the same'; 'You didn't change, when I needed you to evolve and your development to be in line with mine.'

We realize every day that there are no such things as 'good relationships' and 'good communication'. There are only attempts to make adjustments, which, at certain times and in certain relationships, enable us by trial and error to be close to others, to listen to them and feel listened to.

'Let's not look for a good relationships, let's look for a relationship that enables us to be ourselves and to grow.'

FEELINGS AND RELATIONSHIPS

Concerning differentiation, it seems necessary to distinguish the level of feeling from the level of relationships. We shall expand on this topic about which we already talked in the second chapter. When feelings do exist between two persons they are not always able to flow freely or be experienced in the context of a relationship.

> 'I love my father and I think he has tender feelings for me, but we cannot meet without having bitter arguments about politics or the Army. We hardly see each other anymore.'

A relationship between two people can sometimes be sick, tainted, distorted, even destructive, or simply unsatisfying, although both partners experience tender and benevolent feelings. The link has often become rigid for want of listening and because of too many unspoken things, and should be healed and softened.

A couple can become caught in an inextricable relationship where each partner is contaminated by the other's 'poisons', whereas their mutual love seems very real and lively.

> 'He's really the man I want as a life partner; I wouldn't want to live as a couple with anyone else and yet there's something wrong. After 24 hours together, it's like war, as if we needed to run each other down and destroy the good there is between us. I don't know who starts it, but each weekend or holiday, it's hell! I love him and I feel that he loves me, but there are so many disagreements and refusals! It has been going on for eight years . . .'

> 'I feel a lot for my 15-year-old son. I even understand his rebellion and provocations, but the relationship with him is impossible and unbearable nowadays!'

It had become so difficult for this above couple to listen to each other without immediately reacting to justify themselves or talk about themselves that they invented a code for when they started an important dialogue. Each partner took ten marbles and every time one of them wanted to speak, he or she had to drop a marble in a red bowl. When the marble was removed and put in another (green) bowl, this indicated that the other could intervene. The latter would in turn put a marble in the red bowl and speak. Neither of them would interrupt the other as long as the marble had not been moved to the green bowl. In this way each partner was given the chance to speak and ask for the other's attention.

Another couple, who had been complaining and accusing each other as an almost permanent means of communication, decided one day to apply a drastic treatment for a month. They made the following contract which consisted of three bans and three permissions:

- A total ban on making demands. Any need, expectation or wish that is expressed cannot be expressed as a demand. It must be the expression of a personal experience and as such belongs to the one who experiences it.
- A total ban on any blame concerning what one partner does for himself or does not do for the other. Each partner remains responsible for himself.
- A total ban on talking *for* the partner about whatever topic, on interrupting him when he talks about himself, and on making comments about what he says.

- Permission not to answer questions and demands.
- Full permission to tell all one's wishes, dreams, fantasies, needs and expectations and to talk about oneself on any topic (allowing enough speaking time for each, then giving, offering and leaving the partner enough time to himself).
- Full permission for tenderness, cuddles, games, jokes, sharing and glances at each other.

'I love you' does not mean that I shall be able to invent the relational mode in which to place this love. I will still have to find out how I can behave as a father, son, daughter, husband or wife? Which models should I copy, evade or invent? How can I build a relationship with a father who is reserved, a mother so inhibited that I am afraid of making her lose her balance? What structure should I give to the attraction I feel for this man, or this woman?

We blindly shape our feelings into relationships, without a compass or a guide. Many parents believe that it is enough to say 'I love you' to their child when he or she needs words to describe what is going on. Words should help us express not only feelings, but also what is at stake in relationships.

> 'When my son came back from school that day, upset by the headmaster's anger and violence towards his best friend who had imitated his parents' signature, I was only able to tell him about my love, my tenderness and my wish not to see him suffer. I wasn't able to start a dialogue by listening to what had been touched in him, to how he had understood his friend's need to hide his school report from his parents or to the troubles the headmaster had also had as a child. Today, I feel that I am ready to listen to all that . . .'

Some fossilized relationships survive feelings. They go on throughout years and even decades with very little communication so as not to arouse a more lively dialogue that seems impossible. Some loves survive broken relationships and remain alive in the memory, without nostalgia, melancholy or bitterness. Some feelings survive the attacks of time and oblivion; they are like anchors, unaffected by distance.

CHANGE IN FEELINGS

The reason we always remain more or less illiterate about love is because each love goes through changes. We try and live through the changes in our loves like the young boy whose voice is breaking and who clumsily tries to make use of his new voice.

> 'I am 40 and the affection I feel towards my ageing mother has nothing to do with the adoration I had for her at the age of 5. The attachment which binds me to my 18-year-old-daughter is very different from the way I loved her when she was 3.'

'The love I felt for you in the first years of our encounter has nothing in common with the love I now feel for you. I feel that I'm a different man and I see you as a different woman whom I continually go on discovering.'

The law of life is to evolve. Fluctuations and changes in feelings are often badly accepted. Our deep loyalties can hinder change if they are linked with guilt.

'To love each other 20 years later as though it were the first day' appears like an ideal of stagnation. If love is alive, it contains the seeds for its transformation. The strongest and most alienating ties are those whose modifications we accept with most difficulty. We easily cling to some primitive or outmoded stages in our relationships.

A man says: 'If I told my mother about my actual worries, I think she would answer "Eat more vegetables" or "Wash yourself more often".'

His image of the mother–son relationship has not changed, and this may very well be true for her. But he has not checked. He has not told her about his actual preoccupations. He too continues to trap his mother in an image . . . which might be outmoded. One of the greatest obstacles to change seems to be our difficulty to recognize and accept the intrinsic impermanence of life. Life is no long and quiet river; it bubbles, stirs and is projected in a thousand possible directions. But we need stable landmarks. This drives us to classify each relationship once and for all, as if its nature were immutable. However, in the long run, a relationship entails inventing new structures in which our changed feelings can live and in which we can receive those of others.

PARENTAL AND FILIAL RELATIONSHIPS

The parent–child relationship is characterized by continuous modification, gradual evolution and deep or transient changes. In a parental relationship more than in any other relationship, nothing is ever achieved. It is as if improvising without reacting were the only acceptable model.

Many difficulties arise out of fear, out of the refusal to change and out of the wish to cling to a previous stage in the relationship. Any parting with a familiar world and with certainties is a suffering; any transition is painful.

The style of the relationship sometimes survives the stage when it fitted a need. In this way, many parents find it difficult to relinquish a caring and protective relationship with their children and to move on to a relationship of dialogue. Children too reluctantly face the inevitable transformations in their bodies and their way of life.

> 'Daddy, I would like you to go on giving me advice, taking care of me and intervening as before,' says a 20-year-old girl tearfully.

> Another exclaimed angrily: 'That's not fair! You think that I'm big and independent. Well I'm not! I feel small and panic-stricken by the many responsibilities I have to take on. Under the pretext of not intervening, you're not interested in what I do any more. I see you as indifferent and far, impossibly far, away!'

Sometimes roles simply reverse without any change in models: the adult son or daughter is now convinced of the need to take care of his (or her) parents. Now he is the one who knows what is good for the other person, who wants to protect, to guide and influence him, to interfere in his material life and in his relationships.

> 'You're not going to keep this big house on now that there are only the two of you! Mummy, you would be spending your life dusting all the furniture, and you, Daddy, you would be growing vegetables that you would have to give away. Find a small flat and live there, for heaven's sake!'

Our growth is kept in check by our search for security and by our deep wish to return to what we already know, which drives us to repetition. To rely on what we already know and make progress is like walking backwards over our previous tracks. To take the risk of inventing our way also means taking the risk of losing ourselves, of getting lost in quicksands or in directions that are too dangerous.

To change means to modify our path, and therefore implies a risk of moving away from those who are close to us. The birth of a child changes a man and a woman and sometimes transforms them into parents. It changes the woman's relationship to herself, to her own body, to her imaginary life and her future. This is also true for the man. When, in a couple, a man refuses 'to have a child', it is not really the child that he refuses; in fact he is mainly expressing his fear or his uncertainties about his competence and his ability to be a father.

The growth of a child is a powerful agent for change. Our children upset our certainties, compel us to clarify what remains vague, and call into question our images of man and woman, beyond parental roles. In addition to questions, they arouse doubts and make us sort things out; they stimulate our unconscious and permeate our most repressed areas.

To become real adults we have to kill our imaginary parents, those we would have liked to have had, be they idealized parents or monsters we invented. This is the only way to acknowledge our real parents and beyond them to try and meet the man and woman they are and maybe perceive the child that still exists in them.

UNFINISHED BUSINESS

We have something to learn from each stage in childhood, adolescence and adulthood before taking the next step.

Sometimes we are not able to learn or we learn something incomplete. This creates deficiencies and gaps in our development. Later on some relationships will allow for substitute experiences and make up for missed experiences and unexplored discoveries. This sometimes happens in the therapeutic processes, where symbolic mediations release the present from past failings. They help to create a kind of epilogue to situations that remained unfinished: unspoken words, unelaborated breaches[3] and embedded sorrows. Sometimes we lose someone and leave attached to him a part of our imaginary life, which we do not reclaim.

> 'I left my ability to love and my sexual desires attached to the man who left me.'

Sometimes the best part of ourselves will remain with the other person, with the person who left us, or whom we lost. Breach and loss are experienced as real amputations that may split us up or impair us.

In a process of change, we invite people to reclaim the aspect or part of themselves they left with the other person. It is a symbolic process of reunification with the best in themselves.

> 'At the beginning of our relationship, I had given him my love of life, my enthusiasm for music. Ten years later, at the time of our divorce, I had become a hardened woman, allergic to singing and impervious to happiness. Later on, through a symbolic process of mental representation, I "retrieved" the gift I had left him (with which he had not done anything in fact. Nature and music weren't his cup of tea!) It was as if I were getting younger, as if I were finding again a very close and familiar person: myself.'

One of the purposes of change is to regain one's own integrity. Love seems subjected to laws of evolution of which we know nothing but which we put into practice with a constancy that challenges experience. The real love in love lives in the present. It is at ease in the present, on which it sometimes confers a cosmic dimension. But, rapidly, it looks for a future and for safeguards against the hazards of the past and of the present.

Whenever Carmen in Bizet's opera proclaims that 'Love has never known any law', she immediately states one: 'If you don't love me, I love you, and if I love you, beware.'

The only general and often denied law seems to be the law of continual metamorphosis. Many disappointments arise from a confusion between what happens at the beginning and what happens when a relationship becomes established and develops.

Like all significant encounters in life, love opens up new perceptions, awakens dormant areas, and reveals us to ourselves. The vivaciousness of interactions is however short-lasting, and very quickly a structuring relationship pattern sets in, be it enlivening or not. Like a child, the link needs to be fed and stimulated. It needs meaningful words. It changes and exudes waste; it can decline or be enriched; it can be sick or healthy. It is like a child being brought up, taken care of or mistreated by his two creators.

The development of love into a love link is difficult to accept. It is transformed by the loss of idealized images which had been projected onto the other person, and by the reappearance of infantile needs and personal beliefs. It also clashes with invisible loyalties that are deeply engraved in both protagonists.

Love in love has to die to leave room for loving love, which has demands and plans. Once myths have been given up, the link can only be enriched if each partner accepts the need to become constantly more aware of what is inside him.

Nothing is ever acquired for good. No human relationship will ever quench our thirst for the absolute. It remains an infinitely open and fragile adventure.

CHANGE

The only never-ending adventure we have been given to live, amid the gropings and enthusiasms of everyday life, is personal change.

Change is similar to an inner urge. It is an irrepressible and sometimes painful inner motion, to which we sometimes let ourselves go, in the light of our discoveries. We may also, on the contrary, resist it by clinging tightly to our fears and beliefs.

'I have so many skins to shed before at last I find the me which is really me.'

Inner transformation and change in our relationships and in outward events are two aspects of life that are always linked.

If we see life as an opportunity for learning and discovering more about ourselves, the very sufferings and the subtle metamorphosis of maturation that mark it, turn it into something fascinating.

To become who I am in a unique way is the secret code of self-achievement.

Conclusion

This book, such as we imagined, carried, shared and wrote it, cannot end. It remains unfinished, for there are still so many things to say about the extraordinary adventure of human relationships. It remains open to the numerous questions that may dwell in us, in you, reader of these lines. It can also be extended by communication; we remain open to your suggestions, criticisms and discoveries.

And we'd like to remind you that a book always has a minimum of two authors: the one who writes it and the one who reads it.

Notes

1 We use the expression 'talking for' someone to describe a way of talking which is made up of explanations ('If you don't come, it's because you're afraid') and denial ('You're not unhappy, you have everything you need'). It is different if somebody really tells us how he sees us, by offering us a mirror, distorted of course, but nevertheless a mirror. This way of talking can be structuring; it can help us to know ourselves better. The difference lies mainly in the intention of the person telling us about ourselves.

2 Man and woman do not remember their divine origin. At birth he or she is separated, cut off, and therefore in a state of searching and dependent. Paradoxically, the not yet separated foetus is independent. For to be dependent means to feel that you are linked in an insecure way by a link that could break. This explains the anxiety, the intolerance, the fierce and desperate 'clinging' to the link or to the person who symbolizes it. Mystics search for fusion with the Whole so as to regain their independence. And the more they 'submit' (as disciples), the freer they become.

3 We consider a breach to be an abrupt change of state, a discontinuity, such as birth or death. When we use the word 'separation', it is usually in the sense of an evolution or a differentiation from a previous state.